THE LIFE OF AN ENSLAVED AFRICAN IN THE OTTOMAN EMPIRE AND IRAN

The Autobiography of Mahboob Qirvanian

The Life of an Enslaved African in the Ottoman Empire and Iran is a poignant and compelling account of one man's journey through struggle, resilience, and unimaginable suffering. In the early twentieth century, Mahboob Qirvanian recorded his personal experiences of forced migration and enslavement as he navigated his path from captivity in Africa to full citizenship and a reconstructed identity in Iran. Written in Persian and Arabic, this remarkable autobiography serves as a powerful testament to Mahboob's endurance, suffering, and ultimate transformation.

Through insightful analysis, Behnaz A. Mirzai places Mahboob's narrative – the only known account by a former African slave in Iran – within the context of the political upheavals of the Constitutional Revolution in Iran and the Tanzimat reforms of the Ottoman Empire. This book not only sheds light on Mahboob's personal story and the historical injustices of slavery but also engages with broader themes of displacement, identity, and social justice. In doing so, it invites readers to reflect on the enduring legacies of racial inequality and the ongoing struggles for freedom and dignity in the modern world.

BEHNAZ A. MIRZAI is a professor of Middle Eastern history at Brock University and senior guest researcher at Bonn Center for Dependency and Slavery Studies at University of Bonn.

MAHBOOB QIRVANIAN, born circa 1894 in Tunisia, was enslaved and trafficked from North Africa to Iran, where he lived for the majority of his life and was emancipated. He is the author of the only known African slave narrative from that country.

NEW LANDSCAPES IN MIDDLE EAST STUDIES

General Editor: Stefan Winter, Université du Québec à Montréal

Advisory Board

Dyala Hamzah, Université de Montréal
Colin Mitchell, Dalhousie University
Paul Sedra, Simon Fraser University

The Life of an Enslaved African in the Ottoman Empire and Iran

The Autobiography of Mahboob Qirvanian

BEHNAZ A. MIRZAI

UNIVERSITY OF TORONTO PRESS
Toronto Buffalo London

© University of Toronto Press 2025
Toronto Buffalo London
utppublishing.com

ISBN 978-1-4875-6132-1 (cloth) ISBN 978-1-4875-6135-2 (EPUB)
ISBN 978-1-4875-6133-8 (paper) ISBN 978-1-4875-6134-5 (PDF)

New Landscapes in Middle East Studies

Library and Archives Canada Cataloguing in Publication

Title: The life of an enslaved African in the Ottoman Empire and Iran : the autobiography of Mahboob Qirvanian / Behnaz A. Mirzai.
Other titles: Autobiography of Mahboob Qirvanian
Names: Mirzai, Behnaz A., author | Qirvanian, Mahboob, 1894–1939, author.
Description: Series statement: New landscapes in Middle East studies | Includes bibliographical references and index.
Identifiers: Canadiana (print) 20250144271 | Canadiana (ebook) 20250144352 | ISBN 9781487561321 (cloth) | ISBN 9781487561338 (paper) | ISBN 9781487561352 (EPUB) | ISBN 9781487561345 (PDF)
Subjects: LCSH: Qirvanian, Mahboob, 1894–1939. | LCSH: Enslaved persons – Iran – Biography. | LCSH: Slave trade – Iran – History – 20th century. | LCSH: Slave trade – Africa – History – 20th century. | LCSH: Slavery – History – 20th century. | LCGFT: Autobiographies.
Classification: LCC HT869.Q57 M57 2025 | DDC 306.3/62092 – dc23

Cover design: Val Cooke
Cover image: iStock.com/claudiodivizia

We wish to acknowledge the land on which the University of Toronto Press operates. This land is the traditional territory of the Wendat, the Anishnaabeg, the Haudenosaunee, the Métis, and the Mississaugas of the Credit First Nation.

This book has been published with the help of a grant from the Federation for the Humanities and Social Sciences, through the Awards to Scholarly Publications Program, using funds provided by the Social Sciences and Humanities Research Council of Canada.

University of Toronto Press acknowledges the financial support of the Government of Canada, the Canada Council for the Arts, and the Ontario Arts Council, an agency of the Government of Ontario, for its publishing activities.

 Canada Council for the Arts / Conseil des Arts du Canada

 ONTARIO ARTS COUNCIL
CONSEIL DES ARTS DE L'ONTARIO
an Ontario government agency
un organisme du gouvernement de l'Ontario

Funded by the Government of Canada / Financé par le gouvernement du Canada | Canada

To the family of Qirvanian

Contents

List of Maps and Illustrations ix

Foreword xi
PAUL E. LOVEJOY

Acknowledgments xiii

Chronology of Mahboob Qirvanian xv

Introduction xvii
   The African Slave Trade in Iran: An Overview xvii
   The Importance of Mahboob's Autobiography xxv
   Historical Context xxxvii
   The Significance of the Autobiography lxxix

1 In Africa 3
   Genealogy 3
   The Invasion of the Nasara 4
   Fleeing Home (Kidelan, a Village in Sousse) 5
   Enslavement 7

2 Forced Migration: From Africa to the Middle East 9
   To Saljmattyah 12
   From Saljmattyah to a New Town 20
   From the New Town to Sous Aqsa 21
   From Sous Aqsa to El-Obeid 25
   From El-Obeid to Khartoum 31
   Evading British Patrol 32
   From Khartoum to Jedda 34
   British Search Patrol near the Red Sea 37

3 In Ottoman Arabia 40
    Slave Trade in Jedda 40
    From Jedda to Mecca 42
    New Identity 43
    From Mecca to Ta'if 44
    From Ta'if to Mecca: Education 47
    Circumcision 48
    Slave Market in Mecca: Reselling 48
    At the House of the 'Ulama': New Identity 49
    From Mecca to Medina 51
    In Medina 53
    In Najd: Chants and Khayzaran 54
    From Najd to Najaf 55
    Constitutions and the Political Events 59

4 The Departure of Hajj Mahboob to Iran 61
    In Iran: Kurdistan 64
    From Kermanshah to Qom 68
    In Qom 75
    From Qom to Tehran 76
    Customs and Beliefs 78
    In Tehran 80
    Leaving Tehran for Mashhad 85
    In Mashhad 87
    Expelling Mahboob: Moving from Mashhad to Tehran 88
    In Tehran 90
    Imprisonment 91
    Release from Prison 92

5 Leaving Iran for Iraq 95
    The Departure of Mahboob from Tehran to
        Shah 'Abdul 'Azim, Peace Be upon Him 95

6 Returning to Iran 98
    In Shiraz 101
    In Isfahan 103
    Departing from Kashan 103

Bibliography 105

Index 117

Maps and Illustrations

Maps

1. Trans-Saharan trade routes   xxxix
2. Mahboob's trail in North Africa, 1903   xli
3. Tehran and its surroundings in 1910   lxvi
4. The quarter where Mahboob was living in Tehran   lxvii
5. Mahboob's general trail from Sousse, Tunisia, to Tehran, Iran   lxxxiv
6. Mahboob's trail in the Ottoman Empire and Arabia   59
7. Mahboob's trails in Iran and Ottoman Iraq   94

Illustrations

1. Scarification   xxxi
2. Slave trade in Africa   xliii
3. Mujtahid Ishaq Rashti   li
4. Sayyid 'Abdullah Behbehani   lviii
5. Ayatullah Shaykh 'Abdullah Mazandarani and Ayatullah Mulla Muhammad Kazem Khurasani   lx
6. Agha Bahram, the African eunuch, in the palace of Naser al-Din Shah   lxv
7. Mujtahid Shaykh Isma'il Ayatullah Gharavi Rashti   lxviii
8. A genealogical chart of the Iranian Shi'i 'ulama' in the Ottoman Empire and Iran whom Mahboob served   lxxii
9. Aqdas, Mahboob's daughter   lxxv
10. Ma'someh, Mahboob's wife   lxxvii
11. Ahmad, Mahboob's son   lxxx
12. Ahmad, Mahboob's son, with Muhammad Amir Khatami   lxxx
13. Ahmad's wedding in 1964   lxxxi

Foreword

This meticulous, researched study highlights the complex variations in the institution of slavery as seen in a global perspective. Behnaz Mirzai has provided a translation with an introduction and annotations for the autobiography of Mahboob Qirvanian (1894–1939), who was enslaved as a young boy in Africa and eventually recounted his life story in Iran. This account thereby makes accessible an invaluable portrayal of slavery and emancipation within a Muslim context that parallels the many autobiographical accounts of slavery in the European-dominated Atlantic world. The global context of this autobiography focuses on the Sahara, the Nilotic Sudan, the holy lands of the Hijaz, and the emergence of modern Iran, thus straddling regions that are largely overlooked in the global study of slavery. Hence, this is a valuable contribution to the study of slavery in the broader Indian Ocean region.

There were relatively small numbers of enslaved individuals in Iran by the end of the nineteenth century and the first decades of the twentieth, amounting to perhaps no more than 2 per cent of the population and concentrated mainly in the families of wealthy individuals and providing support for administrative services of government officials. This concentration in the households and offices of the elite provided unusual opportunities for the enslaved in terms of education, training, and deployment for men, and relationships of concubinage assured women of the free status of their children and protection for themselves from sale. While these features of slavery in the Islamic context are well known for the Muslim lands extending from sub-Saharan Africa through the Middle East and the Indian Ocean basin, Mahboob's testimony nonetheless stands out as the most detailed personal account of these patterns. Moreover, his life story staddles the divide between the period when slavery still legally prevailed and full emancipation for all enslaved individuals was enacted in 1929, ten years before Mahboob's death.

Mahboob's memoirs convey the therapeutic importance of autobiography. He is able to recount the painful period of enslavement and forced movement over harsh desert trails that were both dangerous and dehumanizing. As a child, who apparently was enslaved as a result of factional conflict, his upbringing required survival, unplanned adjustments to changes in who claimed ownership, and considerable geographical and cultural relocation. Unlike the transatlantic Middle Passage, his trajectory took him across the desert and inserted him into the movement of enslaved individuals that was parallel to and sometimes associated with the pilgrimage to the holy lands of Mecca and Medina, and from there to Persia. The autobiography that Mahboob compiled was his way of remembering the trauma of separation from family and kin and recounting the difficult and dangerous trek that he had to endure. By describing his several masters and the different situations of subordination, Mahboob uses the literacy that he was fortunate to acquire as a mechanism that preserved his memory and allowed him to express the uncertainties and adjustments that he had been forced to experience, which he did so that his family would understand the unique background. The therapeutic dimension unravels the transformations in identity that inevitably reflect the experiences of enslaved individuals, despite the differences in social structure and economic exploitation.

Mirzai provides a detailed introduction that explains the context of the autobiography. She was fortunate to be able to interview Mahboob's son and a couple of his daughters, and thereby establish an ongoing relationship with the family. Through extensive and prolonged interaction, Mirzai has been able to use the autobiography to extend her analysis of the history of slavery in Iran, which she pioneered in her previous work and has documented through video production. In the context of the wider Indian Ocean world, her research stands out as a monumental contribution. She has chronicled an exceptional pattern in the history of slavery in Africa and the Islamic world. Mirzai has successfully revealed a hidden perspective that required not only careful research but also undertook a translation from Persian that makes the account accessible to a wider audience.

Paul E. Lovejoy

Acknowledgments

Working on Mahboob's autobiography has allowed me to journey into the past and connect my memories of, and reactions to, familiar events in Iranian history. The present is the legacy of the past and that history always repeats itself. I belong to a generation that witnessed revolution and war. My family are Turkish Azeri from Tabriz; they witnessed World War II and the Russian occupation of the city. I lived all my childhood in Kurdistan, where my father established the telecommunication system. It was a poverty-stricken province with picturesque mountains and landscapes, rich in natural beauty but also plagued by forbiddingly cold winters.

Everything changed when my family moved to Tehran. The change from rural to city life was difficult for me. On top of this, political unrest was stirring in Tehran, and it erupted when the revolutionary movement broke out in 1978. A year later, the Pahlavi dynasty was overthrown, and the Islamic Republic of Iran was established. It was a period of major political, social, and cultural transitions. I was inspired by the political and socio-economic changes, by my multi-ethnic background, and by my past to understand the experiences of others, which let me bear witness through my research to peace, equality, and justice for all humankind.

In 1997, I moved to Canada and began my graduate studies at York University where I worked as a research assistant at the Nigerian Hinterland Project. The centre was directed by my doctoral dissertation supervisor, Paul Lovejoy. Here, I learned about race, slavery, and the African diaspora, and this is where Babak Ghirvanian, the grandson of Mahboob, brought the current manuscript to my attention. Babak has always been keen to publish his grandfather's autobiography. He continually and willingly provided insights and information about his family. I am very grateful to the Ghirvanian family and especially

Babak for his ceaseless efforts and relentless availability to respond to my questions about Mahboob and to help me contact Mahboob's children. My focus on completing my doctoral degree and publishing several academic books delayed the publication of Mahboob's manuscript for several years. However, I continued to interview Mahboob's family, collected information, and made several trips to Iran to visit Aqdas, his daughter, who has since passed away. She hosted me with so much generosity in Tehran and provided information about the family. She also accompanied me to the cemetery to visit Mahboob's grave.

I have been fortunate to receive opportunities as a visiting professor and visiting researcher at the Bonn Centre for Dependency and Slavery Studies at the University of Bonn, Germany, Unité de Recherche Migrations et Société (URMIS) at Université Côte d'Azur, France, and the Indian Ocean World Centre at McGill University, Montreal. My stay in these academic research centres let me focus on this manuscript and prepare it for publication. I am grateful to Swanie Potot, Marie-Pierre Ballarin, Stephan Conermann, and Gwyn Campbell for inviting me to their research centres. I would like to express my appreciation to Paul Lovejoy, Adam Ali, Ehud Toledano, Janet Afary, Anna Maria Medici, Afua Cooper, Sylviane Diouf, Stephan Conermann, and Hichem Ben-El-Mechaiekh for reading and commenting on the manuscript. I thank Michael Izady for preparing the maps. I wish to thank Muhammad Ridwaan, Mary Lui, Ælfwine Mischler, Sarah King Head, and Judith Nylvek, who provided editorial assistance for the manuscript. Thanks also go to my colleague Andrew McDonald for offering suggestions during the publication process. Special thanks are due to Stephen Shapiro, the acquisitions editor at the University of Toronto Press, for his help and advice. I would also like to extend my thanks to all those individuals who played a role in the preparation of this manuscript. My final acknowledgments and deepest appreciation go to my dear sons, Behrouz and Rouzbeh, who patiently endured my years of study, research, and work.

Chronology of Mahboob Qirvanian

1894	Born in Tunisia
1902	Enslaved, aged eight
1903	Arrived in Jedda, Ottoman Arabia, aged nine
1903	Sold in Mecca to the 'ulama'
1903	Arrived in Najaf, Ottoman Iraq
1911	Arrived in Iran, aged seventeen
1912	Married Ma'someh in Tehran, aged eighteen
1911–18	Lived in Tehran
1918	Arrived in Mashhad, aged twenty-four
1919	Returned to Tehran, aged twenty-five
1920	Went with Ma'someh to Karbala' then Najaf
1921	Returned to Iran, aged twenty-seven
1939	Died in Tehran, aged forty-five
1973	Ma'someh died, aged sixty-nine

Introduction

The African Slave Trade in Iran: An Overview

This short overview outlines the most important issues related to the African slave trade in Iran during a period extending from the imposition of legislation limiting seaborne practices associated with the transportation of slaves in the early nineteenth century to full emancipation of all slaves in 1929. This historical overview seeks to situate Mahboob's autobiography within a temporal and factual context and draws extensively on the author's previous research on the history of slavery, abolition, emancipation, and post-emancipation in Iran.

Slavery in Iran is a little-studied topic that relies on a complex understanding of existing social, political, economic, and cultural factors.[1] The reasons for the dearth of literature about slavery in Iran are that the number of enslaved African people was relatively low in comparison to other parts of the world, the descendants of enslaved Africans lack knowledge about the history of slavery and have shown little interest in learning about this aspect of their heritage, there are few professional studies of the history of slavery, and there are a limited number of documented primary sources such as autobiographies and slave narratives. Although slavery had always existed, not until the eighteenth and nineteenth centuries did the African slave trade intensify along the Red Sea coast and in the Persian Gulf and the Indian Ocean. Dealers responded to the growing demand for labour by the Portuguese in Brazil, the French in Madagascar, and the Omani Arabs who operated

---

1 Mirzai, *A History of Slavery*; Mirzai, *African-Baluchi Trance Dance*; Mirzai, *Afro-Iranian Lives*. For information about the enslavement of Iranian women, see Najmabadi, *Daughters of Quchan*. In her memoir, *Khaterat-i Taj al-Saltana*, Taj al-Saltana includes some references to the enslaved people who were employed in the palace of the shah.

plantations in Zanzibar and Pemba.[2] In Iran this trade was specifically linked to extensive networks in the Indian Ocean with slaves principally being transported by sea from the Swahili coast to areas across the region, including throughout the Ottoman Empire and into the interior of Iran.[3] Most of the slave-carrying ships were Omani and they relied on the direction of seasonal winds.[4]

There were no specialized slave markets in Iran per se as demand was historically not great. Instead, traders known as *dallal* conducted sales in private homes so slaves were often moved between households.[5] Occasionally, the slaves were used as gifts to royal courts or high-ranking officials.[6] In an attempt to regulate the system, buyers received bills of purchase that served as legal proof of ownership. These documents included a description of the slave, the date of purchase, the price paid, and the place of sale.[7]

The slave trade was often justified on religious grounds (i.e., to encourage the conversion of non-believers to Islam).[8] Slaves could be employed in various socio-economic sectors including the military,

---

2 Brazil's economy was dependent on enslaved people procured by the Portuguese, Arabs, and Swahilis for its plantations and cattle farms; the French brought enslaved people to sugar colonies in the Mascarenes; and the Omani Arabs established clove plantations in Zanzibar and on the island of Pemba. For further discussion on the expansion of the East African slave trade, see Hooper and Eltis, "The Indian Ocean"; Allen, *European Slave Trading*; Manning, *Slavery and African Life*, 136–48; Sheriff, *Slaves*; Hopper, *Slaves of One Master*.
3 Dowding to Ross, 11 November 1885, BL, L/PS/20/246; Arnold Burrowes Kemball to Colonel H. D. Robertson and Justin Sheil, 8 July 1842, NAUK, FO 84/426.
4 Kemball to Robertson and Sheil; Arnold Burrowes Kemball, Report on the Persian Gulf, 1847, NAUK, FO 84/692; Robertson to Willoughby, 4 March 1842, NAUK, FO 84/426.
5 Wills, *Persia as It Is*, 75; Bassett, *Persia*, 288. Extract from a French letter from Monsieur Castelli, British agent at Shiraz, to Captain Felix Jones, political resident in the Persian Gulf, 12 August 1859, NAUK, FO 248/183.
6 Samuel Hennell to Justin Sheil, 10 September 1850, NAUK, FO 84/815; Justin Sheil to Ameer-i-Nizam, 16 October 1850, NAUK, FO 84/815; Arnold Burrowes Kemball to Arthur Malet, chief secretary to the government of Bombay, 2 August 1853, BL, L/PS/5/479.
7 Iranian Ministry of Foreign Affairs to the British Consular, box 3, file 4, 1317 [1900], VUK.
8 Noori and Azhar, "Shī'ī Ideas of Slavery"; for example, Muhammad Shah, the king of the Qajar dynasty, who initially was reluctant to ban the trade in enslaved people, argued: "By prohibiting [the slave trade] I will prevent the conversion of five thousand persons into Islam; this will result in [both] my having a bad name and my perpetuating great religious sin." Muhammad Shah to Hajji Mirza Aqasi, 1263 [1846], box 6, file 5, Majmuʻa-yi Bardegi, VUK, Tehran.

public administration, domestic service, and agriculture (maritime and husbandry), based on physical suitability, skills, religious and cultural background, and personal characteristics including intelligence, talent, honesty, and faithfulness.[9] Some even entered the elite and enjoyed higher social standing. Enslaved people employed in the harem (palace) and the royal court enjoyed high status, honour, and prestige. For example, the chief chamberlain, or chief of enslaved people (*qullar aqasi*), and the chief of ceremonies (*ishik aqasi*), or grand chief of ceremonies (*ishik aqasi bashi*), were regarded as part of the ruling elites. The chief enslaved person was in charge of the royal enslaved people and monitored their payments and finances, while the chief of ceremonies was in charge of governmental matters outside the palace.[10] The king's personal and royal bodyguards (the *ghulam-i shahi*) were also regarded as elite slaves who received income. In the harem system, eunuchs, whose tasks included guarding women and children and administrating the harem's matters, also enjoyed authority and prestige and received regular income.[11]

Those who disembarked at the southern ports and worked in maritime activities often established self-sufficient communities. Meanwhile, urban slaves usually could not create such diasporic networks. Their work was limited to gender roles found in the strictly public-private dichotomy of city life. Women were invariably involved in feminine spheres such as public baths and beauty salons or were employed as cooks and nurses.[12] Men were usually labourers (including minstrels, stonemasons, or woodcutters) or worked in the service sector as porters or footmen, for example.[13] Those able to earn salaries or wages in either the private or public sectors in urban settings achieved higher social standing.

The slave-master relationship in Iran was governed by a combination of traditional and local laws and was further regulated by Islamic law.[14] The possession of slaves was a sign of prestige and wealth; consequently, the masters provided for their slaves' socio-economic needs, including food, housing, marriage partners, and, sometimes, education. Most slaves were bought while still young, were given new names, and

---

9 Mirza Sami'a, *Tazkarat al-muluk*, 18.
10 Mirza Sami'a, *Tazkarat al-muluk*, 8.
11 Wills, *Persia as It Is*, 77.
12 Polak, *Persien*, 2:361.
13 Sadid al-Saltana Kababi, *Bandar 'Abbas va Khalij-i Fars*, 157; Landor, *Across Coveted Lands*, 2:80–1.
14 Husayni, *Bardegi az didgah-i Islam*, 29–31.

were converted to the religion of their masters.[15] A common method of punishment was expulsion, which brought great socio-economic hardship to the kinless and unprotected slave.[16] By contrast, those who were granted freedom could more easily transition into society by relying on the kinship network of their former masters. Such networks were established in customary and religious occasions such as weddings.[17] In other cases, freed slaves would remain with their former masters in a personal relationship of clientage (*wala'*).[18] The similar "patronage and attachment"[19] bondage defined the master-slave relationship in the Ottoman societies, where the identity of enslaved and freed slaves was attached to a social group and larger community that included family. As Ehud Toledano states:

> Part of the problem is understanding that enslavement in the Ottoman, Iranian, and Arab societies of the Middle East and North Africa was driven by patronage, grounded in the family, and backed by Shari'a law and socio-cultural norms. This made it in some aspects different from Atlantic world slaveries that have prototyped and stigmatized not only public views, but also modern scholarship on global enslavement. Despite the fact that all types of slavery have a clear core of commonalities – which make them all oppressive, exploitative, degrading, and evil – the differences cannot be brushed aside as irrelevant.[20]

Some slaves did not want to be freed in the Muslim societies, including the Indian Ocean, the Mediterranean, and the Middle East. For example, the royal slave soldiers in the Aden protectorate rebelled against their own freedom when the British freed them so they were compulsorily and forcibly freed in 1943.[21]

Another condition for the liberation of slaves was the penalty a master faced for ill-treating or abusing his slave;[22] however, in such cases,

---

15 Malcolm, *Sketches of Persia*, 1:18.
16 Wills, *In the Land of the Lion and Sun*, 326; Polak, *Persien*, 2:252; E'temad al-Saltana, *Yaddashtha-yi E'temad al-Saltana*, 45; Kemball to Robertson and Sheil; Kemball, Report on the Persian Gulf; Edwards to Arnold Burrowes Kemball, 1842, NAUK, FO 84/426, 207–11.
17 Polak, *Persien*, 1:250.
18 Schacht, *An Introduction to Islamic Law*, 130.
19 Toledano, *As If Silent and Absent*, 24.
20 Toledano, "Enslavement and Freedom."
21 Miers, "Slave Rebellion."
22 Ministry of the Interior, 290/11/384/3, 25/12/1307 [16 March 1929], SAM, Tehran; Husayni, *Bardegi az didgah-i Islam*, 42.

the slave often had to escape and take refuge with higher authorities.[23] Indeed, slaves who lived in Iran but had been born in a British protectorate could theoretically achieve unconditional liberation. For example, 'Abdulrahman Khartoumi was enslaved in Sudan and was brought to Damghan, a town in northern Iran, by Farajullah Khan Damghani. There he was resold and married a *kaniz*[24] with whom he had two daughters.[25] He escaped to the British consulate and demanded his liberation. Faced with the pressure of his owner to return, 'Abdulrahman argued that he was a Sudanese and a British citizen and was entitled to freedom.[26] Meanwhile, his master challenged his origin by stating that he had been purchased in Lebanon, which was under the Ottoman Empire, and then had been brought to Arabia (present-day Saudi Arabia) and later into Iran.[27]

Gender influenced the ease with which liberated slaves could integrate into society. Female slaves inevitably had to rely on marriage to realize such integration as they were limited by social and religious barriers revolving around moral concerns about the sexual exploitation of these unprotected and unskilled members of society.[28] Slave masters also frequently refused to consider releasing female slaves because they considered them their lawful concubines and wives.

In 1807, Britain passed an act banning the embarkation and disembarkation of enslaved Africans within its territories, followed by further legislation in 1811 that outlawed the slave trade entirely.[29] This legislation was enforced through treaty agreements with other nations and achieved through compliance patrols of the Persian Gulf region. The British then banned the sale of Indians, whom they regarded as their subjects, in 1812, and in 1822 banned the sale of any slaves to Christian nations. By 1839, the sale of Somalis, who were Muslim and categorized as *hurr* (free), was also made illegal as their enslavement was against

---

23 The statement of Mas'ud, 26 May 1927, MA 1AB5T402, SAM, Tehran.
24 A female slave.
25 Abbasquli, on the issue of Hajji 'Abdulrahman Khartoumi, 16 Muharram 1323 [23 March 1905], Q1323.3.2, VUK, Tehran.
26 Nasrullah Mushir al-Daula to Sadr al-Mamalek, 4 Muharram 1323 [11 March 1905], Q1323.3.2, VUK, Tehran.
27 'Abdulrahman's master to Nasrullah Mushir al-Daula, Q1323.3.2 [1905], VUK, Tehran.
28 The stories of female runaway slaves, however, do provide valuable insights into the complex ways that gender intersected with the process of emancipation. See Mirzai, *A History of Slavery*, chapter 8 ("Emancipation"), for a detailed discussion.
29 In 1833, the British passed a law banning slavery, and in 1838, slaves were legally emancipated. See Lorimer, *Gazetteer of the Persian Gulf*, 1: pt. 2, 2475.

Islamic law, and in 1887 the territory officially became the British Protectorate of Somaliland. By the end of the century, these laws and treaty agreements increasingly restricted the African slave trade throughout the region.

The British relied on various strategies to enforce compliance. Efforts were made to distinguish newly imported African slaves from more established ones based on linguistic proficiency. If the slaves knew Persian or Arabic, the assumption was that they had entered the country before the firmans had been issued and had not been smuggled in recently.[30] These older slaves were provided with passports indicating their status as Iranian citizens.[31] Meanwhile, those deemed to have been recently smuggled in were sent to Bombay in India and to Zanzibar and Pemba in East Africa, where, as free individuals, they invariably found employment as labourers. Many children were taken to a branch of the Church Missionary Society at Saharanpur, near Bombay.[32]

Even so, the institution of slavery was far from being eradicated. Traders resorted to other methods, including the concealment of seaborne importation activities. To avoid interrogation (and possible seizure) by the British navy, flags of non-complying countries, like France, would often be flown. Similarly, male slaves were often dressed as women using *chadur* (long veils).[33] Another method used by the Omani Arabs was leasing parts of the southern Iranian coast to establish slave-trading ports.[34]

Once on land, transporting slaves was simpler since the traders could rely on well-worn pilgrim and trade routes.[35] In Ottoman-controlled Arabia, the holy cities of Mecca and Medina became important slave-trading hubs. Here, the Ottoman Empire's abolitionist firman in the 1850s was met with fierce opposition by religious leaders. Shaykh Jamal

---

30 Samuel Hennell to T. G. Carless, Bushire, 21 September 1848, BL, L/PS/5/459; Samuel Hennell to T. G. Carless, 21 September 1848, BL, L/PS/9/136.
31 Justin Sheil to Amir Kabir, 1267, box 6, file 24, Majmu'a-yi Bardegi, VUK, Tehran; Lorimer, *Gazetteer of the Persian Gulf*, 1: pt. 2, 2483.
32 Lorimer, *Gazetteer of the Persian Gulf*, 1: pt. 2, 2491; Lord Palmerston to Justin Sheil, 31 December 1849, BL, R/15/1/123; Wilson, *The Persian Gulf*, 230.
33 Précis of Maskat Affairs, 1892–1905, report from the political resident, December 1891, BL, L/PS/20/C245; Felix Jones to Charles Alison, envoy of philanthropy at the Persian court, 7 December 1860, NAUK, FO 248/189; Binning, *Two Years' Travel*, 1:272; Correspondence between the Ministry of Foreign Affairs of Iran and the British agent, Rabi' al-Thani 1300 [February 1883], box 17, file 21, Majmu'a-yi Bardegi, VUK, Tehran.
34 Kemball to Robertson and Sheil, 190–8.
35 Kemball to Robertson and Sheil; Bassett, *Persia*, 4; Burton, *Personal Narrative*, 13, 252.

of Mecca issued a fatwa in 1855 declaring slavery a right provided by Islamic law and the Turks infidels. The ensuing riots resulted in a massacre.[36] Following this event, the Hijaz was excepted from the Ottoman ban on the slave trade. The African slave trade into Arabia and Iran continued legally, but on a smaller scale.

Slavery, a method of control and exploitation of humans by other people for various reasons, is practised in many societies globally in large or small scale. Middle Eastern and North African societies developed distinct forms and non-Atlantic notions of slavery, abolition, and post-emancipation. Studying the experiences of enslaved Africans in the Mediterranean and the Indian Ocean world helps us understand the paradigms of global slavery.[37] Mahboob's journey extended across diverse geographical regions from the Sahara in Africa to the Arab countries and Iran in the Middle East, which shaped his life experience. The hybrid institution of slavery in the Arab world (i.e., the modern states of Saudi Arabia, Yemen, Oman, the United Arab Emirates, Kuwait, and Bahrain) resembled Middle Eastern slavery from social and cultural perspectives, but from the genetics and disease points of view, the Arab system of agricultural slavery was similar to that of the Atlantic world.[38]

In Iran, freed and enslaved African people were employed in various social, cultural, and economic sectors. Some married either Africans or Iranians, resulting in offspring who were called house-born and became members of their master's family. For example, in 1852, about 2 per cent of Tehran's total population was of enslaved and freed people of African descent. The total population of Tehran was 155,736, of whom 756 were Black *ghulams*[39] and eunuchs, and 2,525 were Black *kanizes* and concubines.[40] In 1877, the total population of Isfahan was about fifty thousand, including some enslaved and freed Africans from Zanzibar and Ethiopia.[41]

---

36 Toledano, *Slavery and Abolition*; Hadjia Georjee Kastanti of Hodeida to William Marcus Goghlan, 25 Rabi' al-Awwal 1272 [5 December 1855], BL, L/PS/5/486; Ochsenwald, "Muslim-European Conflict."
37 Toledano, "Expectations and Realities."
38 Toledano, *Slavery and Abolition*; Mitchell, *Rule of Experts*.
39 Male slaves.
40 Sa'dvandian and Ettehadieh, *Amar-i dar al-khalafa-yi Tehran*, 347; Ettehadieh, "Social Condition of Women," 82.
41 Ebrahim Khan, *Jughrafiya-yi Isfahan*, 65, 122; Malcolm, *Sketches of Persia*, 1:19. See the marriage contract of the Black Almas and Kokab Khanum, 22 Rajab 1311 [29 January 1894], 296012411, SAM, Tehran; the report to the Iranian government about Jamila,

Until the end of the Qajar period, the religious capital and centre of Shi'i leadership was located in Ottoman-controlled Iraq at Najaf, close to the shrine of 'Ali.[42] The Iranian Shi'i 'ulama' (or mujtahids)[43] used their religious and political leadership not only to deliver judicial opinion through fatwas and decrees, but also to direct mass movements against the government and foreign interventions in Iran. This position of authority meant that both the Qajar kings and the British deferred to the opinion of 'ulama' on matters of slavery and abolitionism and relied on them to issue fatwas banning the slave trade.[44]

Equality, freedom and justice, and parliamentary government were established in Iran with the opening of the Majles-i Shura-yi Melli (National Consultative Assembly) in 1906. One of the earliest topics of discussion was the banning of slavery.[45] Support came from the Shi'i 'ulama' of southern Iran, who opposed slavery and, in particular, the enslavement of Muslim Iranians who had been kidnapped and shipped to the neighbouring Arab countries.[46] Another vocal supporter was the supreme mujtahid and political leader of the Mashrutiyat (Constitution), Sayyid Muhammad Tabataba'i. He expressed his thoughts in a letter to the shah:

> Last year [government officials] took the daughters of Quchan in lieu of three rays [35.61 kilograms] of wheat tax that [the peasants] did not have, then sold them for a high price to Turkmen and Armenians in 'Ishqabad ... [The establishment of a] *majles-i 'adalat* [parliament of justice] or a council composed of [representatives of] all social groups of people where the shah and beggar are equal could bring justice for the people.[47]

The anti-slavery discourse continued in Parliament until the end of the Qajar period, culminating in Reza Shah Pahlavi's 1929 bill to abolish

---

4 Dhu al-Hijja 1328 [7 December 1910], Q1328.3.1.49, VUK; and Del Afrooz, freedom letter, 7 Jumada al-Thani 1332 [3 May 1914], Q1332.3.3, VUK, Tehran.
42 The first Imam of the Shi'ites, and the fourth caliph of the Sunnis.
43 A mujtahid is a religious authority who may act according to his own judgment in matters relating to religious law. For further information on the position of mujtahids in Iran, see Tabari, "The Role of the Clergy."
44 Justin Sheil to Lord Palmerston, Tehran, 27 April 1847, NAUK, FO 84/692.
45 Kermani, *Tarikh-i Bidari-yi Iranian*, 3:436–43, 481.
46 Sayyid Ja'far to Hesam al-Sadat, 1300 Sh. [1921], MAAB5T403, SAM, Tehran; Ministry of the Interior, the Government of Lingah and the annexed regions, MAAB5T403, SAM, Tehran.
47 Kermani, *Tarikh-i Bidari-yi Iranian*, 2:339, 376; Malekzada, *Tarikh-i Enqelab-i Mashrutiyat-i Iran*, 2:120–2.

the institution of slavery and to emancipate all slaves in Iran.[48] The language of the new policy showed the extent to which the new regime sought to distance itself from the nuances of Islamic law and instead emulate Western epistemologies. As a consequence, Iranian society not only abandoned slavery but embraced a radically different economic system associated with industrial wage labour.

The post-emancipation era, with its transition to socio-economic autonomy and independence, was challenging for many former slaves. Local cultural and socio-economic conditions helped mitigate some of this uncertainty, allowing former slaves to exercise varying degrees of independence, which importantly influenced future patterns of Afro-Iranian community development and individual identity formation. Some former slaves could not sever their attachment to former masters. For financial reasons, they usually remained in positions of servitude. In the same way, differences in regional demographic and socio-economic conditions between the north and south of the country, and between rural and urban areas, affected the experience of freedom for former slaves. In the south, where agriculture, small-scale plantations, and fishing were concentrated, diasporic kinship ties became an important social bond,[49] while in the more urbanized northern regions, many who remained dependent on domestic service were socially linked to their former masters' networks. The experience of post-emancipation varied for former slaves at both the individual and community levels, as well as through the profound impact brought by secularization and Western-style modernization associated with the booming oil industry in the early twentieth century.

The Importance of Mahboob's Autobiography

Autobiographies are a gold mine for authors, and an opportunity for readers to be taken deep into an ocean of secrets. Slave narratives are especially rich treasures. Not only are they an important source of data for understanding the conditions and circumstances under which the institution of slavery existed but they also provide rarely seen glimpses into the lives of those enslaved. As historical documents, they give voice

---

48 Parliament correspondence, Majles, 19 Jumada al-Thani 1325 [30 July 1907];
   Parliament correspondence, Majles, 13 Rabi' al-Awwal 1325 [26 April 1907];
   Parliament correspondence, Majles, 6 Muharram 1325 [19 February 1907];
   Parliament correspondence, Majles, Rabi' al-Thani 1326 [May 1908]; Ministry of the Interior, 290/11/384/3, 25/12/1307 [16 March 1929], SAM, Tehran.
49 The term *kinship* (rather than *tribe*) is a translation of the Persian word *qabila*.

to those who are rarely heard. Slave autobiographies and narratives are rare, and almost non-existent in Iran.⁵⁰ The major challenge was that few enslaved people who crossed from Africa to the Middle East were literate and most had no access to education. What narratives exist are usually oral accounts transcribed by authorities dealing with questions of slavery and the slave trade. Often the narratives are related to the history of the Indian Ocean.⁵¹ In the United States, literacy rates were higher among slaves and former slaves because many Africans who were enslaved by the Europeans were Muslim and literate since Islam emphasizes literacy and education.⁵² The enslaved people in the New World already knew Arabic and they, themselves, wrote their autobiographies, sometimes with help from abolitionists. These autobiographies were published and brought the authors a measure of fame.⁵³ Although slave narratives were written by individuals based on their personal experiences and each held a uniqueness, they shared patterns and traits collectively of sameness.⁵⁴ While many were short, longer African American autobiographies include that of Frederick Douglass, who not only escaped slavery in Maryland but himself became an influential abolitionist. He wrote three versions of his autobiography describing the abolitionist struggle.⁵⁵

---

50 Mirzai has documented a series of slave narratives in chapter 8 ("Emancipation") of *A History of Slavery*.
51 Van Rossum et al., *Testimonies of Enslavement*.
52 Diouf, *Servants of Allah*.
53 Blassingame, *Slave Testimony*.
54 For example, Omar ibn Said (1770–1863), a Muslim scholar from Senegal in West Africa, was enslaved in 1807, sold to Europeans, and taken to Charleston, South Carolina, and wrote many texts including his autobiography in Arabic. See Omar ibn Said, *A Muslim American Slave*; Olney, "'I Was Born.'" Olney, a leading authority on African American slave narratives, shows that many slave autobiographies, narratives, and memoirs start off with the affirmation "I was born." He lists other slave narrative characteristics such as the use of poetic statements, a brief family account, reference to Christian slaveholders, descriptions of food and clothing given to slaves, and the type of work required of slaves, which, interestingly, can also be found in Mahboob's autobiography. Another common feature in African American slave narratives is reserving the first name as a sign of identity continuity but taking a new family name to reflect a new social identity of the free person. Mahboob, however, was given new first names several times, starting with his journey from Africa, and his last name was chosen by himself to reflect the place he was originally from.
55 Lindsay and Sweet, *Biography*; Douglass, *The Life of Frederick Douglass*; Douglass, *My Bondage and My Freedom*; Douglass, *Life and Times*.

Many African Americans, like Mahommah Gardo Baquaqua, were forced to undergo several identity transformations. He was born a Muslim in Benin, and enslaved and taken to Brazil, where he was resold. Later, he fled jail in New York and went to Canada. Here, in 1854, he wrote his autobiography with the help of an abolitionist editor, Samuel Moore, and converted to Christianity.[56] Born an Igbo, Archibald Monteath was enslaved as a boy and brought to Jamaica in 1802. He purchased his freedom after becoming active in the Moravian Church.[57] Similarly, Adrian Atiman was sold into slavery while still a boy living on the Niger River near Timbuktu. He was taken across the Sahara and redeemed by the White Fathers in transit to North Africa. He was baptized, educated, and trained as a doctor in Malta. He returned to Africa, settling in western Tanganyika, before writing his autobiography.[58] Mahboob's experience is not unlike that of Adrian insofar as both were enslaved as children, purchased by religious people, and converted. In the Americas, these memoirs have helped shape the development of a prominent and influential literary genre. By contrast, few memoirs are in the Middle Eastern repertoire beyond a small collection of slave narratives.[59]

The autobiography translated here is a rare example, but its importance is underlined by it being the only African slave narrative written in Iran and one that has not yet been published in any language. Its author was the African-born enslaved Mahboob Qirvanian, who lived in three different cultural, social, and political settings: Africa, the Arab regions under the Ottoman Empire, and Iran. It is a literary legacy and eyewitness account that narrates the compelling personal story of struggle and resilience, and of physical and emotional suffering. It is a tragic story of enslavement and separation. The manuscript traces Mahboob's life from his North African childhood, to the dreadful journey through Africa and the Ottoman Empire, and to eventual freedom in Iran. The author reveals the horrors of slavery and its injustices, as well as his personal transformation in Iran, and offers unique insights into the political upheavals that shook Iran in the early decades of the twentieth century. The autobiography highlights the importance of

---

56 Law and Lovejoy, *Mahommah Gardo Baquaqua*; Lovejoy and Bezerra, *Mahommah Gardo Baquaqua*.
57 Costanzo, "Archibald Monteith"; Warner-Lewis, *Archibald Monteath*.
58 Fouquer, *Le Docteur Adrien Atiman*.
59 See, for example, Toledano, *As If Silent and Absent*; Troutt Powell, *Tell This in My Memory*; Olney, "'I Was Born'"; Alpers and Hopper, "Speaking for Themselves?"; Lee, "Half the Household Was African."

studying the history of the slave trade as well as studying the legacy of slavery and its contribution to the emergence of new societies in the Middle East.

Autobiographies were a popular literary genre in Iran during the nineteenth and twentieth centuries; indeed, during the Qajar period, the elites and intellectuals commonly wrote personal memoirs. Some of these autobiographies provided information about the slave trade and slavery in the context of social change. For example, General Hassan Arfa (1895–1984), who was an army officer, wrote his memoirs about military, political, and social changes in Iran, and the enslavement of many Iranians by Turkmen.[60] Also, the high-ranking general Esma'il Khan Mirpanjeh, who was enslaved by the Turkmen in 1853 and fled a decade later, wrote his memoirs about the enslavement of Iranians by Turkmen.[61] But, it was highly unusual for former slaves to do so because the majority were illiterate or undereducated. It is remarkable that Mahboob's account was written at all. For many years he served religious scholars known as the 'ulama',[62] who were highly educated, as they attended madrasa or traditional and religious schools, and were knowledgeable in Islamic law and science, and were also political activists. They wrote books in every era in accordance with the needs of the society. Undoubtedly, Mahboob was influenced by the 'ulama', who encouraged him to write down his thoughts, which paved a way for writing his autobiography later on. That it was preserved by his family is perhaps not entirely surprising because he transitioned from being a slave to becoming an eminent, educated, religious, and reputable man, who enjoyed close contact with dignitaries and high-ranking political and religious figures of the day. He and his children understood the importance of sharing his story.[63] Mahboob used the manuscript to explain how his journey from enslavement to freedom and his personal experiences shaped his awareness of self and let him transform his status and identity from that of chattel to someone with autonomous self-determination.

Mahboob wrote the autobiography to describe his experiences and explain the trauma of his life aided by words and literature. His manuscript became a healing project through which the trauma of slavery was projected and it created a sense of relief. Writing was a tool for

---

60 Arfa, *Under Five Shahs*.
61 Mirpanjeh, *Khaterat-i esarat*.
62 The term "'ulama'" is an Arabic word derived from *'ilm* or knowledge.
63 The manuscript was brought to my attention by Babak, the grandson of Mahboob.

self-expression used to cope with pain in the healing process. Writing the autobiography had a therapeutic effect on Mahboob that empowered and enabled him to manage stressful emotions of the past and find a path to recovery. Mahboob wrote the autobiography when he was a free and self-autonomous person. He opened a window for readers to get a glimpse of the hardships of his life and the destruction of the bonds between him and his father, mother, and siblings. As an ex-slave, Mahboob used writing, poems, and rhetoric in a powerful way to examine his painful life as he gained full citizenship status and constructed a new identity. Mahboob wrote the autobiography to narrate his transition from slavery to freedom and then to equality in a new society. Writing was employed as a tool to claim his individual and mental freedom and to explain his identity transformations in Africa, the Ottoman Empire, and Iran. The autobiography worked as a therapeutic intervention and gave voice to unspeakable memories and sufferings of Mahboob. He provided guidance, a path of life, and encouragement for his family and readers.

As an expression of identity transformation, Mahboob's autobiography provides a fascinating insight into the mind of an enslaved African who became a free, middle-class citizen of Iran. Descriptions of enslavement, transportation, slave markets, treatment of slaves, forced migration, ethnic identity formation, displacement, and trauma are all found here. A central thread to the narrative is Mahboob's deliberate, self-conscious mapping of his journey of self-determination and identity. For him it was an iterative step-by-step process of interactions with the people he met and the experiences he had along the way. Not only was his name changed several times, but he was also forced to convert from one religion to another, to learn new languages, to subject himself to treatments, to work and live in different places, all according to the culture and religious mores of his masters and their economic circumstances. Mahboob's life story is an exemplar of African-Arab-Iranian identity transformation from bondage to freedom. The conversion from Sunni to Shi'i Islam was among the most important transitions in his life because it allowed him to adopt a new identity and it provided the foundation for a renewed ideological transformation from his past to a new present. The fluidity of identity transformation is also apparent in the way geographical displacement yielded new opportunities, akin to an eco-biography. The memoir also chronicles how natural settings and environments affected his personal journey for his identity.

Identity transformation was conceptualized in this narrative as a trajectory to explore different societal influences. Mahboob staged the relationship of self and other, as well as slave and master, to illustrate how his personal life was shaped within larger cultural, historical, and political contexts. His long journey, from Africa to Ottoman Arabia (Saudi Arabia), to Ottoman Iraq, and ultimately to Iran, occurred during an important period of political transformation in the Ottoman Empire and at the end of the Qajar and the early Pahlavi dynasties in Iran. Mahboob's autobiography transports the reader back to Middle Eastern societies at the end of the nineteenth century and in the early years of the twentieth. He described traditional Middle Eastern societies only just being exposed to the forces of secularization and modernization.

Mahboob extensively uses poetry, Qur'anic verses, metaphors, descriptive words, and analogies. His steadfast faith is an underlying theme; imploring divine help to deal with his many challenges, from separation and frequent despair to the seemingly endless journeys and unclear future. Even though he relies on first-person pronouns, he seeks to avoid the subjectivity inherent among many autobiographies by recounting events in his life and around him as objectively as possible. Consequently, it is possible to verify many of the places he travelled to, the people he interacted with, and the sociopolitical events that affected him.

Mahboob wrote in a lined notebook and often included marginal notes. The old Persian handwriting known as nastaliq is a beautiful script but can be difficult to read given its precise nature and the fading of the ink over time. Although the notebook was torn apart after he died, Mahboob's son Ahmad bound the remaining pages and preserved it. Decades later, this manuscript has become very fragile.

Challenges associated with interpretation of the manuscript include inconsistencies in dating based on the commonly used lunar calendar, that is, the Hijri or Islamic calendar, and the misnumbering of some pages. Confirming the early stages of Mahboob's journey through Africa and the Ottoman Empire has been difficult as some place names cannot be found on historic or contemporary maps. Likely, Mahboob could not recall details of his earlier travels or his later memories. His journey in Iran is easier to trace, as the street names in Tehran's old quarters and neighbourhoods can be identified. He relied on traditional units of measure for length, weight, and distance, and measured time by reference to the astronomical movement of the sun, moon, and stars. Some literary expressions and terminology are no longer used in modern Iran. Similarly, many occupations mentioned no longer exist, nor do modes of transportation that relied on convoys of pack animals and caravans. Despite his life's challenges, Mahboob maintained a sense of humour.

The information in the autobiography is condensed with important events and influential political and religious figures mentioned in passing without reference to historical or social contexts. However, the work

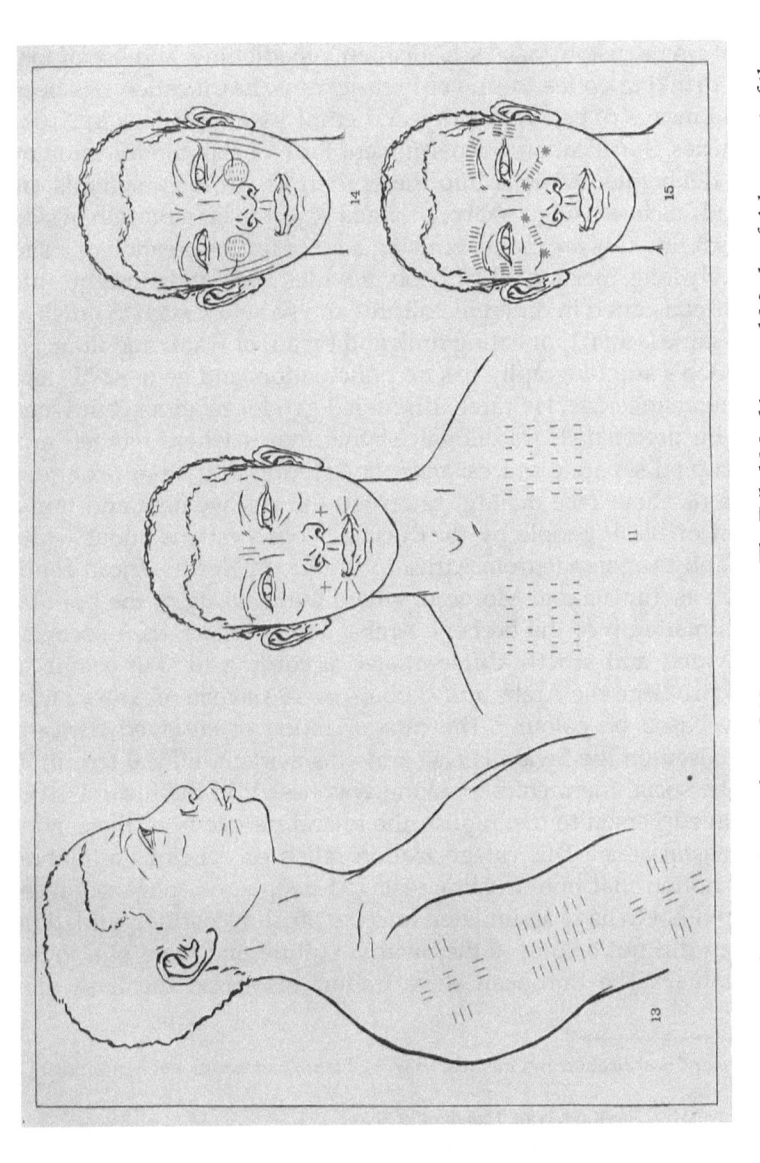

Figure 1. Scarification. Plate iv from C.H. Armitage, *The Tribal Markings and Marks of Adornment of the Natives of the Northern Territories of the Gold Coast Colony* (London: Harrison and Sons, 1924).

is rich with information about the cultural and social lives of ordinary people, their day-to-day lives, customs, and attitudes, and references to local topography and to the economic and political conditions of the era. Superstitions and traditional medicine are described, including the rituals of circumcision, facial scarification, bloodletting, and use of tonics, like drinking coffee to prevent seasickness. Scarification has been used as a means of belief, identity, and ethnicity expressions in Africa for centuries. Scarification is a permanent form of skin modification by making deliberate incisions into the epidermis. Various methods are employed, such as using a sharp, pronged object to lift a portion of skin into which fine cuts are made, or using a razor for the creation of a single, usually long, incision.[64] Mahboob provides fascinating insights into the foods consumed in different cultures and societies, such as crushed sweet sesame (*sekda*),[65] or eating milk and bread, or water and flour.

Mahboob's autobiography has no punctuation, and he used "I" and "we" interchangeably. He rarely discussed gender relations, but when he did, he deferred to traditional Islamic mores where women and men occupied separate spaces: *andarun* (interior) and *birun* (exterior). Discussions about race mainly concerned the enslavement and transportation of Black people by the Nasara,[66] observations about white people, and the passage from Africa to Arabia. In North African countries such as Tunisia and Morocco, where the majority of the population was made up of the Berbers, Arabs, and Africans, their societies were divided and strictly differentiated according to skin colour in order to privilege the Arabs and Berbers, so enslavement was a racial ideology based on colour.[67] The categorization of enslaved Africans was practised on the Swahili coast and was evident in local terminologies. The social hierarchical ranking was based on the birthplace of the enslaved person to distinguish the inland people from those born in the coastal areas. This categorization relied on religious affiliation and the notion that non-Muslim enslaved people, or "pagans," were considered not to have assimilated into the Muslim coastal population; thus, they did not belong to the Swahili culture and were of a lower social status.[68] The European slave traders also used the term *cafre*

---

64 See Keefer, "Scarification and Identity," 539. Mahboob had traditional African scars on his face.
65 Probably halva. See Raghavan, *Handbook of Spices*, 171.
66 The term "Nasara" was used by Mahboob in his autobiography to refer to the people who first captured and enslaved him in Africa.
67 El Hamel, *Black Morocco*, 9–11.
68 McMahon, *Slavery and Emancipation*, 12; Kresse, "The Uses of History," 228. For the classification of enslaved people on the Swahili coast, see Glassman, *Feasts and Riot*, 85–90.

(unbeliever) to categorize Africans.[69] In the Arab world, the environmental conditions required the indigenous Arabs, who were prone to the infectious diseases, to employ sub-Saharan Africans in the moist agricultural lowlands because they had immunity against malaria due to Duffy negativity and haemoglobin S.[70] Similarly, the Ethiopians were used in non-agricultural sectors because of their susceptibility to the infectious diseases. Therefore, the physical and health suitability of different ethnic groups of enslaved Africans, and their preferential use in specific economic sectors, was perceived and interpreted as racial categorization:

> The servile African agriculturalists were identified simply as "Negroes," a blanket term for sub-Saharan Africans. Slaves of Abyssinian (Galla) origin, however, were rarely if ever employed as agriculturalists according to the literature. To a certain degree, this apparent preference for sub-Saharan African slaves as farmers was a function of their price: male Abyssinian slaves were approximately 30–50 percent more expensive than male sub-Saharan African slaves during the nineteenth century. Not surprisingly, ownership of such expensive slaves brought higher status to their owner, and Arabian Peninsula Arabs usually showed off these slaves by assigning them to be domestic servants, bodyguards, or soldiers.[71]

The sub-Saharan Africans possessed a degree of resistance to oasis fevers and malaria. For this reason, "Nubian" slaves of sub-Saharan Africa had a reputation for hard work and physical strength because of their resistance to diseases compared to slaves of Abyssinian "Galla" origin. Similarly, Muhammad Ali, the Egyptian ruler, recruited African soldiers from the plain part of Sudan due to their resistance to malaria.[72]

Various factors determined the classifications, employment, demand, and preference pattern of slaves in the Middle East, including prejudice, reputation, socio-economic functions, and religious attributions. For example, the Oromo people, the nomadic pastoralists in Ethiopia and northern Kenya, were not a preferable ethnic group among the nomads of Taima in Saudi Arabia because of their reputation for being expensive and physically weak.[73] In contrast, the enslaved Oromos were considered to be faithful and kind. For example, they were valued

---

69 Prestholdt, "Portuguese Conceptual Categories," 56.
70 Reilly, *Slavery*, 104.
71 Reilly, 117.
72 Reilly, 117.
73 Doughty, *Travels in Arabia Deserta*, 1:553.

for their strength, intelligence, and height, and were employed as the bodyguards of the rulers in Mecca, Medina, and Boraida.[74] Also, while there were fewer enslaved Sudanese and Ethiopians in Ras al-Khaimah, they were valued in Bahrain as they were excellent soldiers.[75] In nineteenth-century Iran the geographical, religious, socio-economic, and cultural background of enslaved peoples influenced their status.

Conscious of his own racial origins, Mahboob felt a sense of belonging, bondage, and security within the African community. While in Africa and Arabia, he made a clear distinction between the status of slaves and free people when discussing his own experience of resale. Even so, he did not identify specifically when his status changed from slave to free person but characterized it as a gradual transition, although it occurred when he was purchased by the prominent Iranian mujtahids and then in Iran, where he was first employed as a domestic servant and later, ultimately, as a governmental bureaucrat. This important transition from bondage to freedom is not something Mahboob related to race or skin colour but, instead, one that evolved in the context of larger sociopolitical events and financial need. Enslaved people were freed on auspicious occasions, such as weddings, or as an act of atonement based on Iranian tradition. Islamic law also provided conditions to free enslaved people through the payment of zakat, or alms, and granted them rights to marry and ask for freedom.[76] The religious injunctions and customary law facilitated not only the emancipation of slaves but also their assimilation into society. Until the early twentieth century, however, implementing emancipation was up to individual citizens and usually by reference to religious injunctions.[77] These systems of

---

74 Sulivan, *Dhow Chasing*, 177–9.
75 Major David Wilson to the government, 28 January 1831, FO 84/426, NAUK, extract.
76 According to the shari'a, zakat, or alms, were used in eight situations, one of which is the payment of ransom to free enslaved people. See Qur'an 9:60.
77 See Qur'an 24:33; Schacht, *An Introduction to Islamic Law*, 127; Husayni, *Bardegi az didgah-i Islam*, 28. There are several Qur'anic rules in Islamic law through which the liberation of enslaved people is obligatory and the government's responsibility is to implement them (see Qur'an 4:92, 5:89, 58:3); for instance, as religious expiation (*kaffara*) for not fulfilling a Ramadan fast, not acting on undertaken vows (the law of *sadaqa*), if owned by an unmarriageable relative or *mahram* (the law of *tamalluk arham*), an enslaved female who gives birth to the child of her master (the *umm walad*), or after the death of her master (the law of *istilad*). Also, enslaved people had the right to manumit themselves through work (the law of *mukataba*, Qur'an 24:33). See further, Schacht, *An Introduction to Islamic Law*, 129; Hamidullah, *Introduction to Islam*, 127; Husayni, *Bardegi az didgah-i Islam*, 39–43; McDow, "Deeds of Freed Slaves"; Zdanowski, *Slavery and Manumission*, 65.

liberation were also practised in other Middle Eastern countries and those of the Indian Ocean.

According to Gwyn Campbell, the paradigm found among many Indian Ocean societies (contrary to those found in the Atlantic Ocean) stressed the integration and assimilation of enslaved people into society through marriage and manumission and was enhanced by the absence of racial prejudice in Islamic law.[78] In some cases the master-slave bondage evolved into clientage after freedom.[79] Mahboob's notion of his own identity and race was fluid and, as he was transferred from one place to another en route from Africa to Iran, he adjusted to a new setting. His sense of group attachment and belonging was continuously changing. His position and treatment in the new ideological context shaped how he viewed himself and defined the insiders/outsiders and the privileged/unprivileged.

Enslaved Africans experienced different conditions in Iran compared to their kinsmen in the Americas and Europe. Ehud Toledano described the nature of slavery in the Middle East as follows: "Enslavement in non-Atlantic societies was, by and large, more female-dominated, more domestic and less agricultural, more integrative and less exclusionist, and more receptive to gradualist emancipation than to one-step abolition than was its Atlantic counterpart."[80] The differences between Middle Eastern and Atlantic slavery systems were clearly identifiable within economic and socio-religious contexts. Atlantic slavery was an intercontinental system that connected Africa, the New World, and Europe, relying on labour, land, and capital.[81] Because the Middle Eastern societies did not suffer from labour shortages, the surplus of agricultural peasantry resulted in the employment of most enslaved Africans in domestic and service sectors.[82]

The interdisciplinary "asymmetric dependency" concept provides a framework based on which the dynamic processes and multifaceted relations of the slavery system can be analysed in the context of comparative slavery.[83] This concept lets slavery scholarship develop a new method of study based on the connection of all human experiences.

---

78 Campbell, "Female Bondage," 56. See also Erdem, *Slavery in the Ottoman Empire*, 152–84.
79 Schacht, *An Introduction to Islamic Law*, 130.
80 Toledano, "Expectations and Realities," 391.
81 Drescher, *Capitalism and Antislavery*, 5.
82 Segal, *Islam's Black Slaves*, 4; Issawi, *Economic History of Iran*, 3. McNeill, *Europe's Steppe Frontier*, 28. See also Troutt Powell, "Will That Subaltern Ever Speak?," 253.
83 Conermann et al., "Introduction"; Winnebeck et al., "Asymmetrical Dependency."

Conversion can be seen as one shared element within the global slavery context. For both female and male slaves, and even manumitted slaves, conversion to Islam in Iran and the Ottoman Empire provided status, as we see with the case of a manumitted Russian female slave in Jerusalem, the widow of a Greek Orthodox, who chose to convert to Islam for protection.[84] The enslavement of people shares characteristics and structural forms of ownership in the context of global enslavement. Despite shared traits, it is imperative to consider that a unique form of slavery evolves through the interrelationships of local historical, socio-economic, and cultural divergences. This individual hierarchical variation is manifested in the autobiography of Mahboob, who had varied relations with his masters in Africa, the Ottoman Arab countries, and Iran. The asymmetric dependency concept also applies to the experiences of Mahboob in the scope of bondage in the extended geographical, cultural, economic, and social areas that formed his unified character.

The examination of Persian primary documents and sources proves the absence of the racial classification of enslaved Africans; however, sources written by Europeans refer to race and racial affiliation in Iran, which is largely due to their orientalist perception. They claim a correlation between the value and the incorporation of enslaved Africans with race and physical attributions into different socio-economic sectors of Iran.[85] This racial distinction is owing to the influence of the race debates in Western countries that shaped their notion of Middle Eastern slavery. It is important to emphasize that the slave trade in the Atlantic was characterized according to race, whereas Iran, historically, has been home to many ethnic and racial groups, where ethnic identity was associated with culture, social status, class, and geographic affiliations rather than race, colour, and biological variations. For example, various ethnic, racial, and religious groups of Iranian and non-Iranian peoples, including Africans, Turkmen, Kurds, Turks, Azeris, Shirazis, Qazvinis, Isfahanis, Georgians, Armenians, and Circassians were enslaved.[86] In this heterogeneous Iranian society the classification of slaves was not fixed and it provided opportunity for enslaved people of all racial backgrounds to achieve varying degrees of social mobility as seen in the post-emancipation period. The life of Mahboob was not

---

84 Witzenrath, "An Arab in Moscow."
85 See, for example, Wills, *Persia as It Is*, 75–6.
86 The order purchase of three enslaved Turkmen women for Naser al-Din Shah, 1286 [1869], Tehran, 295.2155 and 295/709/1, SAM, Tehran.

exceptional and it perfectly illustrates the nature of Iranian slavery in which skin colour and race did not impede the transition and elevation of the status of the enslaved people. Economics, social status, and culture provided conditions for enslavement, thus all racial and ethnic groups were vulnerable to slavery.

The first word in the autobiography is the name of Mahboob's father, "Rashdan," which is engraved on his gravestone: "Hajj Mahboob, *valad-i* [the son of] Rashdan." Mahboob traces his ancestors to Adam, the first man and the father of all humankind. The story of how humankind was created and began its earthly existence is narrated with some variations in Judaism, Christianity, and Islam, though these three monotheistic religions all agree that Adam was created by God. Mahboob was a devout and pious Muslim who had studied the Qur'an, the holy book of Muslims, under the great Shi'i scholars of Islam. He was familiar with the Qur'anic stories and applied them to his own life story. Beginning with genealogy is traditional in Middle Eastern cultures to ensure knowledge of one's lineage is preserved; however, verifying all the names Mahboob mapped out in this genealogy has not been possible. The last page of the autobiography relates to the data about his journey from Qom to Tehran on 10 September 1921. The manuscript ends abruptly here, leaving us to wonder if he intended subsequent chapters.

Historical Context

Africa

ENSLAVEMENT (TUNISIA)

Tunisia was a French protectorate when Mahboob was born circa 1894 in a coastal village near Sousse.[87] His father's family were wealthy land and livestock owners who hailed from the important Islamic centre Kairouan, where Rashdan was the tribal chief.[88] Mahboob's maternal ancestors were Indian Buddhists. They may have been gypsies, known

---

87 Also known as Ifriqiya, Tunisia was ruled by the Ottoman Empire from the sixteenth to the nineteenth centuries until the country was occupied by the French, in 1881, who remained until independence in 1956; Clancy-Smith, *Rebel and Saint*. On the continuation of the slave trade even after its abolition in Tunisia, see Ibn Abi Diyaf, *Ithaf Ahl al-Zaman*; Mrad Dali, "From Forgetting to Remembrance"; Medici, "Chiudere la porta della schiavitù," 179; Montana, *Abolition of Slavery*; Oualdi, *Un esclave entre deux empires*; Allen, *European Slave Trading*.
88 For information on the social structure of Tunisia, see Green, *Tunisian Ulama*.

as Dom, who immigrated to Tunisia from South Asia in Byzantine times. Mahboob's son Mansour recalled that his father had

> belonged to a tribe in Kairouan, in Sudan. Mahboob's father was the chief of the tribe and a rich person. Sudan was in Africa. Another tribe attacked their village and they fled but, eventually, were enslaved. Mahboob was a child. He had several brothers and sisters in Sudan. They all were separated and never saw each other again.[89]

The name "Sudan" was used to refer to the "Bilad al-Sudan," an Arabic term meaning "the land of Black people." Tunisians and the French referred to slaves in Tunisia as Sudanese slaves, and believed they originated from Sudan, the "French Sudan," or the city-states of Hausa and Kanem-Bornu in Niger, Mali, and Chad, which developed the trans-Saharan slave trade with North Africa.[90]

The eight-year-old Mahboob, his family, and the entire village were enslaved in 1902. He referred to his captors as "Nasara,"[91] white people and infidels, a term in the Qur'an that refers to Christians, but also one generically used by the Arabs to refer to those who followed the prophet Jesus. It is not clear exactly who his captors were.[92] The institution of slavery was abolished in Tunisia by Ahmed Bay on 23 January 1846, but the illegal slave trade continued in Tunisia and, since the traffic was illegal, the information did not appear in the consular reports.[93] There were also a few cases of the French who were secretly involved in illegal slave trafficking such as Resident-General Justin Massicault, who received a slave girl in 1887.[94]

Mahboob wrote that the several hundred slavers and invaders spoke a language he could not understand. Looting and setting fire to the houses, they chased the villagers into the mountains or caves, lit fires, and smoked out their captives with onion skins and dried pepper.

---

89 From the author's interview with Mahboob's son Mansour, who has since passed away. He shared many stories about his father that had been narrated by his mother, Ma'someh.
90 Hamli, "Legal Wrangles."
91 Most likely referring to Europeans.
92 Hamli, "Legal Wrangles."
93 Gordon, *Slavery in the Arab World*, 157.
94 Hamli, "Legal Wrangles," 422, 424. For a discussion on the use of post-abolition compulsory forms of labour, indenture and forced labour, and the exploitative *khammesat* system of serfdom by the French colonial settlers in Tunisia during the French protectorate, see Mrad Dali, "From Forgetting to Remembrance." For a discussion on the *corvée* system of unpaid labour imposed by the French colonial government, see Frith and Hodgson, "Slavery and Its Legacies."

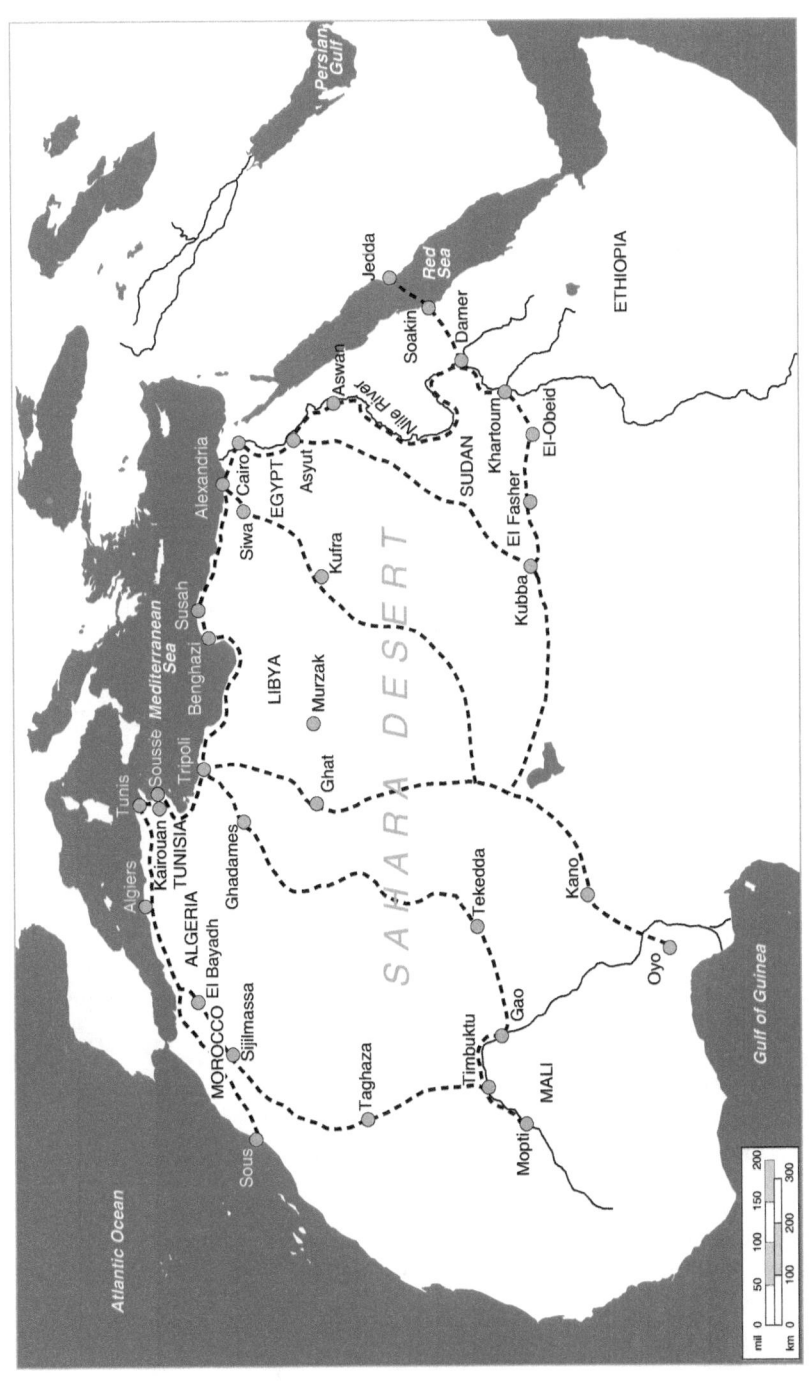

Map 1. Trans-Saharan trade routes

"Most people of the city ran away and some even left their children behind and fled." Mahboob observed the military superiority of the "Nasara" and their use of firearms to help to dominate the "Sudan" and to plunder, enslave, and exploit their commerce. Interestingly, he was aware of the British policy against the slave trade and described that, when he was enslaved, "it was when Britain had yet not dominated Africa, which was not civilized yet." As an African, he believed if the British had been present, his enslavement could have been prevented.[95]

FORCED MIGRATION: JOURNEY FROM AFRICA TO THE MIDDLE EAST

Mahboob's family members and clan were torn apart and sold separately. He himself was sold and relocated several times before arriving in Iran via Ottoman Arabia.[96] His owners were rulers, chiefs, and merchants, who first purchased him as a playmate for their children. He recalled with great anguish the long journey, moving from one place to another and walking in harsh conditions along unsafe roads, through hot, barren deserts and mountains. Mahboob provided a vivid picture and description of the horrors of the slave trade and the treatment of the slaves in Africa. He described the physical hardships and emotional pains of the middle passage, and the forced journey of a caravan of chained enslaved Africans being taken to market. Names of locations and towns along the road reveal that the slavers took the slaves along the infamous North African trans-Saharan camel caravan route of the "Darb al-Arbaʿin" (Forty Days' Road), which passes to the Nilotic Sudan from Egypt.[97]

Walking in extremes of blisteringly hot summers and frigid deserts, many slaves died en route to the Red Sea ports where they were bound for the Arabian Peninsula. Mahboob described that he and his fellow slaves had to walk with heavy, forked pieces of wood around their necks and with their legs chained, traversing barefoot across the scalding desert sand, with ten to twenty people joined by rope. Mahboob recalled that

> ten to twenty Black people [were tied] with two-branched woods around their necks. Each wood weighed ten to twenty *mann*, which one person had to lift and walk with. Some people had their hands cuffed around

---

95 Mrad Dali, "From Slavery to Servitude"; Erdem, *Slavery in the Ottoman Empire*.
96 Mrad Dali, "From Forgetting to Remembrance"; Toledano, *Slavery and Abolition*; Peirce, *A Spectrum of Unfreedom*.
97 Shaw, "Darb al Arba'in"; Roe, "The Old *Darb al Arbein*"; La Rue, "Khabir 'Ali"; Walz, *Trade*.

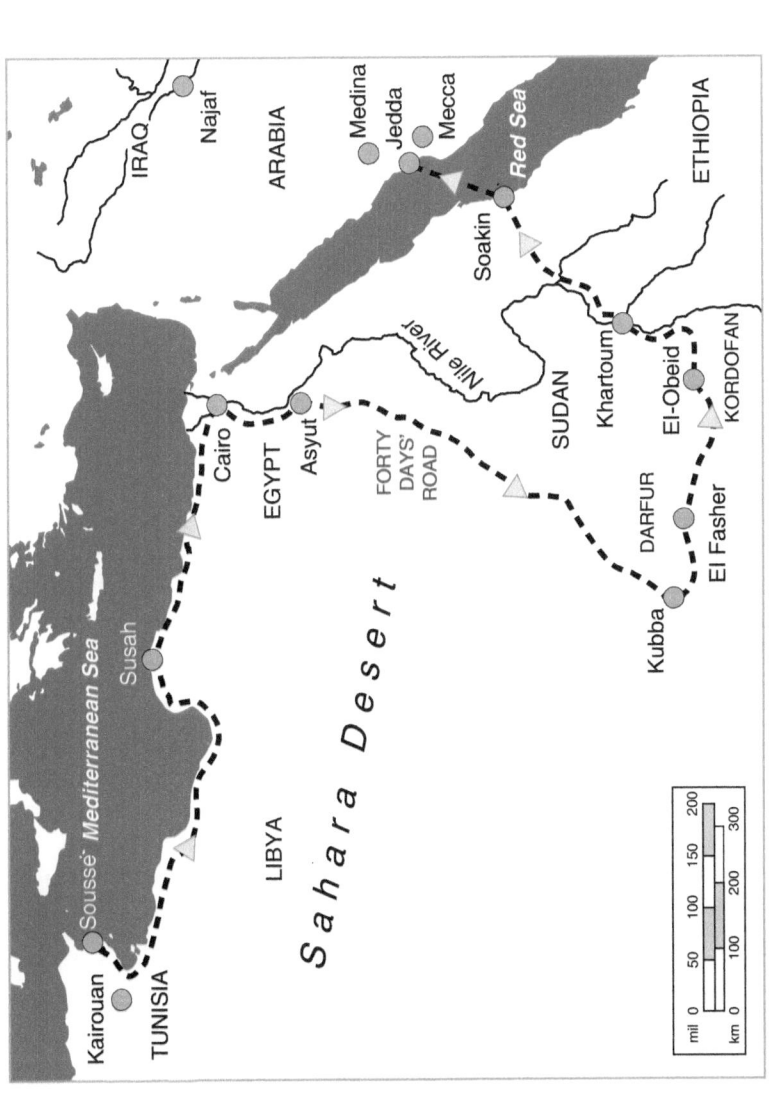

Map 2. Mahboob's trail in North Africa, 1903

the back of their necks. Some of the men were tied up by a two-branched wood and were tied around the neck to another man.

Only women and children were not tied up, but all were expected to walk along in parallel lines: "We, the children, were naked, but the adults, including the women and men, only had a small canvas or animal skin to cover their private parts." The slavers inspected "all our bodies, head-to-toe: mouth, underarms, hands, feet, and private parts," separating the healthy from the sick. He described the hunger, thirst, fatigue, disease, and despair of the enslaved people and their seemingly endless march through the vast desert. There were stories of enslaved people who perished along the way or were buried alive. Food consisted merely of flour and water. Despite the challenges, Mahboob described the local customs he encountered in North and East Africa, such as the circumcision of boys and girls, and the music, dance, and warfare. In particular, he observed how music, singing, and dancing were integrated into African cultures, and described the instruments used in the entertainment, including bugles, trumpets, and large timbals.

In Saljmattyah, Mahboob was sold to the ruler of the town and given his first new name: "Zydagan."[98] After a while, he was transferred to the home of a local minister, who also owned a female slave (*kaniz*). Still only a child himself, it was Mahboob's responsibility to look after their child; he was flogged when he disobeyed.

Mahboob wrote that Saljmattyah was a prosperous town with no poverty. Although its exact location is not clear, it was located on an island, which means it had to have been in the Nile River, probably north of the junction of the White and Blue Nile.[99] Everyone owned property and, rather than using money, goods were exchanged or shared. Everyone helped each other plant, harvest, and hunt. Clothes were made of canvas or animal skins. He described the circumcision of boys and girls: "It is the custom in this country that every year, they circumcised both

---

98 Zydagan is derived from Zayd, the name of the godson of the Prophet Muhammad. Zayd was purchased by the Prophet, freed, and then converted to Islam.

99 Paul Lovejoy commented on Mahboob's itinerary: "At the time, he was a child, and it is possible that he did not remember some locations correctly. Most likely he passed across Libya to the Nile and took the Forty Days' Road south from Asyut to Darfur, apparently branching off the trail before Darfur and going further east to El-Obeid in Kordofan. From there it is clear that he was in various places along the Niger, including at Khartoum, which is a nice fixed-point. He was on Saljmattyah island that had to be in the Nile at some point – where is not exactly clear. But from Khartoum everything is clear." Email message to author, 22 October 2024.

Figure 2. Slave trade in Africa. From Louis Figuier, *Les races humaines* (Paris: Hachette, 1872), 595, via HathiTrust, https://babel.hathitrust.org/cgi/pt?id=hvd.32044024484743&seq=639, and "A Coffle," Slavery Images, 1800s, last updated 6 June 2016, http://slaveryimages.org./database/image-result.php?objectid=24.

boys and girls in every household. They consider it a custom because it is a tradition from the old times. Mainly in the Sudan cities, they perform it on a high area or a mountain."[100] Circumcision is a custom in African societies. Female genital mutilation or clitoridectomy[101] and male circumcision[102] is practised in sub-Saharan Africa and the Arab states.[103] Despite the general prosperity, shortly after Mahboob arrived, Saljmattyah was hit by a famine that lasted until the rains came. He also described internal wars between towns and rulers in this part of Africa.

---

100 See, for example, Silverman, "Anthropology and Circumcision."
101 Clitoridectomy involves removing some or all of the clitoris.
102 Circumcision involves removing the foreskin of the penis.
103 See Mbiti, *Introduction to African Religion*, 96–101; Shell-Duncan and Hernlund, *Female "Circumcision" in Africa*; Caldwell et al., "Male and Female Circumcision in Africa"; Kouba and Muasher, "Female Circumcision in Africa"; Assaad, "Female Circumcision in Egypt"; De Wolf, "Circumcision and Initiation in Western Kenya and Eastern Uganda"; Marck, "Aspects of Male Circumcision."

Told to accompany several merchants[104] to Sous Aqsa,[105] which, according to his testimony, was between El-Obeid and the Nile River south of Khartoum, Mahboob left the town with a *kaniz* whose responsibility was to carry the large water containers. He described the frequent mistreatments inflicted on the female slave by the merchants, and remembered that he too was abused if he refused to massage them. When they arrived at Sous Aqsa, the merchants sold him, the *kaniz*, and another Black person. Here, Mahboob was taken to the ruler's palace to live in the *andarun* with the ruler's wife and servants.

Once again, Mahboob was given a new identity and name: "Zugul." He soon was asked to leave the palace with his master's shepherd. These transitions from one place to another, one house to another, were difficult for a child with no family. Because of his youth, it is not surprising that he became attached to each owner and his family and, equally, how every separation broke his heart. These departures also involved long, challenging journeys through the deserts. In a village near Sous Aqsa, Mahboob's new job was to herd the shepherd's livestock. His meals consisted of bread and milk. Soon after being invaded by a neighbouring tribe, everyone in the region around Sous Aqsa was forced to relocate to El-Obeid.[106]

Mahboob explained that "Saljmattyah is in the north of the Nuba[107] town" and that "we walked from the village of the town of Sous Aqsa that was near the south of Khartoum near the Nile River." He added that, "the distance from the town and village of Sous to the town of Lubayyiz [El-Obeid] was ten days." Even though this and other locations can be roughly approximated, it has not been possible to pinpoint with certainty the towns identified and the distances between them. We know, however, that he began his journey in his hometown in Sousse, Tunisia, before being taken to Saljmattyah and Sous Aqsa, which were towns on one of the most important trans-Saharan slave trade routes. The similarly named town of Sous or Susah is also in the Libyan Desert,

---

104 Mahboob uses the term "merchants" to refer to slave traders.
105 Mahboob wrote that "Sous Aqsa was near the south of Khartoum near the Nile River." There is a town with slightly different spellings of "Susah," "Susa," and "Soussa," in Libya, that might be the town in question, since Mahboob noted that Sous was near Nuba.
106 The closest spelling to Lubayyiz near Khartoum indicated by Mahboob is Al-Ubayyid, or El-Obeid, in Sudan. It was an important transportation hub at the junction of the caravan routes between the Nile valley and the western Sudan, as well as across the desert.
107 Nubia is a region along the Nile River that extends from the Nile River valley to the Red Sea, Khartoum, and to the Libyan Desert.

near Nuba. Mahboob identified no other place names en route except for Lubayyiz in Sudan. His journey in Africa most likely went from Sousse, Tunisia, to Saljmattyah, to Susah, Libya, before arriving in El-Obeid, Kordofan, west of Khartoum, via the Forty Days' Road (Darb al-Arbaʻin) that linked Darfur to Asyut in southern Egypt.[108] This forced migration through the interior of Africa, from north to southeast, involved caravan transportation, either by camel, horse, or on foot, and for the young boy, it was mostly the latter. Even riding on the animals was difficult: "Because of too much riding, my thighs were bruised and I could not walk. The skin on my legs had peeled off."

Despite the suffering caused by the difficult journey, Mahboob remained patient, submissive, and tolerant. At one point, the slavers pitied him, allowing him to ride on the horse and giving him cooked camel liver to eat. The many caravans he saw en route convinced him he was part of a major trade route. In El-Obeid, he lived in the harem with the other servants.[109] His new master ordered new clothes for him and gave him a gratuity. Mahboob also recalled that "since I knew the poems and verses of the land of Sudan, they liked me so much." Soon he was swapped for gifts and was taken to the home of a merchant who already had two male servants, one Black and one white. After Mahboob's arrival, came a female servant (*kaniz*); he travelled with her and the merchant's mother by ship to Khartoum.

Mahboob described the British factories and machineries in Baqaʻ near Khartoum where he encountered a mounted British official inspecting an area not far from the shore. Once his master saw the official, he ordered his servant to cover Mahboob's head with a light veil from the saddlebag. Before the official began to speak with him, the merchant told the servant to "hold this child and quickly take him home to keep him away from the sunlight." Mahboob was taken onto the ship. This strategy was commonly used by the slavers elsewhere, as on the shores of the Persian Gulf,[110] to evade British scrutiny and the risk of their slaves being confiscated as per the abolitionist policy.[111] These officials even asked female travellers to uncover themselves to ensure they were not smuggled African slaves.[112]

---

108 Solieman et al., "Reconstructing the Ancient Caravan Route."
109 Mahboob uses "servants" to refer to slaves.
110 Mirzai, *A History of Slavery*, 148, 155.
111 Sikainga, *Slaves into Workers*.
112 Robinson and Gallagher, *Africa and the Victorians*; Moore-Harell, "Slave Trade in the Sudan."

The final years of nineteenth-century Africa were characterized by European nations scrambling for territory. The British occupied Sudan in 1899, keeping the French out of the Nile valley and its waters until the country's independence in 1956. Khartoum was described as the "capital of Nuba on the coast of the Nile," with the population of about two hundred and fifty thousand Black and white people and Nasara. Mahboob's records were revealing:

> Every day, near the morning, we went to watch the British military exercise and almost all the British soldiers were Black. The city possesses high civilization, sciences, urbanization, a railroad, telegram station, and post office, which were used throughout the Sudan. It means in the newly civilized territories in the Sudan everything in the world such as trees, fruits, booty, and wealth can be found there.

The burgeoning Sudanese nationalist movement led by Muhammad ibn 'Abdullahi, known as Imam Mahdi, which began in 1881, became so popular that four years later, in 1885, the Turco-Egyptian administration was overthrown through a jihad against the infidels.[113] Mahdi sought to bring justice and equity to the world and to establish a treasury known as Bayt al-Mal in Khartoum to collect ransoms and taxes for distribution among his troops and officials.[114] Mahboob noted that

> there is a treasury house which Sultan Mabut Mahdi had built for the people of Sudan during his lifetime. Every day, the Black people would take big drums, kettledrums, bugles, trumpets, reeds, and tambourines and go to the treasury house to play, beat, and sing the Sudanese songs and verses, very respectfully.

Mahboob was repeatedly transferred from one slave owner's household to another. Sometimes he was alone and sometimes he was accompanied by other enslaved Africans. The transitions from one master to another could be unpleasant and stressful as indicated by Mahboob: "My companions and I were crying and we yelled and begged them not to give us to them, but it was useless." One day, his master took him across the Nile River from Khartoum to the home of another merchant. After a week, he was moved again with several other male and female slaves. During the journey, some of them were transferred to

---

113 Searcy, "The Sudanese Mahdi."
114 Abushouk, "Ideology versus Pragmatism."

Hadandawa merchants,[115] the nomadic and pastoral Beja people.[116] Describing this experience, he wrote: "While I was riding, I was crying and sobbing like the spring cloud." In a heartbreaking sentence he added: "My dear father, the breeze that blew now in this dangerous and frightening desert will bring my news to you that your darling child is enslaved in the hands of enemies and has no way to escape." The slave dealers evidently had well-established networks and systems for trading slaves profitably. They were armed and well-equipped. Mahboob described that, further along, more Hadandawa slave dealers carrying enslaved Africans joined their caravan and that the number of slaves continued to increase. Heading towards the Red Sea, he explained the journey and its caravans: "At night, we slept in the deserts, mountains, jungles, and plains, which were frightening and full of threats, and, during the daytime, we were walking hungry, thirsty, and tired. If we stopped walking, they would hit us." When their provisions dried up, the slaves were forced to live on desert herbs until the slavers brought them dates, rice, and milk.

The slave traders were careful not to lose the slaves to disease, animal attacks, escape, confiscation by the British, and so on. In reality, they were concerned not only about these officials but also about bandits and robbers poised in the mountainous areas ready to rob the caravans. In one case, Mahboob was offered to a bandit leader demanding an annual tribute. He refused, saying: "This is a child; [give us] one that is older than this." A *kaniz* was offered instead. The slave traders beat the slaves to make them walk faster. Once they got close to the Red Sea, lights belonging to the British patrol were seen "searching around the sea lest Black people are transported and to prevent their transportation." The route was altered to avoid the risk of inspection. When they arrived at the Red Sea, the slaves were loaded onto a waiting ship and set sail for Jedda. The sea journey was difficult. Mahboob noted that there were about one thousand enslaved Africans on board. Those who got motion sickness were given roasted coffee to chew. Otherwise, provisions included a small cup of water and two to three bites of cooked rice. When they reached their destination, the slaves were disembarked and transported towards Jedda.

---

115 Also spelled Hadendoa or Hadendowa, they lived in parts of Sudan, Egypt, and Eritrea and were known by British troops as "Fuzzy-Wuzzies" due to their elaborate hairstyles.
116 Poussier, "Les représentations identitaires de l'État mahdiste."

Despite all these hardships, Mahboob took time to describe the important role music played in this part of Africa: "It is the tradition here that in all the Sudanese territories, from the old time, men, women, young, and old are having fun. All homes should have drums and musical instruments of all kinds. It is one of the necessities." Traditional music in Africa has played an important role in the daily life of people and highlights their values. African music is rhythmic, conveys a message, tells a story, and has been used for dance and religious practices, festivals, and social rituals. Traditional African music has also been crucial in fighting against colonialism and apartheid by expressing resistance and unity.[117]

Middle East

IDENTITY TRANSFORMATIONS IN OTTOMAN ARABIA

Jedda has been a major port city in western Saudi Arabia for millennia, and from here slaves were transported to the holy cities of Mecca and Medina.[118] Known as Arabia before 1932, the country had then been under Ottoman control for nearly four centuries (1516–1918). Among the many Ottoman influences was the attempted expansion of Sunni Islam, including the Hanafi denominations.[119] Using Turkish terminology, Mahboob described aspects of Arabic culture and society, thus providing important insight into this world in transition. By the end of the nineteenth and early twentieth centuries, the slave trade was active between the coast and the two holy cities as it was an important locus for pilgrims purchasing slaves.[120] After passage of British legislation nearly a half century earlier making abolitionism enforceable at sea, the African slave trade shifted to inland routes. These included those in the Ottoman Empire that extended from Arabia (Mecca and Medina) to Iraq (Baghdad and Karbala') and Iran.[121]

After disembarkation, Mahboob described how the slaves were taken to a village square in Jedda and were lined up. Between ten and twenty slave dealers chose specific male (*ghulam*) and female (*kaniz*) slaves, but those who remained, including Mahboob, went with a merchant who put them in "a large external room. After an hour, they brought us several large trays of cooked rice and lentils. I had never eaten rice and lentils before." He explained that every day two to three of them were

---

117 Mbaegbu, "Power of Music in Africa"; Barz, *Music in East Africa*.
118 Huber, *Channelling Mobilities*.
119 Ochsenwald, "Ottoman Arabia."
120 Hasan, "Arab Slave Trade from the Sudan."
121 Mirzai, *A History of Slavery*, 56.

sold. They came from different backgrounds ("Nubian,[122] Habashi,[123] and others; *ghulam*s and *kaniz*es") and were purchased by local and foreign people including the bedouin. They were also bartered for goods, including livestock and fabric. Mahboob and two other *ghulam*s were taken with three *kaniz*es to the house of an effendi.[124] "The residence for the *kaniz*es was in the interior and our residence was exterior." He soon was separated from the others and taken to the store of a slave dealer in Jedda market where a middleman told the effendi, "This is the slave whom I had recommended and brought." He was then taken to Mecca to the home of a Turkish-born trader, where he lived alongside a Habashi *kaniz* "who was trained in the Hijazi manner." Mahboob was not only cleaned, given new clothes, and taught etiquette but he was renamed again, "Almas" (diamond). He felt at home for the first time in a long time. "Mecca was like my homeland. I had contact with all the dignitaries and nobles there."

Mahboob travelled with the family to Ta'if, a popular countryside retreat for people from Jedda and Mecca during the summer. He described important holy sites like the Jabal al-Noor (Mountain of Light) and he went on a pilgrimage to Uhud, where Hamza, the uncle of the Prophet, is buried. In addition to devotional practices, entertainment played an integral role: "Day and night we had musicians." It heralded the inauguration of pilgrimages as when the residents of Mecca went to Mina[125] and Arafat,[126] "The women take tambourines in their hands and play in alleys and markets until the morning." Similarly, a beating of the drum announced the departure of the caravans. Another insight into the social fabric was how opportunities were provided to male slaves. After spending several months in Ta'if, Mahboob returned to Mecca with the effendi and his family to work in domestic service.[127] He was given his first opportunity to study at the *maktab khana*,[128] the traditional Qur'anic school, and he was circumcised.[129]

---

122 Nubian ethnic groups reside in the Nile valley in southern Egypt and northern Sudan and speak their own language.
123 Habashis or Abyssinians are predominantly Christian ethnic groups from Eritrea and Ethiopia.
124 "Effendi" is a Turkish term meaning "master" or "sir"; Eppel, "The Effendiyya."
125 The city of Mina is near Mecca where pilgrims perform the ritual of stoning the Devil between sunrise and sunset of the last day of the hajj.
126 After leaving Mina the pilgrims go to Mt Arafat on the ninth day of hajj, where the Prophet Muhammad delivered his last sermon.
127 Mahboob uses the term "service" to describe his tasks in the household.
128 Hassim, *Elementary Education*.
129 The established Islamic tradition of *khitan* or *khatna* (circumcision) is performed in childhood although not all denominations deem the practice to be mandatory.

The Life of an Enslaved African in the Ottoman Empire and Iran

Mahboob was offered again for sale:[130] "Take Almas to the slave shop for sale." Because he was not sold the first day, the slave dealer returned the next day with the young boy dressed in traditional "Hijaza clothing" with a turban[131] to "the [slave] shop, which was a special place for the sale of *ghulam*s and *kaniz*es. We arrived at the door of the shop. They brought me a chair. I sat. I saw slaves; the female slaves were placed in rows: best, intermediate, inferior." Crying, "the [slave] dealer, whose name was Hajj Sa'idi, came and took me with him to walk to the court of God's house [the Ka'ba] for sale." Continuing to cry, the slave dealer took Mahboob to a house "where all Black people were for sale. I watched and saw two Habashi *kaniz*es who were trained in the Hijazi tradition and had been brought along with me for sale." Still not sold, "Almas" was taken back to the home of the effendi.

The life-changing event occurred when Mahboob was purchased by the prominent Iranian Shi'i religious and political leaders Ayatullah Shaykh Mulla 'Abdullah Mazandarani[132] and mujtahid[133] Shaykh Ishaq Ayatullah Gharavi Rashti, also known as Gilani, Amlashi,[134] who were then in Mecca on holy pilgrimage; later they would lead the historic

---

130 Mahboob's description of his sale by his first owner in Mecca alluded to a well-established organization and method for selling slaves at market during this era. He identified clearly that the person who took him to market was a slave dealer and that there were specialized slave markets and slave shops. In spite of agreements with the British to implement abolitionism, the slave trade was practised in the Hijaz due to the popular uprising following the denunciation of the prohibition of the slave trade by the Ottoman Arabian 'ulama'. Slavery became illegal in Arabia in 1962.
131 The costume was banned by Saudi authorities in 1964 in an effort to implement cultural hegemony.
132 Ayatullah Mulla 'Abdullah Mazandarani was a foremost Shi'i mujtahid and one of the main religious and political leaders of the Iranian Constitutional Revolution who issued fatwas (religious decrees) advocating for the establishment of a parliamentary government. He studied in seminaries in Iraq, Najaf, and Karbala' and went on to become a mujtahid. After the bombardment of Parliament by Muhammad 'Ali Shah Qajar, which was supported by Russia, he issued a fatwa and wrote letters to the Muslims in Russia asking them to help the revolutionaries in Tabriz. He also issued fatwas against the Russian occupation of Tabriz and northern Iran.
133 A mujtahid is a religious authority who may act according to his own judgment in matters relating to religious law. For further information on the position of mujtahids in Iran, see Tabari, "The Role of the Clergy."
134 Shaykh Ishaq Ayatullah Gharavi Rashti (also known as Gilani, Amlashi) (d. 1940) was a high-ranking Shi'i mujtahid. He was the son of 'Allama Mirza Habibullah Gharavi Rashti (Gilani, Amlashi), one of the greatest Shi'i mujtahids during the Qajar period. Ishaq Rashti was a student and the son-in-law of a supreme Shi'i

Figure 3. Mujtahid Ishaq Rashti. Courtesy of *Hadith Parsay-i: Ghulshan Abrar* in "Biography of His Holiness Grand Ayatollah Hajj Mirza Habib Amlashi" [in Persian], Gilkhabar.ir, 15 December 2015, https://gilkhabar.ir/news/i/136097.

Constitutional Revolution in Iran and advocate for freedom and equality. Mahboob described the transaction: "After the greetings and the conversation about my purchase, they counted the amount of a hundred and fifty tomans[135] and gave it to Mr. Effendi, the master." His first encounter with the mujtahids was interesting because they asked him why he was crying. "We are your fathers. Don't be sad," they consoled him. Mahboob noted that, "whatever they were saying to each other, I did not understand, because my language was Sudani and Hijazi, and

---

mujtahid, Ayatullah Shaykh Sha'ban Divshali Langarudi (Gilani) (1858–1929). Also, Divshali was one of the students of Mirza Habibullah.

135 About 94 dollars. All currency equivalents are given in Spanish dollars or cents. For the exchange rates, see Mirzai, *A History of Slavery*, x.

I could not understand the Iraqi Arab language. … After half an hour, they started speaking Farsi with each other."

Even though he was still very young, Mahboob was forced to adapt once again, not least of all because he needed to learn the language of his new masters. Also, "they changed my name over dinner. After *istikhara* with the Great Qur'an, they named me Mahboob." The 'ulama' chose this name because it means "beloved" and was considered a good omen. Hereafter, his name never changed again. Renaming practices were an important way for masters and slaveholders to reconstruct their slaves' identities. Mahboob had already been subject to two identity transformations in Africa: first to "Zaydagan" and then to "Zugul." In Mecca his name had been changed to "Almas," and then finally he was given the name he kept for the rest of his life, "Mahboob." An integral part of Mahboob's identity transformation was faith-based conversion. Thus, in addition to learning to read in Mecca, he was also sent to the school to learn the Qur'an and converted to Sunni Islam. His second conversion into the Twelver Shi'i Ithna 'Ashari, or Ja'fari, occurred when he was bought by Ishaq Rashti and Hajj Shaykh 'Abdullah Mazandarani,[136] for whom Iranian national religious identity was highly important. As before, the identity shift involved linguistic, cultural, and religious transformations, but this time the shift would shape a future mostly spent in Iran.

After being purchased by the religious scholars, Mahboob's status gradually transitioned from slave to domestic worker and servant; however, it is impossible to determine precisely when this transition occurred. The 'ulama' treated the young boy well. He was taken to the home's interior, where the women cared for him and kept him calm. One day he "wanted watermelon, which in the Hijazi language is called *habhab*. All of a sudden, I saw a watermelon as big as his head!" had been brought for him. The 'ulama' taught Mahboob and instructed him to emulate them in religious practices and morals: "When I wanted to pray with folded hands, they prohibited it." He described how the son of the landlord of the 'ulama' "was coming and telling me every day to pray like they did and I was not listening at all." Still only a child while in Arabia, it was difficult for him to understand why he needed to adopt these new customs, but gradually he came to appreciate that his new masters belonged to a different cultural and religious

---

136 Twelver Shi'i Muslims believe in the leadership of the twelve Imams, the first of whom is 'Ali ibn Abi Talib and the last Muhammad ibn Hasan – whom they believe is in the state of occultation.

background than what he had known. Before then, he would have called them "ʿAjamis," a racial pejorative that meant "mute" and Arabs had used for the Persians during their conquest of Iran.

With the ritual of pilgrimage finished, it was time to return to Najaf, where the ʿulamaʾ lived. The caravans were prepared and the ʿulamaʾ, their families, and Mahboob left Mecca after visiting the historic religious sites of Fatema Zahra, the daughter of the Prophet Muhammad, and Khadija, the Prophet's wife. They also visited the Fadak garden and the mosque of Qoba. But while en route to Medina, the caravans were attacked by bedouin raiders who demanded tributes and were possibly driven by sectarian motives.[137] Many died.

At Medina, the group stayed at a beautiful house. Here Mahboob described the tradition of carrying the carriage of the Prophet Muhammad's daughter Zeynab from Medina to Sham in Syria and then its respectful return, accompanied by several thousand marching soldiers. He recalled a similar procession for the carriage of the Prophet's wife ʿAʾisha, which was taken from Medina to Egypt, but noted the Egyptians did not return the carriage to Medina.[138]

After Medina, the group travelled to Najaf, where Hajj Shaykh ʿAbdullah Mazandarani and his family lived. While camping in the Najd mountains, Mahboob wrote, "At every location where we arrived, I had toys like monkeys, donkeys, goats, and others so did not get homesick." He was taken to a palace to visit by Ojan Qasim Kermani, one of the camel loaders. Again, he was fascinated by the different cultures and described the musical instruments, dances, and performances he saw:

> The ruler himself was sitting next to the window that overlooked the entire plain where the Hajj had set up the camp, and under his palace about five hundred people sat and had the *khayzaran* cane in their hands, chanting something in their own language. They honoured their ruler by tapping the *khayzaran* on the ground.[139]

---

137 Pétriat, "Caravan Trade"; Peters, *The Hajj*.
138 In 1927, the bedouin military warriors known as the Ikhwan (Brethren), who were trained the fanatical Wahhabi interpretation of Islam in Arabia, issued a fatwa demanding Ibn Saʿud to ban "the tradition of the Egyptian *mahmal*. This was a splendidly adorned camel litter, accompanied by an Egyptian armed escort, that traditionally led the Egyptian pilgrimage caravan to Mecca. In 1926, the Ikhwan attacked it. Over the following months, the Ikhwan repeatedly reproached Ibn Saʿud for having protected the *mahmal* from further damage. For more information, see Amin et al., *The Modern Middle East*, 57–61.
139 *Khayzaran*, or *ʿasa*, is a wooden cane or stick used in traditional dances in some Middle Eastern countries, especially by the African diaspora there.

The ruler of Najd questioned Mahboob's gender identity when he asked whether he was a *"kairh* or *antalo*. This was an idiom used by the Arabs to ask, 'are you a eunuch or not a eunuch?'" The camel loader replied on his behalf: "No, he is not a eunuch." Eunuchs were highly valued and fetched a much higher price in the palaces and among the elites in Arabia than the other slaves, largely because as few as only one in ten survived after castration.

In Najaf, Ottoman Iraq

EDUCATION

Najaf is one of the most important Shi'i holy cities in Iraq, which, until the Lausanne Treaty in 1923, had been a province of the Ottoman Empire since 1534. In the town is the shrine of 'Ali, the first Shi'i Imam, son-in-law, and cousin of the Prophet Muhammad, and it is an important pilgrimage destination along the route from Iran to Mecca. It has also been the site of the first important Islamic seminary (*hawza*) for international Shi'i religious scholars, including prominent and high-ranking Iranian 'ulama' and mujtahids, for more than a millennium.[140]

Arriving in Najaf by caravan with the 'ulama', Mahboob first was entrusted to Sayyid Muhammad 'Abdulnabi Shushtari for a while so that the 'ulama' could make a pilgrimage to 'Ali's shrine. As was tradition, a rooster was sacrificed in thanks for a safe return from Mecca. People in Najaf welcomed the arrival of mujtahid Ishaq Rashti. It was in this circle of honourable Persian 'ulama' and mujtahids, learned religious scholars, and leading Qajar political reformers that the nine-year-old Mahboob found himself. But as he did not yet understand or speak the Persian language, it was difficult for him to integrate easily:

> That day, I was very scared. I had not seen such strange people, women and men, who were jubilating and yelling for us. They took me above the sash and entertained me in their own traditional ways, but I did not know their language and only still spoke the Hijazi language.[141]

This stage of identity transformation was challenging: "During this one month, my sleep, behaviour, speech, and deeds were foreign and I was

---

140 Nakash, *The Shi'is of Iraq*; Heern, "Islamic Education in Najaf"; Sindawi, "*Ḥawza* Instruction"; Al-Janabi, "The Holy City of Najaf."
141 Hijazi Arabic, also known as West Arabian Arabic, is spoken in the Hijaz region of what is today Saudi Arabia.

not at all familiar with the people and did not know them." It was a gradual integration into the new society and culture that improved as he became acquainted with the household and played with the other children. It was also through interaction with an elderly and knowledgeable male nurse (*lala*) who had been assigned to care for him that Mahboob began to learn about this new culture, language, and society.

The nine-year-old Mahboob was passionate about education and study: "The kids of the sir's aunt were going to the women's *maktab*. When the servants or the concubines were going to bring the kids home, they were holding my hands, took me with them, and brought the kids back. I was going and watching their *maktab khana*s but did not understand what they were saying." So enthralled, Mahboob insisted that he too be allowed to attend school and was sent to the *maktab khana* near the Indian mosque. His teacher was one of the great 'ulama', Shaykh Asadullah Shushtari. Even in 1903 there were only a few modern schools in the entire Ottoman Empire, so the traditional *maktab khana*s were the only places where children could receive an education, which focused on teaching the Qur'an along with basic writing and etiquette. For the mujtahids, these schools were also seen as an important place for children to receive a basic educational grounding as part of the modernizing reforms they advocated.

Mahboob attended the school in Najaf with another slave boy from Mecca who was owned by his neighbour, Ayatullah Sayyid Husayn Bahr al-'Ulum, known as Hajj Aqamir Bahr al-Ulum Rashti, another prominent mujtahid who supported the Constitutional Revolution in Iran. Sadly, his companion passed away, and while he lamented his loss, Mahboob wrote that, "I remained determined and busy to study and be educated to become a tool to help my spiritual and material life." Later, under the *'alim* Shaykh Mirza Ibrahim Hamadani, he learned to read and write, and was given instruction in Persian language and literature as well as mathematics. Soon Mahboob was helping the other students. Recognizing his promise, he was sent to the 'Alawi school in Najaf where he learned a wider range of subjects including geography, higher mathematics, and French. This multilingual skill served him well later in Iran.

IRANIAN AND OTTOMAN CONSTITUTIONAL REVOLUTIONS

Mahboob explained that he was in Najaf "until the Iranian Constitution and after the Ottoman Constitution, and all the events and their impact on Najaf, the people, and the 'ulama', and the damage to Najaf, its surroundings, and some of the regions of the honourable Najaf." The close relationship between Iran and the Ottoman Empire was not only characterized by border disputes but also population displacement and migration across the borders as so many Iranians were either living in the Ottoman Empire states or crossing the Ottoman land for pilgrimage. Both countries shared a common frontier and religious principles. The language of the Qajar court and the Ottoman Empire was Turkish and both practised Islam (though different denominations) and, due to being similar, any socio-economic, political, and cultural changes affected both. They also adopted a similar strategy for banning the slave trade and freeing enslaved people according to Islamic law. A series of reforms in the Ottoman Empire, known as the Tanzimat (reorganization), were introduced from 1839 to 1876 to change and improve various parts of the Ottoman citizens' lives through political, military, socio-economic, and administrative systems that followed European models. The reforms resulted in the promulgation of two edicts: the Gülhane Hatt-i Şerif (Noble Edict of the Rose Chamber) on 3 November 1839 and the Hatt-i Hümayun (Imperial Edict) on 18 February 1856. The Young Ottomans, a group of intellectuals, criticized the Tanzimat reforms as ineffective and emphasized the implementation of reforms within the context of Islamic law to succeed. They played an important role in the Ottoman Constitution and the opening of Parliament, the First Constitutional Era (Birinci Meşrutiyet Devri), which was in effect from 1876 to 1878. Following the policy of modernization in Istanbul, intellectuals, politicians, and reformers acquainted with the Ottoman sociopolitical and judicial transformations demanded similar changes in Iran. Protecting the Qajar and Ottoman states from foreign influence was one of the main goals of these reforms. In the same vein, reformers advocated for the suppression of the slave trade through the establishment of a court and justice system based on the Western model.[142] For example, Mirza Husayn Khan Sepah Salar was the Iranian ambassador to the Ottoman Empire from 1858 to 1870, which coincided with social and political reforms associated with the Tanzimat period.[143] He was appointed as prime minister when he returned to Iran and implemented a series of reforms, such as the establishment of a parliamentary system of government to improve the judicial system.[144] He created

---

142 Taylour Thomson to the Earl of Derby, Tehran, 13 May 1874, FO 84/1397, NAUK, London; Nashat, *Origins of Modern Reform in Iran*, 44, 49.
143 One key reform was the removal of the legal distinctions between enslaved people, freed people, and free people. Durugönül, "Invisibility of Turks"; Durugönül, "Construction of Identity," 286.
144 Kermani, *Tarikh-i Bidari-yi Iranian*, 1:105–8; Adamiyat, *Fekr-i azadi*, 57–59. The nine ministers were accountable to the prime minister and the shah. Mustaufi, *Sharh-i*

the Supreme Court in 1873 and the "Box of Justice" in 1875.[145] Malkum Khan, a Christian Armenian who converted to Islam, advocated constitutionalism for Iran.[146] He was also influenced by the Tanzimat reforms he observed in Istanbul between 1863 and 1871 and the calls for equality for all Ottoman subjects, including enslaved people, which underpinned the Constitution of 1876. One of the main debates of the constitution was implementing anti-slavery policy in both the Ottoman Empire and Iran.[147] Malkum Khan wrote *Daftar-i Tanzimat* (The Book of Reforms) and over two hundred other treatises related to the subjects of law, equality, the judiciary, freedom, and governmental reform.[148]

The prominent 'ulama' in Najaf, including Mahboob's masters, Ishaq Rashti and Hajj Shaykh 'Abdullah Mazandarani, were actively involved in supporting the Iranian Constitutional Revolution (1906–11), which demanded a parliament, a transparent legal system, limits on executive power, as well as freedom and equality.[149] Historically, the 'ulama' and mujtahids were independent authorities, who played an important role in directing the Iranians on issues related not only to religion but also to politics. They helped influence the decision-making process of internal matters and foreign affairs at higher levels. This strong network of 'ulama' and mujtahids opposed Iran's Qajar dynasty[150] and were closely allied with their colleagues based in Qom, Iran, and Najaf and Karbala', Ottoman Iraq. Mazandarani, along with the two prominent mujtahids Akhund Khurasani and Mirza Husayn Tehrani, helped inaugurate the movement when they telegraphed from Najaf a fatwa to support drafting a national constitution. In 1906, Mozafar al-Din Shah issued a decree to create a constitution and parliament. Another great leader of the movement, Sayyid Muhammad Tabataba'i, passionately sought the establishment of an equitable and democratic justice system. His compatriot and famous mujtahid and scholar Sayyid 'Abdullah

---

zendegani-yi man, 1:120–4; Kasravi Tabrizi, *Tarikh-i mashruta-yi Iran*, 8; Adamiyat, *Fekr-i azadi*, 79–85.
145 Mustaufi, *Sharh-i zendegani-yi man*, 1:135.
146 Hairi, *Shī'īsm and Constitutionalism in Iran*, 37.
147 Erdem, *Slavery in the Ottoman Empire*, 125.
148 Hairi, *Shī'īsm and Constitutionalism in Iran*, 38–43; Algar, *Mīrzā Malkum Khān*, 29, 187.
149 For more on the Iranian Constitutional Revolution, see Afary, *The Iranian Constitutional Revolution*; Bayat, *Iran's First Revolution*; Browne, *The Persian Revolution*; Keddie, "Iranian Politics"; Katouzian, "Liberty and Licence."
150 Kramer, *Shi'ism*.

Figure 4. Sayyid ʿAbdullah Behbehani. Courtesy of "Who Was Ayatullah Sayyid ʿAbdullah Behbehani and How Was He Martyred? Who Participated in His Martyrdom? How Did He Persuade Muhammad ʿAli Shah to Relent?" [in Persian], Jamaran.ir, 20 February 2021, https://www.jamaran.news/fa/tiny/news-1497408.

Behbehani[151] supported the constitutional government.[152] The latter also played an important role in this movement by resettling in Najaf until the shah signed the decree for the constitution in 1906.

From Najaf, Mahboob observed "the destruction resulting from the Iranian constitution, and the arrival of Sayyid ʿAbdullah Behbehani to

---

151 Sayyid ʿAbdullah Behbehani, also known as the "Black King," was one the prominent Shiʿi leaders of the Iranian Constitutional Revolution. He was born in Najaf. His grandfather was from Bahrain who immigrated to Behbehan. His mother, Fatema, was a *kaniz* from Ethiopia who was given to Ismaʿil, the father of ʿAbdullah, as gift. For this reason, he was of dark complexion. He was also the representative of the Jewish community in the first term of Parliament. "Pictures, Jewish Representatives in Parliament."

152 Hairi, "The Persian Constitutional Revolution."

Iran." He described a trip he took with Shaykh Isma'il Rashti, Ayatullah Mirza-yi Shirazi,[153] 'Abdul Karim Kermani, and Behbehani to Karbala', Baghdad, Samarra, and Kazemiyah. The latter did not return to Najaf until later, but Isma'il Rashti went on to India. Shortly after signing the new constitution, the shah died, but his Qajar successor, Muhammad 'Ali Shah, revoked the document and, with the support of Britain and Russia, bombarded Parliament in 1908. Mahboob described how the news of the bombardment affected his mujtahid masters in Najaf. Iran was a deeply divided country, not least because of the meddling of Russia and Britain, both of which attempted to extend their spheres of influence in Iran. A large part of the populace sought to free Iran and reopen Parliament. The English reporter Arthur Moore and American missionary Howard Baskerville, who supported the freedom fighters, were killed. Taking control of Tehran, Parliament was reopened, and Muhammad 'Ali Shah was deposed and fled to Russia. His successor, Ahmad Shah, was the last Qajar ruler. The Iranian Parliament's second term, from November 1909 to December 1911, was dissolved under foreign pressure. The subsequent civil war brought further bloodshed, including the assassination of Behbehani in 1910, whose body was transferred to Najaf for burial.

The Young Turks in the Ottoman Empire, another group of reformists made up of the elites, army officers, and intellectuals, led the Young Turk Revolution in 1908, which was followed by the Second Constitutional Era from 1908 to 1922.[154] Inspired by the success of the Iranian Constitutional Revolution two years earlier, the Iranian 'ulama' in Ottoman Iraq supported the Young Turk Revolution in 1908. Mahboob has recorded that when his masters Mazandarani and Khurasani met with Ottoman officials, they declared the unity of the two Muslim nations, the Ottomans and Persians, illustrating the extent to which political change in Iran and the Ottoman Empire was intertwined and that it relied on the involvement of Iranian 'ulama' and mujtahids who were living in Ottoman Iraq.[155] This uprising led to the organization of the Committee of Union and Progress, which forced the Ottoman sultan 'Abdul Hamid II to restore the Ottoman Constitution and recall Parliament.[156]

---

153 Mahboob does not indicate the first name of Mirza-yi Shirazi, but according to historical documents, he was mujtahid Mirza Muhammad Taqi Shirazi (1840–1920), also known as Mirza Junior. He was the student of Ayatullah Muhamad Hasan Shirazi, Mirza Senior, the supreme Shi'i leader of the Tobacco movement in Iran.
154 Bozdağlioğlu, *Turkish Foreign Policy*; Cetinsaya, *Ottoman Administration of Iraq*.
155 Atamaz, "Constitutionalism as a Solution."
156 Sohrabi, *Revolution and Constitutionalism*.

ix   The Life of an Enslaved African in the Ottoman Empire and Iran

Figure 5. Ayatullah Shaykh 'Abdullah Mazandarani (right) and Ayatullah Mulla Muhammad Kazem Khurasani (left). Courtesy of the Institute for Iranian Contemporary Historical Studies (IICHS), Tehran.

Mahboob's recollection of events from 1903 to 1911 are remarkable. He recorded important turning points and moments that shook both the Qajar dynasty in Iran and the Ottoman Empire, forever restructuring traditional social and political orders and transforming their populations. He witnessed the impact of political upheavals in Iran on the mujtahids in Najaf and the prominent 'ulama'. At the centre of events, he recorded:

> the arrival of the Friday imam of Tehran, and afterwards, the events of Khurasan, the emigration of all the 'ulama' and Muslims for jihad, the return of the great 'ulama' of the honourable Najaf, the emigration of the Iranian people, the arrival of the telegraph from Hajj Shaykh Ismail from Tehran, and the departure of the caravan to Iran.

Mass emigration between 1905 and 1906 of religious leaders and common people from Iran to take sanctuary elsewhere was a show of protest against the Qajar government.

The Departure of Hajj Mahboob to Iran

FIRST JOURNEY FROM OTTOMAN IRAQ TO IRAN

The section entitled "The Departure of Hajj Mahboob to Iran" by Mahboob himself describes an important chapter in his life. Separating this period of his life from the previous narrative indicates the significance he placed on his journey to Iran, where he started a new life, married, and had children. In 1911, some of the 'ulama' and their families returned to Iran. Arriving in the politically unstable country at age seventeen was profound; Mahboob saw first-hand how Russian pressure forced the dissolution of Parliament's second term and brought Russian troops into Tabriz and the northern regions of the country.

Mahboob's journey from Najaf began at the holy Shi'i city of Karbala', where he and the others visited the shrines of Husayn, the third Imam, and 'Abbas, the son of 'Ali, the first Imam. His account of the towns and sites they passed along the way from Ottoman Iraq to Iran was detailed and can be easily pinpointed. From Karbala' they went to Kazemiyah, where again they made a pilgrimage to the shrines of the seventh and ninth Imams of the Twelver Shi'ites. Here Mahboob obtained a passport from the British consulate since without one, as a Black man, he could be detained under the terms of the Brussels Conference Act of 1890. With his passport, Mahboob was able for the first time to travel freely and cross national borders.

Their caravan was treated with respect along the route by influential residents and dignitaries. The Salmasi family were well respected in Samarra and Kazemiyah, having emigrated from Iranian Azerbaijan, and they were guardians of the shrines. When one of Mahboob's masters, Ishaq Rashti, separated from the group near the Iranian border, he "asked Mr. Hajji Mirza Ahmad to look after me and take good care of me," referring to the son of the prominent mujtahid 'Allama Mirza Habibullah Rashti and brother of Ishaq Rashti; it was in the latter's house in Tehran that Mahboob lived for nearly seven years. When it was announced that mujtahid Ayatullah Mirza Ahmad Kafaee Khurasani,[157] the Najaf-born third son of Ayatullah Akhund Mulla Muhammad Kazem Heravi-yi Khurasani,[158] had arrived in the Diyala province of Ottoman Iraq, the ruler of Qazal Rabat came to welcome them. An

---

157 Mahboob refers to him as Ayatullahzadeh, meaning the son of the grand religious scholar.
158 The distinguished political and religious leader was buried in the shrine of Reza, the eighth Imam of the Shi'ites, in Mashhad, when he died in 1971. Farzaneh, *The Iranian Constitutional Revolution*.

important Shi'i mujtahid, Mirza Ahmad worked tirelessly alongside his father during Iran's Constitutional Revolution and against the British in Iraq with Mirza-yi Shirazi.

Mahboob described this journey in great detail, providing distances between various locations, descriptions of the natural environment, people, and customs, and observations about political security and infrastructure. The entourage of twenty people travelled in three rented carriages with pack animals along the caravan route. On several occasions, the carriage's wheels came off, thus delaying their journey. They stopped at the coffee houses to rest, drink coffee and tea, and to use the hookah. The caravanserais, remnants of which still exist in Iran today, were designed as rest stops for passengers but also as places where horses could be changed.

Mahboob described the "Arab and 'Ajam Khanaqin" caravanserai in which they stayed after entering the Kurdish province of Iran: "We entered and settled in the caravanserai of the customs [office]. From Qazal Rabat to Khanaqin was five *farsang*s. I got one of the rooms in the upper level of the customs caravanserai. The friends each got a place and residence for themselves." After the governor of Khanaqin welcomed Mirza Ahmad and distributed gifts, border guards checked their passports. The border was described as a huge mountain with a large tower at its pinnacle: "From Khanaqin up to there is the border of the great Ottoman government, and from there to Qasr-i Shirin, itself, belongs to the great government of Iran." There were many similar towers from which guards could monitor the roads and where fires could be lit to warn the others in case of danger.

Mahboob added: "One day in Khanaqin, several pilgrims arrived and stayed at the same customs caravanserai. Several masters, servants, and women settled near our room." He agreed to deliver a letter for them, written in French, to the Alliance school in Tehran. He also saw Kurdish people with their horses travelling on the mountain and a man with his *kaniz* in the coffee shop. When they realized Mirza Ahmad was staying at the caravanserai, the people and dignitaries of Qasr-i Shirin approached him and kissed his hands as a sign of respect. They also discharged gun shots into the air, as a traditional show of celebration. All the gentlemen were invited to the home of Shaykh 'Ali mujtahid. When "Mr. Davood Khan Kalhor with his group came to visit Mr. Hajj Mirza Ahmad Ayatullahzadeh, he brought many sheep as presents and gifts as tributes for him." The gifts presented by the leader of the Kalhor clan, who had played an important role in Iran's Constitutional Revolution, were not accepted by Mirza Ahmad. Mahboob quoted his decision: "They all belong to the Muslims. They are stolen and looted. They are haram. I do not want them. I do not need them." Religious observations and etiquette were important for the passengers, who viewed themselves not as ordinary people but as examples and representatives of Shi'i society. In that context, Mahboob was aware of social, moral, and religious boundaries, and, in response to a Kurdish person who offered him "beautiful local women," he replied: "I do not need one; I am a eunuch."

In Pol-i Zahab, Mirza Ahmad was greeted by people playing small drums on horses. Invited into a tent, the group first rested before gifts such as sheep, fruit, and rice were offered, and again, not accepted. The 'ulama' of Kermanshah invited them to the home of the merchant Sayyid Habib, with its *"biruni* and *andaruni,* two sets of backyards, outside for men and inside for women." A group of nobles, dignitaries, local rulers, and 'ulama' were sitting to see Mirza Ahmad. The son of Shaykh 'Abbas Lari Karbala'i, also from Najaf, arrived in Kermanshah and lived with the family. Mahboob described the Kurdish as religious people and fighters.

After leaving Kermanshah, they arrived at Sar Zanjar, where their passports were again inspected. Mahboob described the road from Sahneh to Kangavar as dangerous and frightening, where people were often robbed and killed, as had recently happened to a sayyid. Having to stop at a coffee shop en route, several Kurdish guards demanded a protection payment of four qirans[159] for travelling along the road. Mirza Ahmad and the group were welcomed in Husayn Abad by a group of 'ulama' including the prominent Shi'i mujtahid of Hamadan Shaykh 'Ali Hamadani. He entertained them all night. A similar welcome met them at the next stop in Sultan Abad, where "the honourable gentlemen of elders, dignitaries, and nobles had lined up sitting on the other side of the city and were waiting for the wagon and carriage." Again, they ate, drank tea, coffee, and water, and were entertained.

Qom is one of the holiest Shi'i cities in Iran with its shrine of Fatema, the sister of the eighth Imam, and the country's largest theological college. Here, along with 'ulama' 'Abdul 'Ali Dashti and Mirza Ahmad, the group went to the house of the shrine's custodian. Mahboob described the house with its *biruni* for men and *andaruni* for women. He travelled with the women to Tehran the next day while Mirza Ahmad stayed in Qom. At Zanjirh, their passports were checked and, as was customary, the horses were changed. Mahboob took special care to conceal the identities of the women with whom he was travelling since they were the relatives of Ayatullah Akhund Mulla Muhammad Kazem Khurasani, explaining that "this family has so many enemies."

---

159 About 0.64 cents.

At a nearby village, a girl getting water asked Mahboob where he was from and "what are these scars on your face?" He explained that "it is a custom in my land and they have a rule that they cut the face of all men and women with a blade." The girl was also interested in having one of his rings, which were *dorr*, agate, and turquoise. She explained that she had been a "little girl, ten years old, when they kidnapped and enslaved me from my country and brought me here. They bother me a lot and beat me." After hearing the story and seeing the bruises on her legs, Mahboob gave her the turquoise ring. Then they continued their journey to Shah 'Abdul 'Azim and then to Tehran.

IN TEHRAN

Tehran has been the capital of Iran since the Qajar period. After their passports were verified at the city's gate, Mahboob met his master's nephew. At the army's wagon house centre, a well-dressed man with a tie arranged a place for the women and children to rest. Later a stagecoach took the servants, the women and children, and Mahboob to the master's house. It was in one of the oldest districts of Tehran, in "the alley of Hajji Mirza 'Ali Harir Forosh, Pamenar, across the mosque and the *ab anbar* of Bahram Khan, the late eunuch,[160] to the alley known as the Kashiha." Mahboob described Mashq Square, where people played music. In the *biruni*, he entertained visiting dignitaries. Several days later, Mirza Ahmad arrived at the master's house from Qom. The gathered dignitaries and the 'ulama' went to different places: to Shemiran (Mirza Ahmad, Mirza Ibrahim, his paternal cousin, and two of the servants, Shaykh 'Abdul 'Ali Dashti, the son of Shaykh Muhammad Dashti, and Hajj 'Abdul Rasul); a group returned to Najaf (Muhammad,

---

160 Agha Bahram Qarabaghi was a favourite enslaved African eunuch of Anis al-Daula, Naser al-Din Shah's wife. Agha Bahram was considered trustworthy by the kings of Qajar and assigned as Amir-i Divan Khana (Chief Justice) to investigate if any disagreements arose among the women of the harem. He built the eight hundred-square-meter mosque and school of Agha Bahram in the Shah Ghulaman Quarter in Pamenar (known as Ayatullah Kashani) around 1849, and during the Pahlavi government the mosque was renovated by Ayatullah Kashani, whose house was located behind the mosque. The two hundred-square-meter *ab anbar* (water reservoir) of Agha Bahram was in the north of the mosque, with the *sara-yi* (market/rest place) and *takiya* (religious centre) of Agha Bahram located in the district of Shah Ghulaman in the Pamenar street in the 'Odjilan neighbourhood. The mosque was renovated later by Ayatullah Kashani during the Pahlavi dynasty. Mu'ayyir al-Mamalik, *Yaddashthaei az zendegani-yi khususi-yi Naser al-Din Shah*, 18; Taifa, *Agha Bahram*; Murad Khani, *Sara-yi Agha Bahram*. It was here, in one of the oldest streets of Tehran, where Mahboob with mujtahid Isma'il Rashti and his family resided. The Agha Bahram Mosque was near the Pamenar market. The Pamenar street is in southern street of today's Amir Kabir (Chiragh Barq).

Figure 6. Agha Bahram, the African eunuch, in the palace of Naser al-Din Shah. Courtesy of Gulestan Palace, Albumkhana-yi Kakh-i Gulestan (the Photo Collection Centre of the Gulestan Palace), Tehran, Iran.

Bazaz the merchant, Hajj ʿAli, and Shaykh ʿImad al-Din, the son of Shaykh Muhammad Rashti, the son of the Ayatullah); to Rasht (the daughter of Hajj Aqa Bozorg and her servant and helper); and to Shahrud (Shaykh Ahmad Shahrudi, his brother, mother, and son). After they had all left, Mahboob noted that "I and my uncle's wife, with her two sons and one servant, remained in Tehran." In Tehran, Mahboob lived in the house of Zahra Khurasani, known as Kafaee, who was the only daughter of the prominent Shiʿi mujtahid Mulla Muhammad Kazem Heravi Khurasani, and her husband, mujtahid Shaykh Ismaʿil Gharavi Rashti (Gilani).[161]

---

[161] Mujtahid Ismaʿil Gharavi Rashti (Gilani) (d. 1914) was the son of the prominent mujtahid ʿAllama Mirza Habibullah Rashti. He was one of the best students and the son-in-law of Mulla Muhammad Kazem Khurasani, one the greatest mujtahids.

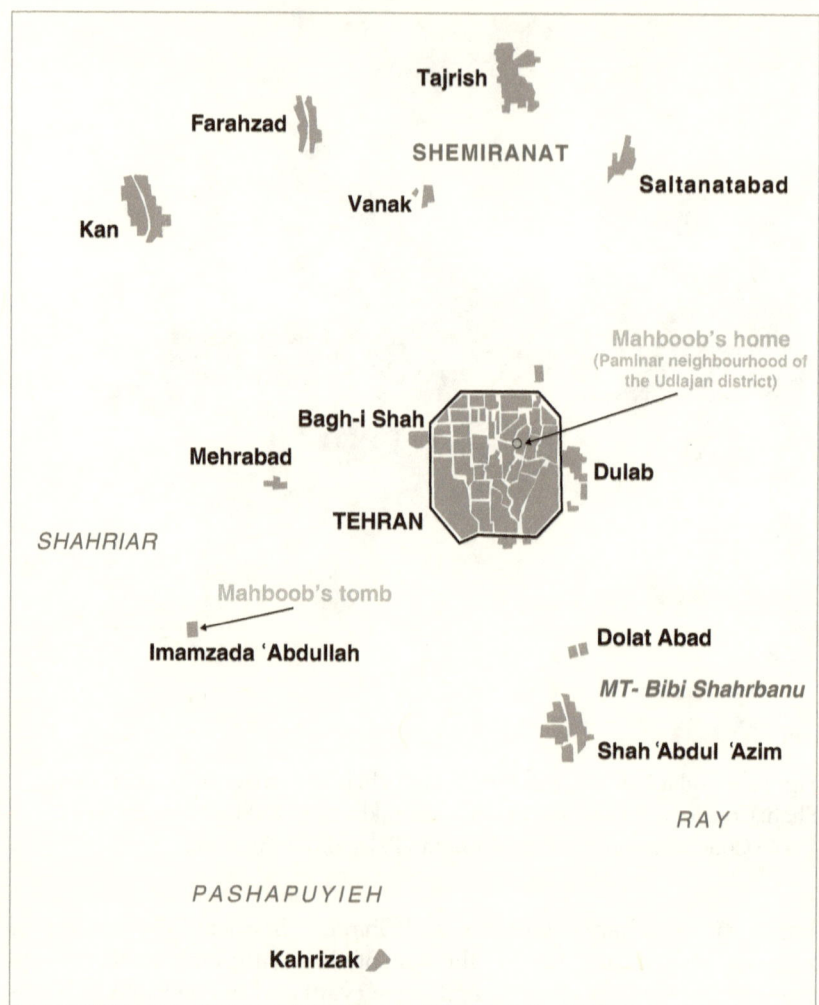

Map 3. Tehran and its surroundings in 1910

By this time, Mahboob was no longer a slave. Even so, he still called his masters Shaykh ʿAbdullah Mazandarani and Ishaq Rashti and other ʿulama᾽ "aqa" meaning "noble" or "Mr." as a sign of respect.[162]

A constitutionalist, he studied in Najaf before returning to Tehran and becoming active in politics. He became a member of Parliament representing Gilan.

162 Mahboob uses the terms *aqayan* (pl.) and *aqa* (sing.) as honorific titles to refer to the ʿulama᾽. The words literally means Messrs and Mr.

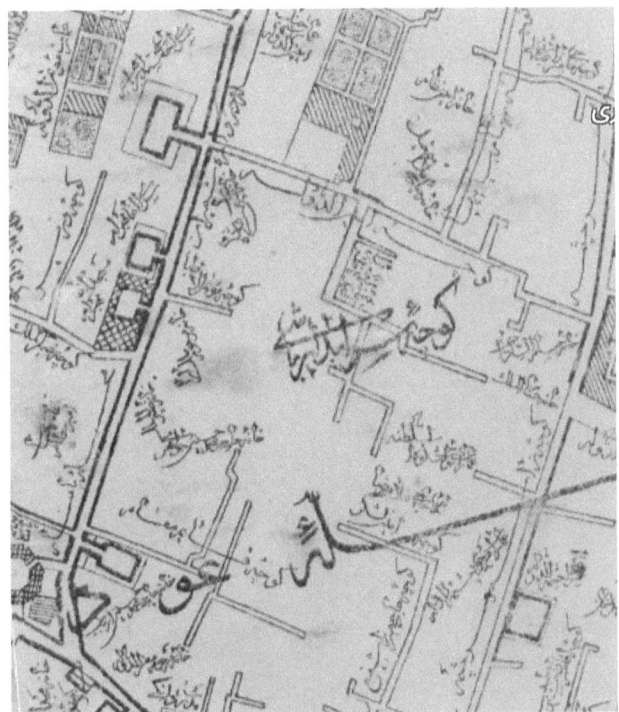

Map 4. The quarter where Mahboob was living in Tehran. Based partially on A.F. Stahl, *Karte der Umgegend von Teheran*, 1900, 20 × 66 cm, the University of Chicago Map Collection, https://luna.lib.uchicago.edu/luna/servlet/detail/UCHICAGO~2~2~525~1239931.

He called mujtahid Isma'il Rashti "his uncle," although it was understood to be a spiritual not biological relationship. Despite this change in status, he described the difficulties he faced in the household, including unfounded accusations of dishonesty. He consoled himself by noting: "Hajji Mahboob, you have suffered so much in the world, this is not worse than slavery in those deserts, and will not be."

While he was living in this first home in Tehran, Mahboob chronicled the major political changes in Iran and the challenges brought on by rapid social change. Turmoil and civil war were centred in Tehran. When the pro-constitutionalists and freedom fighters captured the city on 13 July 1909, Muhammad 'Ali Shah Qajar was forced into exile in Russia. Although he was deposed, he attempted a coup d'état in 1911 with the support of Russia when he landed in Astarabad; soon defeated, he returned to Russia. To restore the monarchy, the anti-constitutionalist

Figure 7. Mujtahid Shaykh Isma'il Ayatullah Gharavi Rashti. Courtesy of *Hadith Parsay-i: Ghulshan Abrar* in "Biography of His Holiness Grand Ayatollah Hajj Mirza Habib Amlashi" [in Persian], Gilkhabar.ir, 15 December 2015, https://gilkhabar.ir/news/i/136097.

military commander 'Ali Arshad al-Daula was appointed to regain Tehran, but he was defeated and killed by Yapram Khan. Supporting their deposed brother, both Abulfath Mirza Salar al-Daula and Shu'a al-Saltana attempted to take Tehran but were defeated by the constitutionalists. Mahboob listed the unfolding events:

> Arshad al-Daula's murder by Yafar Khan; the arrival of Salar al-Daula to Kurdistan, Luristan, and forming an army for the intention of capturing Tehran; the departure of Yafram Khan Armani to fight with him; and after the war so many were killed; the arrival of Shu'a al-Saltana intending to capture the capital and his defeat; the arrival of Rashid al-Sultan from Mazandaran and his murder by the mujtahids intending for the capital; lots of news spread that Muhammad 'Ali Shah intended [to capture] the

capital but he was unsuccessful; and the arrival of news from the provinces, surroundings, foreign countries, and so on.

Around this time, Mahboob and the family of mujtahid Isma'il Rashti moved to their second home in Tehran. Then came the news from Najaf that the prominent Shi'i jurist and political activist Akhund Mulla Muhammad Kazem Khurasani, the father-in-law of mujtahid Isma'il Rashti, had died on 12 December 1911.

Even though he focused on political upheavals in this section of his autobiography, Mahboob also found time to note household conversations about his marriage to Ma'someh Yosufgar, a white Persian from Tehran, who was nine years younger than her eighteen-year-old husband. The match was arranged by their friends and the married couple settled in the house of mujtahid Isma'il Rashti in Tehran. This personal information is noted in the margins of the autobiography:

> In the year 1330, on the night of Friday 11 Rajab [26 June 1912], I got married. God bestowed upon me three children; two of them died, they were girls, and one son survived, [born] on Tuesday 24 Dhu al-Hajja al-Haram [...] [4 December].

Continuing to describe the political crisis, Mahboob focused principally on the Russian support of the Qajar regime. In its attempt to restore Muhammad 'Ali Shah in November 1911, Russia issued ultimatums against the constitutionalists and occupied northern Iran, which led to the dissolution of Parliament and the execution of their opponents. In response, many Iranians boycotted Russian goods, tore their Russian-made clothing, and banned the consumption of its sugar and tea. Many people from the Caucasus, Armenia, and Georgia lost their lives by joining the constitutionalist cause against Russia.[163] Samsam al-Saltana, who also served as prime minister (first from 3 May to 16 July 1909 and again from 23 December 1912 to 17 January 1913) and represented Tehran in the Fourth Parliament, mobilized the Bakhtiyaris, led by his brother, 'Ali Qoli Khan Bakhtiyari, to fight against the supporters of the former shah. Mahboob described the events:

> [Then] was the ultimatum of the Russians, who said that people should not use Russian goods, and the animosity of the gentlemen. Every day I went to the Majles Parliament to discuss security, and after that, we

---

163 Berberian, *Armenians*.

discussed the murder of the Qafqazi Mujahedin. The Mujahedin with the gentlemen, Samsam al-Saltana, wanted many Bakhtiyaris to be at the door of the house of the Mujahed gentlemen to protect and safeguard them. There was a bread shortage and Russian food shortages, and a boycott of sugar and tea; however, people were using these secretly![164]

In 1911, the Iranian Parliament was forced to resign under internal and external pressures, and in 1912, Russia bombarded the holy shrine in Mashhad. Mahboob described that although peace was ultimately established, the economic struggle of the people remained: "I wish it was not that the Muslims' blood was shed unjustly. They imposed tariffs on the people who did not deserve them in each quarter, and in the alleys, markets, and mosques." He wrote of the coronation of Ahmad Shah on 21 July 1914, an auspicious event that coincided with the beginning of World War I. He explained how this foreign war affected Iran with an Ottoman invasion and further territorial gains by Russia. Mahboob was eager to keep in touch with friends so he knew their whereabouts and ensured their well-being. During the early part of World War I, the family of Isma'il Rashti and Mahboob moved to their third home.

Mahboob described how many 'ulama', mujtahids, and dignitaries were killed, including the former member of parliament and mujtahid Mirza Mohsen in 1917. His assassination was part of the activities of the so-called Punishment Committee, a secret organization whose goal was to remove traitors and foreign agents. The situation was dire and there were many deaths as a result of widespread starvation and famine,[165] as well as a typhoid epidemic that killed Mahboob's own daughter. After mujtahid Isma'il Rashti's death in August 1914, Mahboob lamented that he too

> was infected [with] typhoid, and [witnessed] the death of people and the death of my own little daughter, and my friends and buddies, and the sickness of my uncle [mujtahid Isma'il Rashti] after one year [who] also died after so much suffering.

He was deeply affected by all the miseries inflicted on Iran including the economic crisis. He articulated concerns about his own financial

---

164 For more, see Deutschmann, *Iran and Russian Imperialism*.
165 Majd, *The Great Famine*.

situation, having amassed a debt of 2,500 tomans[166] that was owed to the government but which he finally paid off.

Mahboob lived in Tehran for about seven years, from June 1911 to October 1918, when the 'ulama' of Najaf urged Zahra, the wife of the late mujtahid Isma'il Rashti and the daughter of Mulla Kazem Khurasani, to move: "Certainly, you should depart from Tehran to go to the Holy Land [Mashhad]. Shortly, we will send several people to Tehran to help you depart." Mahboob explained that he had also received telegraphs and letters from "the Holy Land" to move to Mashhad as living in Tehran was considered too unsafe and uncertain. As he, his family, and the late Isma'il's family prepared for their departure, he drew up and gave an inventory of all the household items to the legal guardian of the late Isma'il.

Even after Isma'il Rashti's death, Mahboob had continued to serve the family. But at the age of twenty-four, in 1918, the young man and his family, together with the late Isma'il's family, left Tehran with only two tomans[167] in his pocket. The road from Tehran to Mashhad was dangerous even though the lands en route were fertile and prosperous. This paradox was noted: "It cannot be expressed that God has bestowed His blessing upon the people of Iran and the people of Khurasan, but alas! They do not know the value of God's blessing." At the village of Toroq near Mashhad, the family joined the son of Mulla Muhammad Kazem Heravi Khurasani, Mirza Muhammad, who, with several servants and relatives, was awaiting his sister, Zahra, and her children on a stagecoach. Mahboob and his family followed their stagecoach to Mashhad. They stayed at Mirza Muhammad's home for ten days in a private house.

Working as a servant, Mahboob earned two hundred[168] tomans in Mashhad. Because he was still in debt and had to borrow more money, false allegations began to circulate about him. So bad were the rumours that the family was asked to leave Khurasan. Even though his innocence was not disputed by Mirza Muhammad, Mahboob still was told: "Tomorrow you and your family should move out of here and go to Tehran."

---

166 About 4,000 dollars.
167 About 3.2 dollars.
168 About 320 dollars.

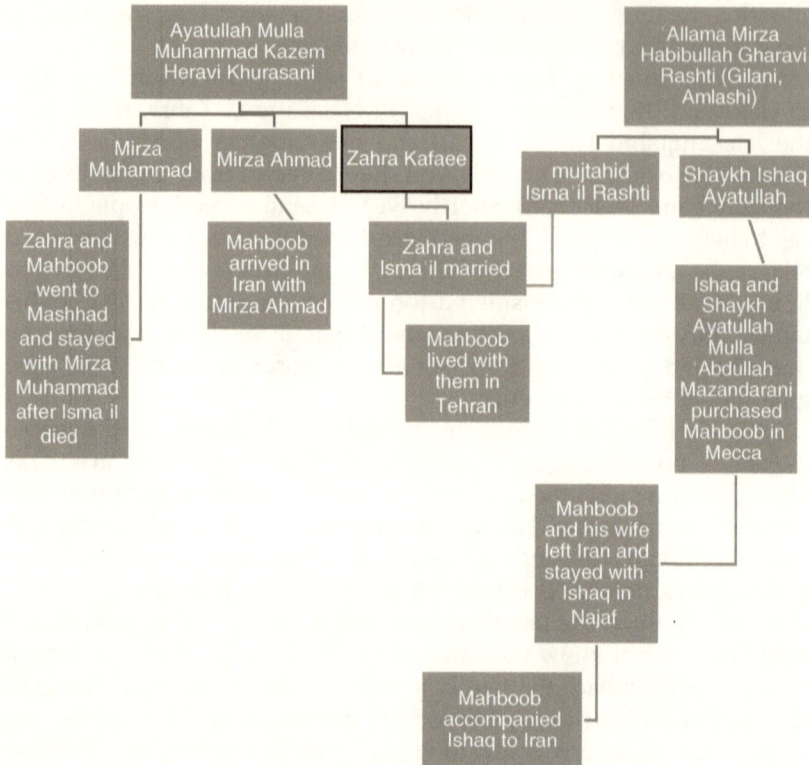

Figure 8. A genealogical chart of the Iranian Shi'i 'ulama' in the Ottoman Empire and Iran whom Mahboob served

MAHBOOB'S EXPULSION

In July 1919, Mahboob, his wife, and their child left Mashhad for Tehran. This was the first time he was not associated with a household and was left to his own devices. Faced with considerable financial hardship and constraints during this journey, he could not pay rent or repair his carriage. Still, their caravan returned to Tehran where the family went to their home. They could not remove their belongings from the wagon until Mahboob raised enough funds to cover the cost of the trip by borrowing money from a friend. He described his feelings of despair about the financial privations; he and his family continued to suffer from ill health. They were thrown out of their first dwelling when the lawyer hired by the landlord ordered: "Throw him to the ruins." The reason given was that if they had been expelled from Mashhad for wrongdoing, then they could not stay. The family then moved to a nearby house that belonged to Ma'someh's family but after about two months, out of despair, Mahboob left Iran and returned to Ottoman Iraq: "After eight to nine years when I journeyed to Iran, Khurasan, and its districts, it did not take long before I had enough and, for me, moving towards the holy shrines was the priority instead of staying in Iran." The family in Mashhad wrote a letter to their legal executor to help with his trip back to Ottoman Iraq. He sent his family to the shrine of Shah 'Abdul 'Azim to wait for him; however, just before his departure, a creditor came with a government officer, and Mahboob was sent to the debtors' prison. After several days, Ayatullah Sayyid Muhammad Behbehani[169] sent money to secure his release, instructing his attendant to take money to pay down the debt. The creditor waived five[170] of the twenty[171] tomans that were owed, which finally reduced the debt to twelve[172] tomans. Several people had given money, but it seems that, in the end, the legal executor resolved the issue by paying off the debt.

The next section of Mahboob's memoir, entitled by himself "The Departure of Mahboob from Tehran to Shah 'Abdul 'Azim, Peace Be upon Him," indicates again the importance of this new stage in his life, saying "goodbye to that damn ruined Tehran and [I] left." Mahboob rejoined his worried family at Shah 'Abdul 'Azim. At the age of twenty-five, he wanted to begin a new life outside Iran. Being winter, flu and illness spread through the caravan. He was captured en route to Ottoman Iraq, but only for a while, by the British, who questioned if he was a slave or freeman. In Karbala', the family first stayed with Mirza Hasan Nori and then with Ishaq Rashti, the brother of the late Isma'il. After a couple of months, Mahboob happily returned to Najaf after a ten-year absence.

SECOND JOURNEY FROM OTTOMAN IRAQ TO IRAN

Two years later, in 1921, Mahboob accompanied Ishaq Rashti and the grandchildren of mujtahid Shaykh Javad Behbehani and returned to Iran but this time from a different direction, in the south, arriving at the port of Mahshahr on the Persian Gulf. From here he travelled from

---

169 Ayatullah Sayyid Muhammad Behbehani (1874–1963) was the son of Sayyid 'Abdullah Behbehani, the prominent leader of the Iranian Constitutional Revolution. He studied under Ayatullah Muhammad Kazem Khurasani, was involved in politics, and was appointed as a representative of Tehran for Parliament. Muhammad Behbehani supported the nationalization of oil by Dr. Muhammad Mossadeq.
170 About 8 dollars.
171 About 32 dollars.
172 About 19.2 dollars.

Khorramshahr to Bushehr. Identifying each merchant, the dignitaries, and 'ulama' who welcomed him during his stay at the home of mujtahid Shaykh Muhammad Dashtestani, he explained that he was given a five-to-six-toman allowance and that his wife in Najaf was sent cloth as a gift.

The governor of Dashtestan, Asif al-Mulk, supported their journey from Bushehr to Shiraz. Ishaq Rashti was invited by the governor of Fars, Nusrat al-Saltana, to a military reception when they arrived at Kazerun. Seeking his opinion about whether to accept the offer, Mahboob told Ishaq Rashti: "Your position is spiritual, it is good to let them go." So the offer was not accepted, and they continued their journey. Still, they were welcomed at Fars by Nusrat al-Saltana, Sulat al-Daula, and a group of dignitaries. After visiting historic monuments and important places in Shiraz, they continued on to Isfahan. Here, they stayed with Hajj Nour al-Din and then with the prominent Shi'i jurist Sayyid 'Abdul Husayn Sayyid al-'Araqain for several months. In Kashan, Mahboob referred briefly to witnessing the murder of pilgrims and the event of Yar Muhammad Khan. After staying with the mujtahid of Naraq, Mirza Shahab al-Din Mujtahid, also known as Naraqi, the group moved on to Qom.

The last surviving page of Mahboob's autobiography described his arrival in Qom before being reunited with his family, who were still in Najaf. We know that he continued to face many financial challenges and bore witness to the ongoing horrors of political transformations that gripped Iran. Again, he was determined to leave his adopted country, but displacement was difficult. After losing another child in Najaf, his wife was keen to return to her family in Iran.

Mahboob's Family[173]

Mahboob always treated his wife with respect and kindness, and she praised him for being a good husband. Ma'someh learned some Arabic while living in Najaf and taught her son Mansour too. Soon after their

---

173 The autobiography was brought to my attention when I was a graduate student researching slavery and the African diaspora in Iran as a research assistant working with the Nigerian Hinterland Project on slavery at York University, Canada, by Babak, the grandson of Mahboob. After graduating, I began gradually working on the manuscript. I scanned, transcribed, and translated the autobiography. I also collected information about Mahboob from Babak, who also helped me contact Mahboob's children. I travelled to Iran in 2015 and interviewed the late Aqdas (Mahboob's daughter). I also interviewed Mansour and Fatema in 2019. It is noteworthy that Babak continued providing important information even up to the time of publication of this manuscript.

Figure 9. Aqdas, Mahboob's daughter

return to Iran, Mahboob first got a job in Qoorkhana, the arms manufacturing factory near Toopkhana Square in Tehran. Soon, he was hired by the Roads Ministry under the Department for Roads and Streets (Toroq va Shavareʻ), where he remained employed for the rest of his life.

Several of Mahboob's children died in infancy, but six survived to adulthood and carried his legacy. The eldest, Masʻoud, died in 1961 and is buried near his father in the cemetery of Imamzada ʻAbdullah; the youngest, Ahmad, was born only four months before his father died in 1939. All were born in Tehran and were given Qurʾanic names chosen by their father. Although they were all issued identification documents in these names, they later adopted modern names.

Education

The role that education and linguistic proficiency played in Mahboob's social ascendancy is abundantly obvious. Though still a small child himself, Mansour remembered when his father was hired by the Iranian royal court to serve as translator at the wedding of the sister of the king of Egypt, Fawzia, to Muhammad Reza Shah Pahlavi in March 1939:

> When Fawzia, the first Egyptian wife of the king of Iran, came with her relatives and entourage to Iran, the court was looking for a *dilmaj*, a

translator who could speak both the Arabic and Persian languages, for the people who had arrived from Egypt to Iran for the wedding. That is when Mahboob was employed by the court as a translator for the dignitaries.

In all walks of life, personal and social, Mahboob emphasized the importance of education, and undoubtedly because of his own difficult childhood, he was determined to ensure his children achieved success in their lives. His opportunity to study at the oldest and one of the most important Shi'i seminaries in Najaf (known as al-Hawza al-'Almiya) was linked to a belief that only through educating its children could a nation prepare for its future. With this mindset, and none of the prevailing gender biases, Mahboob sent both his daughters and sons to school; they all worked and were active in the public sector. Mansour remembered that when his father enrolled him in the traditional school (*maktab khana*) he learned the Qur'an. He also described how students would take a piece of animal skin to sit on at school, and that the teacher would sit above them on a dais, reading from the Qur'an, which rested on a wooden stool. He was later enrolled in one of the oldest schools in Tehran, Amir Atabak. Mansour also remembered that during the reign of Reza Shah, his father took him to Tehran's Jalalia Square to watch the athletes and the military processions of guns and cannons.

Mahboob's Legacy

In addition to education, Mahboob's enduring legacy to his family was his tireless work ethic. With no relatives from their father's side, his children's closest kin were through their Tehran-born mother. By the 1930s, the family lived near Sarcheshmeh in Tehran on Sirus Street. When working as a government official in the Roads Ministry, Mahboob became unwell and after only two days of illness, he passed away in late 1939. He was buried in the cemetery of Imamzada 'Abdullah.[174] His children were still young, with the eldest, Mas'oud, in high school and the youngest, Ahmad, only four months old.

Mahboob had planned ahead so that his wife would receive a monthly pension that allowed his family to live a comfortable life. Like most people at that time, they lived in rental accommodation. At the time of his death, the family was living in "Aqa 'Aziz alley behind Sirus

---

174 After interviewing Mahboob's daughter Aqdas in Iran, she showed me his grave and that of his son Mas'oud in the Imamzada 'Abdullah cemetery. She provided me with useful information including family photos.

Figure 10. Ma'someh, Mahboob's wife

Street, but they moved to the alley of Sa'adat Akhavi and then to the Bazarcha Nayib Saltana. They moved several more times in Tehran's old neighbourhoods: south to Bazarcha Imamzada Yahya, Sirus Street, near the Jewish Quarter; to the east of the city in Sarbaz Street; to the northern districts in Se Rah-i Zindan in Shemiran; then east to Narmak Street, Tehran Pars; and north to Deza Shib in Shemiran.

Ma'someh, Mahboob's wife, died on 13 January 1973 of a heart attack at the age of sixty-nine.

Mahboob's Characteristics

A tall and strong man, Mahboob bore facial scarifications induced by his captors. He described that, while still in North Africa, "One day, they brought me and a few others who belonged to my own racial group.[175] We lay down and they cut my face and their faces to prevent illness." A hard worker, he possessed the qualities of consistency, determination, and resilience. These characteristics are seen often in his autobiography along with his commitment to learning and building a new life on his own despite his hardships. He moved forward no matter how challenging life was.

The surname that Mahboob assumed was Qirvanian, which referred to his place of origin in Qairawan. A city in northern Tunisia, the

---

175 Mahboob uses the expression "people of my own racial group" to refer to the Black racial groups from Africa.

name has various English spellings, such as Ghirvan, Kairouan, and al-Qairawan. In the mid-1920s, the Iranian state abolished honorary and honorific titles and made family names mandatory. The main reason for this onomastic reform was conscription; to know the identities of the young men. The reform was part of the state-building efforts following the weakening of the central government after World War I.[176] It was customary for family names to reflect the person's occupation or origin. In Iran, he was also known as "Sudani," referring generically to the large geographical area in Africa, not necessarily the country of Sudan. (Qairawan was also a Sudanese city.) The honorific title "Hajj Mahboob," by which he was known among friends and acquaintances, referred to his having made the pilgrimage to Mecca; thus, he was considered a pious man who was owed special respect and spiritual importance. His children called him *"aqa joon"* meaning "dear sir" or literally "dad."

With links to both Arab and Islamic traditions, Mahboob was strongly influenced by Arab culture as seen in his choice to wear traditional Arab clothes. Fluent in Arabic, he spoke the Persian language with an African and Arab accent. He also knew some French. Mansour remembered a family photo of his father in Najaf wearing the symbolic Ottoman headdress, known in Turkish as a *"fineh"* (or "fez") and in Arabic as "tarbush," with its black tassel attached to the top.[177] He also recalled a photo of his father wearing a turban.[178] Another Arab tradition he followed was to address his wife by the name of their eldest son, Mas'oud. A pious and spiritual man, who had memorized the Qur'an, Mahboob's strong attachment to Islam could be seen in his commitment to daily prayers. He was so respected and revered in the community that neighbours often came to him at night asking him to consult the Qur'an and tell them what the meaning of events were. "Is it good or bad?" they asked. Mansour recalled that "My father was a good person. He was known in the old neighbourhood. They addressed him as 'Hajji Mahboob.' As a child, everyone respected me too." He remembered that:

> People from the neighbourhoods, streets, and alleys would come to talk with Mahboob and ask for his guidance. Then he would open the Qur'an and interpret their life matters, advising them to be faithful.

---

176 See Chehabi, *Onomastic Reforms*.
177 Metinsoy, "Neither Fez nor Hat."
178 Unfortunately, the family were not able to find photos at the time of my interview.

Mansour recounted a dream his father had told his mother about shortly before he died:

> One night Mahboob had dreamed that his wife had worn a wedding dress and was standing among fifteen Arabs. He told them, "You should not be near my wife, my honour." The Arabs said: "We want to take your honour with us."

Mahboob then told them, "I cannot come with you. I will come in fifteen days." When he awoke, he told his wife that, since he would soon die, he needed to perform morning ablution and prepare for prayers. He then asked for forgiveness from everyone and requested that his Qur'an student 'Ali Asghar conduct the prayers over his body.

Ahmad: The "Golden Eagle"

Mahboob's youngest child, Ahmad, was only four months old when his father died. Adhering to his father's wishes regarding education and hard work, Ahmad enrolled in the air force after high school and pursued a university degree to become a pilot. Through his dedication and talent, he received a bursary to study in the United States. When he completed his training, he worked as an F-86 instructor in Iran and Pakistan. Known as the "Golden Eagle," he was also a talented volleyball player who played with Muhammad Amir Khatami, the commander of the Imperial Iranian Air Force and son-in-law of Muhammad Reza Shah, the last king of Iran. One of his friends, Muhammad 'Atiqechi, an F4 Phantom pilot, recalls that Ahmad was brave and supportive, and in two cases when the Iranian pilots did not follow the instructions of their commander during training at the air force station in Risalpur, Pakistan, Ahmad intervened to resolve the issues.[179] His and another jet plane tragically crashed in the Karkas Mountains in April 1972. He was only thirty-three years old.

The Significance of the Autobiography

The original manuscript of the autobiography is 185 pages long. It has no punctuation marks. The pages of the manuscript are fragile. A few

---

179 Mehr News Agency, interviews of Sadeq Vafaei with General Muhammad 'Atiqechi, 19 Bahman 1401 [8 February 2022].

Figure 11. Ahmad, Mahboob's son

Figure 12. Ahmad, Mahboob's son, with Muhammad Amir Khatami

Figure 13. Ahmad's wedding in 1964

pages are missing and some have torn edges. Sometimes the author wrote on the margins. It covers the period between 1894 and 1921, that is, until he was twenty-seven years old. The manuscript is a chronicle of hardship that leaves the reader with a feeling of sympathy and with a broken heart. This autobiography is authentic and was written by Mahboob himself. Mahboob was an intelligent man, fluent in Arabic, Persian, and French. He penned the narrative of his enslavement in Persian with some Arabic. He knew many poems of famous poets and the Qur'an, the Islamic holy book, by heart; he used these as metaphors to express his feelings and emotions. The manuscript confirms that some slaves in Iran were educated.

The editor's intention in this translation is to bring this important autobiography to the wider scholarly community. The project is a departure from, but also builds on, previous anthropological, ethnographic, and archival research that has focused on identity transformation in the trade of African and indigenous slaves in Iran. This important ethnocultural narrative will not only enhance our understanding of the changing pattern of enslavement, slave marketing, and slave use in Iran and throughout the Middle East from the nineteenth century to the present day, but it will add an important dimension to studies on the global African diaspora.

This autobiography is unique and has not hitherto been published in any language. It is an important primary source and provides invaluable historical evidence for teaching. Analysing this narrative as a historical text will help students appreciate the institution of slavery comparatively throughout the Islamic world and make connections between the slave trade and its diaspora from Africa to the Middle East and elsewhere in the world. This autobiography contributes to the growing literature on global slavery.

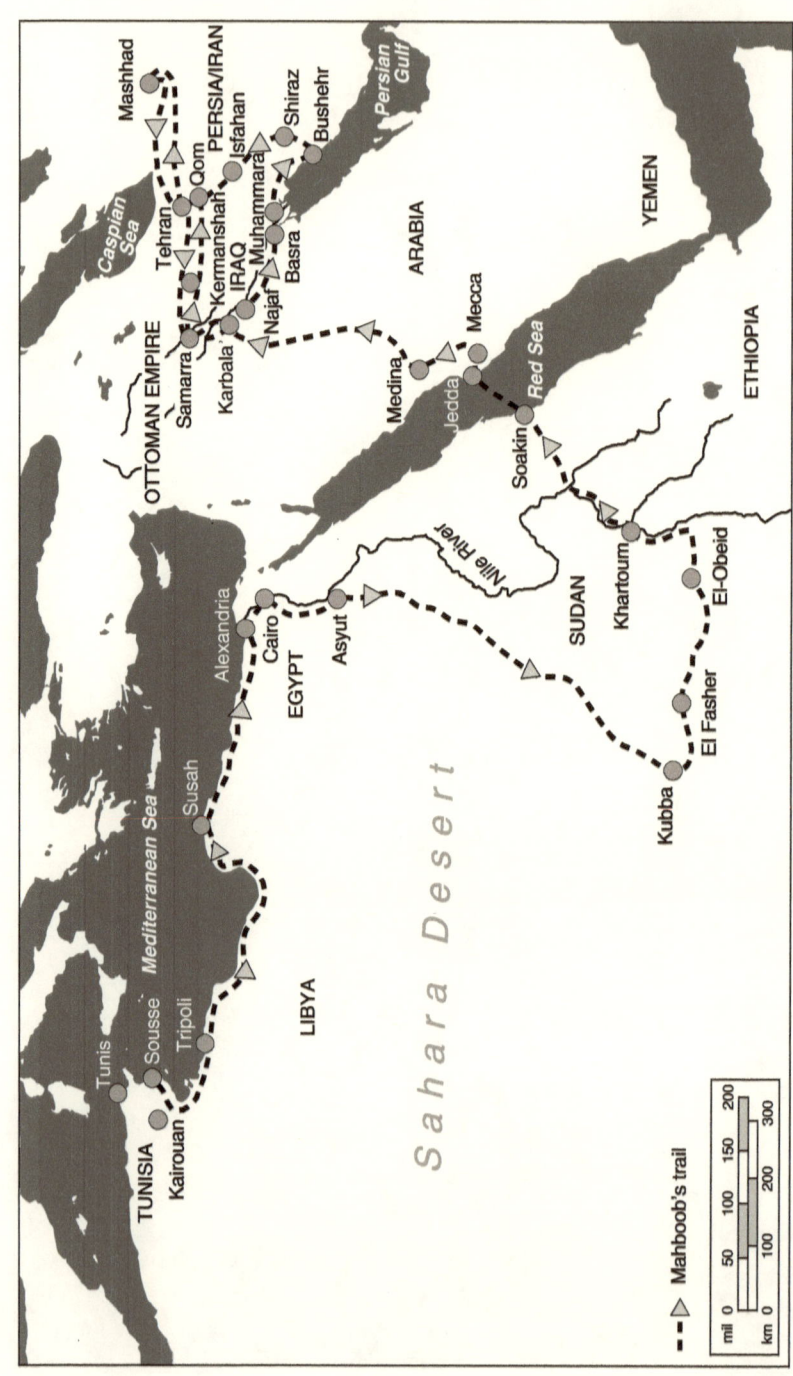

Map 5. Mahboob's general trail from Sousse, Tunisia, to Tehran, Iran

THE LIFE OF AN ENSLAVED AFRICAN IN THE OTTOMAN EMPIRE AND IRAN

1 [In Africa]

[Genealogy]

Rashdan, son of Tuskan, son of Qys, son of Tisan, son of Baqysan, son of Naqysan, son of Rostkan, son of Armian, son of Ramian, son of Aswadan, son of Qasvadan, son of Shahoyan, son of Shapoyan, son of Nashry, son of Shanpa, son of Rahich, son of Marahich, son of Baqariyon, son of Marqiyon, son of Shaqiyon, son of Janty, son of Zangi, son of Dangy, son of Chiran, son of Hayolan, son of Maymon, son of Tyolan, son of Barenkan, son of Torenkan, son of Sorenkan, son of Naqshan, son of Yaqshan, son of Baqshan, son of Nalis, son of Vilamis, son of Balamis, son of Karshna, son of Barshina, son of Karmish, son of Ashna, son of Bashna, son of Dashna, son of Havon, son of Mavon, son of Tavon, son of Chobidon, son of Mabidon, son of Tabidon, son of Farbidon, son of Shonizon, son of Havizon, son of Kavizon, son of Ranizon, son of Hali, son of Kali, son of Savas, son of Nivas, son of Riqa, son of Morqa, son of Moʿareqa, son of Qazemkesh, son of Karvankesh, son of Kashvadeh, son of Nashvad, son of Dashne, son of Badkazi, son of Sivan, son of Arhoman, son of Tachi, son of Marnato, son of Kanton, son of Qihosh, son of Manosh, son of Shanosh, son of Kashosh, son of Daqbosh, son of Him, son of Anis, son of Nafis, son of Lafis, son of Da […],[1] son of Qelis, son of Kamlafis, son of Rodsiyanfis, son of Himan, son of Nohiman, son of Kahiman, son of Yahiman, son of Shahiman, son of Sahiman, son of Anlis, son of Belfis, son of Him, son of Ham, son of Noh, son of Mehlaʾil, son of Lamak, son of Shalah, son of Akhtoʿ, son of Edris, son of Albazer, son of Mehlaʾil, son of Qinan, son of Anosh, son of Shays,

---

[1] A bracketed ellipsis signifies whenever a word or more was illegible or missing from the original manuscript.

son of Adam, peace be upon him. This is my genealogy, which has been said.

My father is from Qayrawan,[2] in northern Tunisia, and it was the capital in the old days. He is originally from the Chahar Yari. His mother, Tayyan, is the daughter of Fandok, the chief of the clan. My mother, Chanpina, is from Saljmattyah,[3] and is the daughter of Qays. Her mother is Vargàn, a Buddhist originally from the Buddhists of India, who has numerous family members, kinsmen, tribes, and clans – not ten, not a hundred, but thousands – and they are owners of agricultural lands, herds, cows, and booty. They are brave and warriors.

[The Invasion of the Nasara[4]]

The reason for my enslavement was that, in Muharram al-Haram 1320 [April 1902], I was a child, had just turned eight, and was living in the village of Kidelan of Sousse.[5] I was inexperienced and unaware of the past and future. It was when Britain had not yet dominated Africa, which was not yet civilized. The Nasara [Christians and Europeans] were invading this territory often and were plundering and looting everywhere. They were killing and pillaging wherever they arrived in the countries of the Sudan until they eventually arrived to the surroundings of the West Coast of Nubia. Since guns and cannons were not available in most parts of the Sudan territories in those days, the Nasara took advantage of the situation and placed all the Sudanese at the centre of their commerce and they did whatever they could, until, in Muharram 1320 [April 1902], they arrived around the Sousse village. On Thursday morning, 13 Muharram al-Haram [22 April], I had come out and stood in front of the house […]. The sky became dark and strong winds started blowing […].[6] I was unaware. In the midst of this, I saw several chiefs of the Sousse village, one Arozankan, and Sayvas, and Sahyat, with a large number of armed people; group after group and crowd after crowd with so much tumultuousness, and women from behind were ululating and running frantically. I was thinking, what has happened that the people of the village are so restless this day? What would happen next? Shortly after, I went home. I still had no clue about

---

2 Also spelled Kairouan. The city was founded in 50/670.
3 Identification of Saljmattyah is uncertain.
4 The term usually refers to Christians and Europeans.
5 Sousse, or Sousa, is an important port and commercial centre in Tunisia. There are also places in Libya with a similar name.
6 The corner of the document has been ripped, thus some sentences of this paragraph are not available.

anything that was happening and that would happen. Remember these words until I write later.

My father had travelled a couple of days before this event to the village of Qaysariyah for trade, and four of my brothers had gone to herd the flocks. Two of them [...] would go every day, early in the morning, and return at sunset. Sometimes, I [...] would go to the garden to plant and farm and sometimes [...] I was with my brothers [...] or I was home with my mother [...]. From early in the morning until now we were defending attacks from the Nasara but that has not been useful so far. And it was almost clear to us that they numbered about six hundred or more and they wanted to invade the village to kill, ravage, and plunder. And God willing, with God's help, we will fight and defeat them to be victorious; and if they overcome us, then there is no other choice but to run away. At sunset, we announced that whoever is able should flee to other villages from this village because this village is no longer safe, lest they raid us and our village at night. In this regard, there is a saying:

> Do not trust fate/time [even] for a blink of an eye for fate/time has vicissitudes and two tongues and two faces.

After the incident, it was not long before I saw my brothers were back home from the pasturage and they learned of the situation. The four brothers planned that the eldest brother, Zamalah, and the second brother take the cows (about three to four hundred good ones) and a herd of fifteen hundred other animals and escape in the night. And it was planned that we go to the village of Riri. If it became safe, we would return from the village of Riri, and if it was not safe, we would stay there until it was safe. After saying this, they bid farewell and left and fled the same night. At this time, I saw my sister, who was the eldest of us, as she came from her house. After [exchanging] greetings, our mother said, "You did such a good thing by coming. I was about to send someone to get you here but saw you came yourself." Her mother asked her, "Where is your husband?" The daughter replied, "It has been several days that I have no news of his whereabouts. He had gone to the Riri city and has not got back yet." Her mother said, "Just now your brothers fled to Riri; perhaps you have heard of today's incident?" The daughter replied, "Yes, I know."

[Fleeing Home (Kidelan, a Village in Sousse)]

Two of the brothers told my mother that it would be a good idea if we fled too. My mother agreed. Then I saw my mother get up and close the doors of the storage room where there was a year's worth of grain. She filled a two-*mann*[7] leather container with sesame seeds and took an axe. We left the house and closed the entrance door securely. When we went out, it was dark and most of the people of the village had already left the same night. My mother said, "To which village do we escape now?" My brothers replied, "It is night now and everywhere is dark. It is too far to go to a village. It would be good to go to the vast mountain that is near the village of Sousse in Azunjan, near the Qerqiat Island, where the nearby spring water supplies the village. It would be good to go there."

My mother agreed. My mother, my sister, my brothers, and I, all together, left the village. When we were two *maydan-i asb*[8] from [our] village, we descended the mountain. Our village was at the top of the mountain. After we made our way down the mountain, we arrived at a narrow valley between two mountains, one of which was non-cone shaped with green land. I saw one side was the mountain, which supplies the water to the village, and the other side was a pleasant jungle and a spring. Twelve months a year, water falls from the mountain. In the surroundings of our town, there had not been a mountain as big and vast as this. Once we arrived at that mountain, my mother hugged me and went in the cave. I heard a tumult, like a beehive, coming from inside the cave from women and children and, occasionally, from men who had come to hide in that cave because of the fear of the Nasara. And that cave is so large that it could hold up to five or six hundred people. A few of the older and younger men were standing at the cave's entrance watching and guarding it, lest anyone trespass. If the inhabitants of the city wanted water, those few older and younger men who were guarding the cave would go as a group quietly and get us water, lest the Nasara notice. That night in the cave we had so much fear and agony until dawn. After sunrise and when the praising rooster sang with the permission of God, my mother woke me up and we waited until the sunlight brightened everywhere. We and the people of the village, all of us, left the cave. We saw that nothing had happened. All of us, men and women, elderly and young, began moving towards the city. Once we arrived in the city, we realized that nothing had happened in the city and we all became happy. That day everyone went back to their own routine of work, business, and farming. That day was Friday

---

7 Equivalent to six kilograms.
8 Two *maydan-i asb* equal three kilometres; one *maydan-i asb* (1.5 kilometres) is one quarter of a *farsang*. Dehkhoda, *Lughatnama-yi Dehkhoda*, vol. 13, s.v. 'meydan'.

14 Muharram al-Haram [23 April], and we were at home till dusk and nothing happened. And we were unaware of the end of the unpleasant day and did not know what would happen; and we were ignorant as to how the turning firmament would affect us. Do not be heedless of the consequences of deeds. But the men of our city, who had gone to defend it, were still fighting. They were informing us continuously of what was going on and about the details of events. At sunset, after eating supper, just like last night, we locked the door of the house and came out. We saw it was dark:

> The moon appeared when it became night
> The Mercury star broke the inkpot

[Enslavement]

We went again from the village to the same mountain until we reached that very same cave and entered. Once we entered the cave, we realized that the noise of women could reach the sky as they were talking and screaming. My mother and others were yelling, "Oh women, be a bit quiet lest something should happen." It was useless. That night was Saturday 15 Muharram al-Haram. We were in the cave until the brightness of the morning. With the rise of the world-brightening sun, I woke up with the sound and noises of the men and women. The noise was to the extent that it could make one deaf, like it was the Resurrection. I looked and did not see my mother, nor my sister, nor my brothers. No one was there. I got worried. God, what has happened?! Then I looked at the cave. I saw a great amount of smoke had filled it. I saw one of the white men standing in the cave and putting onion skin and Indian pepper he was holding into the fire; all around the cave were fire pits, and this man was throwing onion skin and dried pepper into the fire. We were not able to see each other. I didn't know what was happening. Then I saw men, women, and children, young and old, coming out of the cave. Amid this, I saw my old aunt coming out of the cave. She spotted me and grabbed my hand and together we left the cave. One person, who was from the Nasara, remained in the cave until everyone left it. He created the smoke in the cave to make us choke, so whoever was in the cave would leave. Once we exited the cave, I opened my eyes and looked at the narrow valley between the two mountains and noticed what fate had done!

> The killer arrow became paired with the snake
> Destiny both smiled and said, "Well done!"

I looked and saw, what a world! What resurrection has happened! Several of the Nasara had sat and were sewing clothes for themselves. Some were gathering the Black people, and others were holding guns and shooting in the air to scare the Black people. Suddenly, my eyes caught something above the city. I saw smoke was going up to the sky and that they had set fire to all the houses and looted whatever treasures and valuables there were. I asked my aunt what had happened to my mother and my sister who were with me last night. "Where did they go?" She replied, "It seems that your mother and sister fled last night. Most people of the city ran away and some even left their children behind and fled. It seems that your brothers were enslaved." Then I asked my aunt, "What can we do? There is no way to flee and no way to escape. They will enslave us too."

She replied, "Yes, my child. These creatures, whom you see, will enslave all men and women, young and old." While my aunt was shaking like a weeping willow, I was also crying. Those days, whoever you could see was shouting "oh soul, oh grief, oh regret" for themselves. Amid thinking, "Oh God, what would be our fate," I saw one of the Nasara come up to me and my aunt and ordered us to go. We said nothing and, out of fear, started walking until we arrived at the line of the Black people who belonged to our own village and were enslaved. He said, "Stay." We stood. We did not know what they would do to us. We were waiting and had lost hope. Tears dried out in our eyes. God! May no one be tearful and see misfortune. As we were standing, suddenly we saw a group of the Nasara arrive and they ordered us to walk. We started walking. After walking two *maydan-i asb*, we looked and saw about five to six hundred of the Nasara on a hill with colourful flags running and saying things in their own language and chanting happily, meaning they had conquered. We walked past from there. We were enslaved that day, Saturday 15 Muharram al-Haram[9] [24 April], six hours before sunset, in that province, in that city, and in the village of Sousse Azunjan, near the Futenjalun mountain, near Qerqiat Island, near the West Coast of Nubia.

---

9 He was enslaved in 1320/1902 according to his memoire.

2 [Forced Migration: From Africa to the Middle East]

We said our goodbyes to that province, departed, and migrated from there. I had no news about my father and my brothers, nor any news about my mother and my sister. We put our faith in the hands of God and continued walking: I trusted in the One who is alive, He who does not die.

I heard a few words. We walked past the village of Sousse, about half a *farsang*.[1] I got tired. At this time, I saw one of the Nasara come and put me on his back and put me down after an hour. While I was walking, I saw my brother, the fourth brother, who was older than me, and he had also been enslaved. And ahead of him was a flock of around three to four hundred sheep that the Nasara had entrusted him to shepherd. Once my brother spotted me, he hugged me, kissed my face, and turned his face to me and said, "Do you see, brother, what has happened to us? That we were enslaved by the infidels? Dear God, what was our fault that we deserved this kind of cruelty by the infidels?!"

As we were walking, we were complaining about our faith and whether we would ever again see our father, mother, sisters, and brothers. Three hours after sunset, we arrived at a house made of wood that had several rooms. It was old and located between a mountain and a jungle and, by the side of it, was plain land. They placed all the Black people, who were thirsty, hungry, and tired, there. My brother and I sat in one corner. After a short rest, I saw that the Nasara took several wooden bowls filled with water and mixed with flour then ordered all the Black people to eat. Since they had not had any food or bread to eat,

---

1 Half a *farsang* is about three kilometres. A *farsang*, or *parsang*, is a Persian unit of measure. Each *farsang* equals six kilometres, or about four miles. Dihkhoda, *Lughatnama-yi Dehkhoda*, vol. 10, s.v. *'farsang'*.

all of a sudden the Black people rushed like sheep and started eating. While my brother and I were sitting, I saw the very same Nasara who had put me on his back. He came and held my hand and brought me to a room. He told me to sit down. I sat. I saw he brought some food and put it next to me and asked me to eat. I ate a little then got up and came out and sat in my previous spot. My brother ate some food and came. We were sitting next to each other and were talking. I saw one of the Nasara come and take my brother away. I started crying. While I was crying for my brother, I saw one strong Black man onto whom the Nasara had attached a [forked,] two-branched piece of wood, like a *zonnard*, around his neck, and his legs were tied with chains. While he was sitting, he suddenly turned his face to me and said, "Son, do not cry, do not be afraid; your brother will come back now." While he was talking to me, I saw the same Nasara come. He held my hand, took me away, and I had no idea where he was taking me. Then he brought me next to one of the lines that the people of our city were standing in. I stood in the line where they inspected us. I looked and saw that all the Black people they had brought were lined up. Men were separate. We, who were children, were separate, and women were separate. While I was looking at the line, I saw my brother who was older than both of us was in the line. They had enslaved him too and his head was injured. They had wrapped up his head. Once his eyes fell on me, he called my other brother over from the line, and he went to see what he wanted. He gave him something and said, "Give this to our brother. I am worried he might be hungry." Then, my brother brought it and gave it to me. I looked at it and noticed it was crushed sweet sesame, which the Black people call "*sekda*." I ate it and then he returned to his line. Shortly after, the Nasara ordered everyone in the lines to move on two by two, so they could determine who was a better walker. Everyone in the lines walked past, then it was the turn of the little ones. They ordered us to march in pairs, and we began walking. We walked for ten or twenty steps, then they ordered us to run. We began running, then they told us to stop, and we would stop. They were inspecting all our bodies, head-to-toe: mouth, underarms, hands, feet, and private parts. Then, they selected and separated the good ones from the bad ones until all the lines were reviewed. It did not last long; they beat the departure drum. We migrated from the first stop the same day, Saturday 15 Muharram [24 April], in the afternoon. We marched all the way until sunset, when the sun dipped to the horizon. After an hour in the dark, we arrived in a jungle. They kept us there. That night, my brothers and I were exhausted; we spent the night next to each other in that jungle with thousands of difficulties. With the rise of the world-illuminating sun, which embellished the world with its own light, we departed from the stop.

For six nights and days, we marched and walked past the rest stops through deserts, plains, mountains, and jungles in a suffering state and, whenever hunger dominated us, we ate the same jungle fruits and desert herbs to survive. At night, wherever we were stationed, the Nasara would light a fire till the morning, lest we escape or some wild animals like lions and tigers eat us. The Nasara were guarding the area around us, to protect and safeguard us until morning. On the seventh day, 21 Muharram [30 April], early in the morning, when the sun illumined the world, they lined us up again. This time, they brought many ropes and attached every ten to twenty people to one rope and then ordered us to walk. We said "In the name of God" and started walking in the desert.

There is no one in my heart except the Friend [God][2]

After marching about one *farsang*, we arrived at the foot of a high mountain. We made our way up and down the mountain. As we walked a little, I looked behind. In addition to the ropes tied around the neck of the Black people, ten to twenty of them were also tied up with two-branched pieces of wood around their necks. Each piece of wood weighed ten to twenty *mann*, which a person had to lift and walk with. Some people had their hands cuffed behind their necks. Some men were tied by two-branched pieces of wood and were tied around the neck to another man. Only women and children were not tied up.

One who wished us to be burn out
I wish was here to watch afar

Since I found myself in the desert, all that my eyes could see was the desert and [more] desert.

May I be sacrificed for your closed door, Majnun!
Wherever I look is the desert

It was a desert with no water and no grass. The land was sandy, and the sun was so hot we were almost dying of thirst. Our sweat was dropping from everywhere [on our bodies].

If an avian puts its beak on the ground
Its beak will turn red from fire

---

2 Attributed to Husayn ibn Mansur al-Hallaj, a Sufi mystic who was executed in 309/922, and believed to have been his last words.

On the one hand was the intensity of heat, and on the other hand was the hunger and thirst that dominated us. We did not wear proper clothes. We, the children, were naked, but the adults, the women and men, only had a small canvas or animal skin to cover their private parts, and that was all. While walking, I suddenly heard the Nasara raise a tumult and shout, "Oh you Black people, why do you not shut your infants up?" [...][3]

I woke up at the crack of dawn. At once I saw that a young person came, brought some breakfast, and put it before me. After eating, the young man turned his face to me and said, "Get up. We will go together to the garden. Have a look and take a walk so you do not get homesick. You will get homesick by staying indoors." We went out of the house towards the garden. We arrived at the garden after walking a short distance, about two *maydan-i asb* away from the village. We entered the garden, and I looked around. What a garden! It was breathtaking!

> There is a garden like heaven
> Wherein all kinds of colourful flowers have bloomed

I saw a very pleasant green garden. I ate some fruits, which were so sweet, until I was full. I drank some water and washed my face and hands with the water from the canal. I got up and continued strolling. That day I was busy playing in the garden until sunset. We returned home at dusk. He entertained me like the first night.

I enjoyed my time for one week and experienced nothing but kindness and benevolence, except one day when they gathered me and a few others who belonged to my own racial group. We lay down and they cut my face and their faces to prevent illness. Also, someone who was the same race as me died in that village. They grabbed the naked man's hands and feet, dug a ditch, threw him in, buried him, and returned.

[To Saljmattyah]

After one week, on 1 Safar 1320 [10 May 1902], at sunrise, the young man wearing black came and placed breakfast before me. After I ate it, he turned his face to me and said to get up, so we went. I quickly left my seat, and he grabbed my hand. He brought me to a small place and said, "Sit." I sat, and he left. Then I saw that about (twenty) people who were the same race as me were gathered there, most of whom were

---

3 Pages 20–3 are missing in the original text.

naked. A man about sixty or seventy years old, with a grey beard and a white turban on his head, was sitting in a corner. Once he saw me, he turned his attention to me and showed kindness. While talking to him, I saw a tall and muscular man armed with a weapon in his hand, whose face projected bravery. He came and said hello to the old man with the grey beard, who replied hello. Then, he started asking questions. I was sitting in the corner and wanted to know what would happen. After a long conversation, I heard the old man tell him, "I have assigned you to take all these Black people to the island of Saljmattyah, to the mountainous ruler, near the Dez Castle of the Nuba town, in the north of the Nuba town." He instructed him on what was supposed to be done. Soon, after half an hour, that man told us to get up. It was early in the morning on 1 Safar that we departed from that village. We said "In the name of God" and made our way into the desert.

There is no one in my heart except the Friend [God]

And I was fighting with my own destiny saying, "Oh destiny, for how long should I be the captive of the sufferings of life, helpless towards the desire of the enemies?"

I was crying like rainfall: "Oh the traitorous world, and oh the misbehaved sky, until when do you not return from this path and [cease to] play and fight so much with one? You do the wish of the others, [yet] you do not do my wish. Oh destiny, if you behave this way, turn upside down, and I'll ask God for my death, and death will not be coming to me. Oh, see the misfortune, that one should wheedle death to come."

We did not stop anywhere as we walked past one rest stop to another. We were not aware of anything and did not know where they were taking us to. For one month, we were in the dangerous and scary deserts, mountains, plains, and jungles, where there were ferocious animals, ghouls, demons, the drumming of the jinn,[4] and wild animals, where, if the flesh of a human is thrown there, each piece will be shared with thousands of wild beasts.

About thirty villages and communities were ahead of us, and in each village and jungle where we arrived, we could only have some rest, and that was all. The person in charge of us was leading us like a shepherd guiding his flock. We had got used to marching so we did not feel the exhaustion. Our feet formed calluses, so if we were walking over a thorny bush, we would never feel it. We were marching in a state

---

4 A spirit.

of hunger, thirst, and fatigue. We survived by eating mostly jungle fruits and plants grown on the ground and were thanking God. In two days, we had two rest stops[5] left to the end. We had not yet arrived at Saljmattyah Island. Near noon, the blackness of the jungle appeared from a distance. We moved towards that jungle and were sweating all over our bodies. We continued walking until we arrived at the foot of that jungle. We arrived beneath the jungle with thousands of difficulties. I looked at the other side and saw a pleasant jungle with tropical green trees rising to the sky, the green and pleasant ground with colourful and different plants, and a cool breeze touched our bodies, and we were refreshed. A spring was under the trees. We sat, then we got up and walked around in that jungle for a while and ate from the jungle's fruits, and we were relieved from hunger. We sat again under the tree where there was the spring. I was deeply thinking what my fate would be. Then again, in the afternoon, we departed from there. We were marching in that desert until sunset. [Despite seeking] refuge from the suffering of the long way, that night until the morning we spent with a thousand difficulties and fatigue in that jungle. The next day, in the morning, we departed again from there. We walked until sunset. The darkness of night had covered the world, when the person in charge told us, "God willing, tomorrow in the morning, we will arrive at Saljmattyah Island." We spent that night in the jungle with thousands of [more] difficulties until the morning. We woke up at dawn, when the sun brightened the world with its radiance. The sun's rays radiated and a beam of light flashed at us.

We started marching towards Saljmattyah Island. We walked all the way until we arrived at the foot of a mountain. We climbed up the mountain. A town came into our view. We walked faster and arrived at the gate of the town. We entered the gate of the town. We said "In the name of God" and entered the town. What a town I saw! Very nice buildings! The lands were green like emeralds; trees and fruit trees reached the sky! The town seemed to us heavily populated. We walked until we arrived at the square where I saw people who belonged to the same racial group as me. The person in charge of us ordered us to stop. We stopped to see what would happen, and he left. Shortly after, he returned, divided us, and sent one person to each house. He took me to a house and left. When I entered the house, I thanked God, that

---

5 The original word is *manzel*, meaning house or place. Mahboob uses *manzel* as a stop location, which is sometimes a village, city, station, or simply a location. "Rest stop" has been used throughout the translation to maintain the original meaning.

praise be to God, I am relieved from those deserts and roads. When I entered the house, by chance, there was no one in that house except two people, one man and one woman. I said, "Greetings," and they replied. They got up and the man held my hand and brought me up to the top of the chair, and sat me next to himself. The man and woman started hosting me in their own customs. They said, "Oh young one, you are very welcome. We are pleased to meet you. Your steps in this house are congratulated." They started asking questions: "When did you arrive in this town?" I replied, "We entered the town just now. I did not go any other place except here." Then they said, "Oh young one, tell us your history. From which region and community are you?" I started telling them about my account from the time I stepped out of the gate of Sousse Azunjan, how we were enslaved, and the arrival to that island and that village, until I arrived at Saljmattyah Island. I explained whatever had happened. After, I saw that the man and woman were looking at me with surprise. They said, "Indeed, you, at this young age, have suffered a lot that we have not seen up to now." Then, the man turned his face to me and said, "Oh son, know and be informed that this is the town of Saljmattyah, and it has a great ruler, and we all, most of the residents of this town, belong to the same race as you, and it is very diverse. It seems they brought you to this town for the ruler and divided you among the homes until you want to go. The person who was in charge of you has handed you over to me to look after you until the ruler wants you. Now, we have no children. Be our child. We will take care of you for a thousand years. Do you accept us as your father and mother?" I replied, "Of course. It is my great honour to have such a father and a mother to take care of me. I am indebted. It is my honour." They liked my response very much and said, "Oh child, do not be sad. Talk and laugh. Go and come. Say whatever you need. Do not be shy. Now, you are so tired, hungry, and thirsty." He told his wife, "Get up. If there is any water and bread, bring it." The woman got up. Shortly after, she came back with some water and bread and put it before me. She offered, "In the name of God, have it." I said "In the name of God" and started eating, and I became full. I got a little energy. I thanked God. I spoke a little with that man and then he said, "You are tired. Go over to the bed and rest." I got up and slept on a corner of the bed until sunset. At dusk, I awoke and sat up. The woman came and sat next to me and started talking about life until half an hour into the night. Her husband came. I said hello. His wife got up and he sat. We started chatting until three hours into the night. The woman had gone to prepare the supper. She returned after three hours and said, "Supper is ready. You let me know whenever you want me to bring it." Her husband said, "Bring the supper quickly." After only a very short time the spread was set. After having supper, we got up and slept. At dayspring, I woke up. After breakfast, dad came, held my hand, took me to the spring, and washed me. Then we returned home. After three days, dad told me, "Child, it has been several days since you got here but we have not gone out for a walk and tour. If you want, let's go together to the garden, so you do not get homesick." I accepted. We left the house. We walked twelve and a half *farsang*s and arrived at a garden.

> There is a garden like heaven
> Wherein all kinds of colourful flowers have bloomed

I saw a very pleasant and green garden. I ate some garden fruits and sugar cane until I was full. I drank some water using my hand. I washed my hands and face with the water of the canal. I got up for a walk in the garden. That day, I strolled in the garden until dusk; then we returned home.

They hosted me as usual every night. I was continuously served in the house of that dad for two months. In this period, I got to know all the streets, markets, quarters, and the house of the great people, men and women, and young ones. Most of the time, I would go with dad to the garden for agriculture, plantation, and sowing seeds. Sometimes, I went with dad and sometimes I did not go. I spent the night and day according to my wishes. I was always having fun and walking around. I was invited to houses, gardens, parties, and meetings and did not realize if it was day or night. All the residents liked me very much. I used to go play with the kids of the neighbourhood during the day. Little by little, slowly, I started playing with the sons of the ruler and we became friends, to the extent that I used to go to their house day and night. Sometimes, I did not return to dad's house. When he asked, "Where were you, son? Why were you late?" I would reply, "I went to play with the ruler's sons. Therefore, I am late. Some days and nights, they would not let me leave earlier." Then he would say, "Wherever you go, come home early."

The ruler had a palace protected by strong ramparts and towers that surrounded it. In that palace and castle, there were fifty to sixty households, all of which were the ruler's children and wives. Whenever he, his wives, children, and sons spotted me, they would hold my hand, take me, and treat me with kindness and compassion. Especially the ruler himself; whenever he saw me, he took me to the palace and treated me with kindness and said, "You are like my own child and there is no difference between you and my other children. Come and go here every day." He would serve me water, which was plentiful in that country.

The lifestyle in this country is different. All of them, men and women, old and young, are used to fun, joy, and entertainment. Not a single poor person can be found here. Everyone has their own land, agriculture, plantation, property, cows, sheep, and wealth. Money is rare and cannot be found here. Their market is different; it is like a square space. Men and women bring their goods; if it is grain, it is weighed by a kilo, and if it is something else, it is exchanged for goods. Their plates for both elites and commoners are made of clay and wood. They do not even have a shower. If they need water for washing and cleaning, they will go near springs and canals to wash. Their arms are all spears, swords, bows and arrows, maces, shields, and perhaps very few guns, which they may or may not have. They have good horses, which cannot be found anywhere else. If they want to harvest, whoever's garden, either commoner or elite, they will invite a group of about ten to twenty people. They bring food and drink to the garden and get busy harvesting. Or, if they want to go hunting, it is the same. They invite about sixty people and leave with special weapons and hunting tools. Whatever they catch, they share among themselves. Most cloths in the country are either of canvas or of wild or non-wild animal skins. The boys do not cover their private parts until the age of ten or fifteen, or before twenty, except for a few. It is the custom in this country that, every year, they circumcise both boys and girls in each household. They consider it a custom because it is a tradition from the old times. Mainly in the cities of the Sudan, they perform it on a high area or a mountain. The town of this ruler, where I was in, is mountainous.

After seven months, an officer who was sent by the ruler came to dad and said, "The ruler orders that you and your son should come to the palace." He said this and left. Then, dad held my hand, and we walked all the way until we entered the ruler's palace. Some nobles of the town had been sitting and talking there. Dad said hello. He replied. Then he turned his face to dad and said, "Leave this Zydagan here and go." Dad said, "Very well," and took the ruler's permission to leave and returned to his house. After an hour, the people were dismissed from the ruler's meeting and everyone left. The ruler himself, too, went inside his harem. He had ordered that I should be taken care of: "That Zydagan, he should be looked after." I remained there between ten and seventeen days. I was having a good time and enjoying myself. They were all my friends and fellows. A lion was given to the ruler along with other gifts and presents. For many days and nights that animal spent time with us and slept with us and never hurt us.

I stayed in the ruler's house for a number of days and was having fun. Days were passing with feasting and drinking, and I was not aware of the future and what would happen next. One day, in the afternoon, the ruler called me. I went to the ruler and bowed. After some questions and answers, he told his officer, "Take this Zydagan and a wild sheep to the house of my minister and return." I took permission to leave and left with the officer. We walked all the way until we arrived at the house of the minister. The officer handed me over and left. When I entered the house of the minister, I saw there was no one except him, his wife, and one *kaniz*. They hosted me a lot. After two to three days, his wife made me responsible for a child I had to look after. After a few days, I became frustrated. I put the child down and escaped to the house of the first dad. Then, they found me and returned me. Sometimes, they asked me to do some work, and at other times not at all. I escaped to the streets and deserts all the time. Then the wife of the minister would come after me and flog me. I bothered them so much that they got frustrated.

After five or six months, I heard people crying of hunger, for a severe famine had come, to the extent that "friends forgot pleasure." It lasted between five and six months, so all the stored food of the people was gone, and most people escaped to the surrounding areas, deserts, and regions to get grains. Some were going to the deserts and jungles and were bringing back herbs and jungle fruits to survive. Shortly after, the minister of the ruler went to the town of Jahdiyyeh for grains. His trip lasted one month. Upon his return, he brought back many things, including a hundred sheep and ewes, wheat, and other things. Then he divided some of it among his friends and kept some for himself. Then I and the remaining fifty to sixty sheep and ewes were handed over to a shepherd of the town. I had to take several herds of sheep and ewes to the pastureland during the daytime and return them at dusk. I was so happy to get this work. Whatever it was, it was much better than staying home.

The famine gradually ended. Rain came pouring down, plants grew, prices dropped, and people were relieved from their difficulties. People were so happy. I was busy with the work of herding. The direction and location of our movement was on the main and back routes that were about two to three *farsang*s. I was always moving around not knowing what would happen next. Until the world changed and an order was received from another city. A ruler sent a letter to the ruler of Saljmattyah that said, "I intend to fight with you." He replied, "I gladly accept!" Now, I did not know what the fight was for. I did not know. There is a proverb that kings know best where the interests of their country lie. The ruler ordered the ministers to prepare the troops and army. The ministers opened the door of the treasury and gave them guns, a salary or stipend, and sent them out of the town's gate. After seven days, the ministers gathered at the court and bowed. For seven days, we paraded seven thousand soldiers, who were camped outside of the town waiting for the order of His Excellency to leave. The ruler admired them greatly and ordered the robe of honour be given to the ministers.

On the same day, the ruler and all the ministers and commanders rode their fast horses from the town, entered the camp, and positioned themselves in his own pavilion. The ruler determined a good time to depart from there early in the morning. The next day, with the break of day, they beat the drum for departure and the army left. The ruler put his son, Karrshid, in charge of the town and left the town with some of the commanders. That day, I did not go to the pastureland with my friends. I went half a *farsang* to watch. Then, I saw some officers were beating women and men, forcing them to bring food supplies and drinks for the ruler, which they then took, and returned since they had no choice. The next day, we got busy with our own work. The town was quiet. The distance from the town of Saljmattyah to the town of the ruler was about five to seven *manzel*. Every day reports were received from the ruler about what had transpired.

The war lasted for two months. After that, a messenger arrived. The ruler had written a victory letter to his son, Karrshid, "Oh son, know that after two months, praise be to God, the victory and triumph is ours for we have defeated that ruler and seized all the booty. Wait for five to six more days until we return. Decorate the town and prepare to welcome us." The next day, following the order of the ruler's son, a herald announced in the street and bazaar, "Oh people, get ready from now until six days, since the ruler will return with victory and triumph within the next few days." People became so happy by hearing the news. Following the order of the ruler's son, people started preparing the welcome reception and decorating the town. On the sixth day, people, group after group, and crowd after crowd, would greet them. Each community was sitting apart by twenty steps and had different musical instruments, including bugles and trumpets, and they played and sang according to their own custom. That day, my friends and I went to the greeting. We were half a *farsang* away from the town, when we saw the ruler and his commanders, ministers, chiefs, and heads mounted on horses, and the infantry was coming to the town with glory and greatness. He entered his palace with so much honour. That day, about two to three hundred cows and sheep were sacrificed for the ruler and someone played a large timbal; the sound reached one *farsang* away. The celebration reached the extent to make one unconscious.

Because after drinking, friends became happy

[From Saljmattyah to a New Town]

The ruler told the ministers, "From today, for seven days, people will have joy and will celebrate." After seven days, the herald would announce in the streets and bazaars that the ruler intends to leave this town to go to that old town where he was residing before. Whoever wants to move to that town must get a house and furniture for himself. Because this town is too small, it is not suitable for living in and should be evacuated. In short, during the seven days, people from the surrounding areas, who heard that the ruler had returned, were bringing presents, gifts, and offers to him, including one person who had brought several heads of horses as a present. After seven days, following the order of the ruler, people, group after group, batches and batches of people, went towards that old town. Everyone fixed whatever required repair or renovation and returned, and if they liked it there, departed for the old town. Shortly after a month, all the residents of the current town departed and the town was evacuated. The minister whom I was with also took his wife, children, everything, and departed with us.

From the town of Saljmattyah to that old town was about two *farsang*s. After a year living in that town, I said goodbye and moved towards the old town. We walked all the way until we arrived at that town.

> I want a world different from this world
> So that I traverse in another world

Once we entered the old town, I thought, "What a city! Vast and great!" Although it was not completely renovated and fixed, it was much better than the previous town. This town was both mountainous and higher than the first one and had tropical and cold climate trees! It was a very pleasant town. The minister provided us with a house and we settled there. I was doing the same job again as usual. I would go to the pastureland during the day and return home with my friends at dusk. We used the main and back roads as our path. The area around the town was a good location for traversing, sightseeing, and hunting.

I did not have a bad time there, but from the moment I entered that town, it was as if all the world's sorrow and grief had settled in my heart. No one saw me with a smiling face. I do not know what bad event happened to me. It was not my fault. From the beginning of the world, it has been my fate. No one knows except my God. Of the many troubles, sufferings, and agonies that were inflicted on me by people, one was about the many wells, water springs, and canals there. In the new town, near sunset, I went out of town and to a nearby well. I saw a group of people standing, looking confused, and not knowing what to do. I asked, "What has happened to you folk that you are standing by this well at night?" They said, "We are scared to go down into this well to fill up these water containers and bottles," which were made of animal skins. "Come here. We will harness you up with ropes and you will go down to the bottom of the well and fill all these water containers then we will pull you up. Once everyone's thirst is slaked, we will pull you up from the bottom of the well." They surrounded me, fastened a rope around my waist, and threw me to the bottom of the well, which was about fifty to sixty *zarʿ* deep.[6]

> They struck my foot with the axe of injustice
> Now my place from top of the moon is at the bottom of the well

At the bottom of the well, the loud noise of the animals could make one deaf. I quickly filled the containers, tied them to the rope, and they pulled them up. Once everyone's thirst was slaked, they pulled me up from the bottom of the well. I said goodbye and went home. They really liked me so much in that new town. I planted the seed of goodness. I was there until early in the spring. Whatever I was doing, following the order of the wife of that minister, they gave the work to someone else to do.

[From the New Town to Sous Aqsa]

Soon, the wife of the ruler [minister] travelled to the town of her father. No one remained in the house, except the minister and I, his daughter, and a *kaniz*, who was cooking. The ruler [minister] and his wife had horrible behaviour. They had very bad temperaments. I hated their behaviour very much. Secretly, a few merchants of the town planned to travel and trade in the town of Sous Aqsa and the ruler [minister] instructed them to let me know if they intended to go for trade. I was not aware of anything that would happen to me, or what would be my fate, and where life would take me. Soon after sunrise, when day-spring lit the world, I saw several well-armed young people come to the door of the minister's house. They knocked on the door. I saw the minister appear at the door of the house. After greeting and saluting with the two or three merchants whom the minister had previously instructed, the minister told the merchants, "Now that you are departing today, I

---

6 A *zarʿ* is a unit of measure equivalent to 104 centimetres.

entrust this Zydagan to you; take him with you." Once I heard this, I became very sad. The minister said to me, "You must go." Any excuses I made were not accepted. [I thought,] "Whether I want to or not, it does not happen by force or insistence. I must leave." Then, I kissed the minister's hands and asked for his forgiveness: "Please forgive any of my wrongdoings." Near the morning, I said goodbye to the town and from there left with those merchants.

> One cannot fight with fate
> One cannot complain about life

We went all the way until we left the town's gate. We said "In the name of God" and started walking. I said:

> We went, and you and my sad heart know
> To where bad fate takes our destiny

Hear these few words. That day we were walking in the desert until we arrived in a jungle at sunset. We spent that night in the jungle with thousands of difficulties and hardships until the morning. At the crack of dawn, when the sun brightened and decorated the world, we departed again from there to go towards Sous Aqsa. We walked past house after house, valley after valley, and stopped nowhere, except in some villages to get food supplies. What mountains and deserts full of danger and fear! What strange and unseen places that eyes had not seen and ears had not heard of! If one sees those strange things that God has created, one will faint! At every village we arrived at, two to three merchants joined us. One merchant who was with us had a *kaniz*. The job of carrying a very large water container was handed over to the *kaniz*. He mistreated the *kaniz* so much. One incident that happened to me on our way was that, one day, when we arrived at a village and were tired, one merchant told me, "Come give my foot a massage." In reply, I said, "Am I your wife to massage your foot?" Once he heard that from me, he got up and struck my face with a pistol. I fainted from the pain. When I became conscious, some people ran and said, "Don't cry. He is older. It is okay." I got up with difficulty and gave the merchant a foot massage, then stopped.

Near the evening, we again migrated from the village. We walked past about thirty villages. We were walking on that road, in the desert, mountains, plains, valleys, up and down, for one month. The last station was the thirtieth village. We arrived in the last station, the village. It was near noon. We stayed there and ate bread and drank water. After resting and becoming full, while we were talking, the sound of a drum came from one *farsang* away. I asked the people of the village, "Where is this sound coming from?" They said, "It is coming from Sous Aqsa." I said, "From here to Sous Aqsa is about one *farsang*." We stayed there until three hours before dusk, then we moved out of the village for the town. We went on until half an hour had passed, the sun had set, and we arrived near the gate of the town. We walked past the town's gate, proceeded, and arrived in a place and settled on its corner. That night the sky was very dark and cloudy, and the weather was very windy. We spent that night with thousands of troubles and difficulties in the rain under a fur cloak until the morning. After the break of day, the stormy weather was over. The merchants found a place for us and took us there. That day, the merchants brought us water and bread.

We stayed three days in the place the merchants had prepared for us. On the third day, near the evening, the merchants took us to the door of a large house. Then the other merchants who were with us took the *kaniz* and left, and I had no news about them. They brought and entrusted me to someone who was of the same race as me. Then the merchants left. Several assistants of the ruler of Sous came and took me and the person who was with me to the ruler's palace. After seeing us, the ruler liked us and ordered, "Prepare a place for them to stay." He especially asked them to look after me and entertain me very well. In the *andarun*, they prepared a place for me. When I went inside the *andarun*, the ruler's wife and his servants came and surrounded me. They started asking questions and welcomed me: "Young one, you are very welcome. Your arrival to this house be blessed. Where are you coming from? To what community and region do you belong? Young one, tell us your story." Willy-nilly, I started explaining whatever had happened to me during the period before I arrived at the town of Sous. They became very surprised: "Indeed, young one, you suffered a lot at this early age. We have never seen someone like you up to now. We have seen very few endure such hardships and difficulties." After half an hour, the ruler's wife and others left my side and everyone got busy with their own work and jobs. At night, they brought me supper. After supper, I went to a corner which they had prepared for me to rest. I spent that night as best I could. At the break of day, I woke up, went and washed my face, then came back and sat in the yard.

I was in the town of Sous Aqsa for ten days, and during the period I was there I did not have a bad time. I was strolling, talking, and conversing. It was not bad there for me. All the men and women were kind to me. When I arrived there, they changed my name. The ruler asked them to give me the name "Zugul." Whenever they called me, they called me Zugul. One day when I was in the town of Sous Aqsa, it was near the evening and I was standing in front of the ruler's palace. A young handsome person dressed in white approached me. After greeting me and asking how I was, he asked, "What is your name?" I said, "My name is Zugul. Brother, you came here asking about me, who is a stranger. Who are you?" He replied, "I am your friend. What is wrong if I ask how you are doing? I saw you look like a stranger, who has come from far, so I thought to ask how you are. How are you doing, my kind brother?"

> One who has ended up here
> No one knows his feeling except God
> From the time I moved away from here too
> My burning, alas, has passed nine skies
> Until I am alive and sorrowful
> I mourn the separation from my kind father

Then, the young person asked me, "Dear brother, show me your hand." He looked a little at the lines of my hand then said, "You have very good luck. There is hope that you will reach high positions and status. Do not despair. Your condition will be better than this." After half an hour passed, he said goodbye and left. I do not know where he went. I was surprised. "God, who was he? Was he a jinni, or an angel disguised as a young person?" I was there until the eleventh day when, near noon, I saw two people enter the ruler's palace. It was obvious from their faces that they were shepherds. After an hour, they came out and asked me, "What is your name?" I replied, "Zugul." They said, "The two of us, whom you see, are the ruler's shepherds. The ruler has ordered that we take you to the village. What do you think?" I said, "Okay, I have nothing to say. Give me two minutes so that I can go and ask permission from the ruler, then I will come with you." They said, "Okay, go." I entered the ruler's palace, greeted him, and bowed. Then the ruler and others replied and greeted me. The ruler said, "Son, what do you want to say?" I said, "The ruler be safe. I have nothing to say, except the two shepherds are standing in front of the door of the house and said that the ruler has ordered them to take me with them to the village. What do you order? Whatever is best for you, please order." He replied, "Yes, son. I told them to take you to the village so you don't get homesick here. Those two are my shepherds. Go." I said goodbye to the ruler and others, came out of the ruler's palace, and left with those two shepherds. I said goodbye to the friends and the town of Sous Aqsa and moved out. I said "In the name of God" and proceeded, exiting through the town's gate. I said,

> There is none other than Him [God] in the land

I cried from the bottom of my heart, "God, what was my fault that this became my fate? I am not at ease for a moment. God, give me either death or salvation. Until when should I walk in the towns, deserts, mountains, and endure these ups and downs? God, I entrust myself to You." It was six hours before dusk when we left the town of Sous Aqsa. The weather was so warm. We walked until the sun had reached the horizon. We arrived at a village. When we arrived, I saw that they had just brought the sheep and herds from the pastureland and the small lambs were with their mothers. I saw there were no more than two or three households. One of the shepherds took me to his own house. It was clear what the condition of a village house would be. He hosted me. I ate bread and milk that night. I was so tired. They had prepared a corner for me, and I rested. I spent that night there. At day-spring, I awoke and got up. There was a water canal. I sat, refreshed my hands and face, then I returned and sat in a corner. After a moment, they brought me some bread and milk, known as *loqmat al-sabah* [breakfast], and placed it before me, and I ate. After eating, I looked outside and saw they were milking all the sheep. After milking, two of the shepherds moved the sheep and the herds and separated the small lambs from their mothers and they left. Then, the wife of that shepherd asked me, "Can you graze these two to three hundred lambs nearby?" I replied, "Of course, that I can do." She said, "Good, take them." I held a stick in my hand and started herding the lambs towards the pastureland. Almost for two *maydan-i asb*, the grasses were so thick and the land was green. The grasses were two to three *zar*ʿ tall, green like emeralds, the beauty of which would make one unconscious. I paused and told myself, "Since I am new and foreign, I cannot proceed. I will stay here to graze the lambs and I will watch." I returned the lambs near the evening. That day, until about sunset, I was in the desert. Near dusk, I went towards the house. They were so kind and entertained me a lot. I spent that day and night there. The next day, like the day before, I took the lambs to the pastureland. I was in the village for seven days. During this time, I did not have a bad time, and was unaware of what would happen.

[From Sous Aqsa to El-Obeid]

On the seventh day, a messenger from the town of Sous Aqsa arrived and said, "Get ready to move out, since the ruler wants to fight with another ruler and wants to evacuate this town. So, all the inhabitants and residents must move out towards the town of Lubayyiz and this town will be vacant." The messenger left. The next day, near the morning, the shepherds had prepared several camels and packed everything and put all their belongings on the backs of the camels. The same day, we walked from the village of the town of Sous Aqsa, which was near the south of Khartoum, near the Nile River. We said goodbye to that town and that village and left. We said "In the name of God" and proceeded to move out towards the town of Lubayyiz. That day we walked in the desert until sunset. I was unaware as to where we were going. At sunset, we arrived in a reed land. We camped there. After having some rest and eating some bread and water, we spent that night with thousands of difficulties in that desert. At dawn, we woke up. After breakfast, we put the belongings on the backs of the camels. They had entrusted me with the cattle to herd and also one mare that the shepherd had mounted his son on. Early in the morning, we moved out from there again.

The distance from the town and village of Sous to the town of Lubayyiz was ten days. We did not stay anywhere and walked past one place after another and passed through dangerous and frightening places, including strange and odd deserts, mountains, valleys, jungles, and plains, and went up and down until we arrived at the ninth camp. We stayed in that place that night. At the first light of day, when the sun brightens and decorates the world, we ate breakfast. While talking with those shepherds, dust rose from the distance. We waited to see what it was. I looked carefully and saw an Arab riding a camel and approaching fast. We waited until he arrived. He laid the camel down and came under the tree where we were sitting. He greeted us. We replied. They asked him to sit. He sat. After welcoming him, the shepherds asked, "Oh friend, where are you coming from? Where are you going to?" The person was the shepherds' friend, and they knew each other. He said, "I am coming from the town and going towards the town of Lubayyiz." They asked, "Do you have any news about the town?" He said, "I swear to God, no one is in the town, except a few, and they too are leaving." After an hour, he got up. They said, "Now that you are leaving towards the town of Lubayyiz, take this Zugul to sit on the camel with you. Since the day we left the village, he has not had a ride. Mount him, and take him with you, and get him to the ruler's camp." He said, "All right," and pointed to me and said, "Get up to mount." I kissed the shepherds and asked for forgiveness: "Forgive me for these several days that I was with you." I said that and sat on the carrier with the person who was on the camel. The camel stood up and we proceeded. Then, the camel owner started asking me questions about my past and present and what had happened to me. Then, he removed cooked camel liver from a leather container on the camel pack, divided it and gave me half of it, and he ate the other half.

While we were riding, we were continuously seeing caravans on foot and mounted camels coming from the town of Sous Aqsa and going to the town of Lubayyiz. We took the back road when we left the village, and these caravans were taking a different road. Among them, I saw a woman sitting on the back of a horse and two attendants running on foot behind that prestigious woman. We walked all the way. Many tents became visible from a distance. I asked the camel owner, "What are these tents?" He replied, "Apparently, they belong to the ruler's camp." We arrived quickly to the tents. When we arrived near a very large tent, he laid the camel down, held my hand, and brought me to the large tent. We both entered. I saw that several high-ranking officials of the ruler were sitting, gathered around and talking with each other. We greeted them. They replied. The camel rider entrusted me to the officials and told them that I belonged to the ruler. He said goodbye and left. They asked me to sit. I sat. They started talking to me and said, "What happened to you during this period?" I replied, "Thank God, I had a good time; it was not bad."

After an hour passed, those people and the high-ranking official said to me, "Oh dear brother, we intend to move out to get to the ruler's camp. You should come with us." I quickly got up and came out of the tent and asked, "Were these not the ruler's tents?" They replied, "No, all these tents you see belong to the harem of the ruler, who is coming behind us slowly." We said "In the name of God" and all four of us moved out on foot from there. It was noon when we left there and started walking in the desert. Wherever we arrived, every twenty to thirty steps, we picked sweet sugar cane and ate, talked, laughed, and walked. We walked in the desert until dusk. At sunset, when the sun had reached the horizon, a large crowd of people appeared from the distance. We started walking fast to reach them. They were five to six hundred men and women, white and Black, young and old, who were part of the caravan. When we arrived at the caravan, I saw they were camped near a water canal. I sat near the water canal, drank water with my hand, washed my hands and face, and then got up. The official told me, "Oh dear brother, you walked a lot today and are tired. Now it is dusk. It is good for you to mount the camel." I said, "Whatever you say." He held my hand, brought me over, and entrusted me to a girl who was around eighteen or nineteen years old. He told her to take good care of me: "Mount this Zugul on the camel and take him with you to the town of Lubayyiz." I went. The girl said, "Okay." The girl was a resident of the town of Sous Aqsa. I saw the saddle on the camel was slightly dispositioned. The girl fastened the camel saddle tightly, then two or three other kids and myself mounted and the camel started moving.

> How good it would be with one gesture to get two results
> One, the death of the rival, and the second, reaching the loved one

We walked all the way with the caravan, and, almost three hours after sunset, we arrived in the town of Lubayyiz. The girl brought me to the ruler's palace. She helped me dismount and entrusted me there and left. Then an attendant of the ruler held my hand. That night he brought me to a room that was for the servants. I entered the room and saw all the servants were sleeping. I was so tired and slept in a corner until sunrise. At the crack of dawn, when the sunlight brightens and decorates the world, I woke up, went out of the room, and left to wash the dust from my face and hands. After washing, I returned and again sat in the same room. All the Black and white friends were gathered. We were brought breakfast, and my friends and I ate; then we went out of the room to the yard. The yard was so vast that in the middle of it a large tent was set up. They had placed a chain around the tent for the ruler, who sat there for judgment and for resolving issues related to people, day and night. While walking in the yard, the officials came from the government office and said, "Now, the ruler is coming out of the harem." While we were talking, the ruler came out of the harem and went inside the tent. The ministers, officials, and chiefs were seated. I was coming and going and talking with the companions. That day, the ruler was working until noon on matters related to the politics and economy of the country. At noon, the meeting was over. The ruler went inside his harem, and the chiefs and ministers all kept busy with their own business. In the evening, again, they all gathered, the same as in the morning. It was the summer season. They had set up the tent in the yard.

Three days passed and it was near morning when I was walking in the yard and the chiefs and ministers were sitting. In the midst of this, the ruler saw me and called me over. I replied and entered the tent and greeted him. He returned my greetings. The ruler then asked me, "Son, when did you arrive?" I replied, "Your Majesty, it has been two or three days since I arrived." He said, "So, why did you not come to see me during these three days?" I said, "Your Majesty, I was busy praying for Your Excellency until now; otherwise, I would not be late in coming to your service. Today, I came to visit you and kiss your feet." He admired me a lot. After some questions and answers, he told his treasurer, "Make sure to get an appropriate cloth for my son Zugul today."

The treasurer said, "Of course, today I will provide it for him." After half an hour, I asked permission from the ruler and came out of the tent. It was near the evening when, following the order of the ruler, he provided me with a robe and gratuity. I became so happy. I thanked God for changing the worn-out cloth, which was given to me when I was staying with the minister of Saljmattyah's ruler.

While I was in the town of Lubayyiz, the ruler and other servants, men and women, were so kind to me. They looked after me with so much kindness. Since I knew the poems and verses of the land of Sudan, they liked me very much. It had not been ten days before one of the merchants of this region, who was a close friend of the ruler and had seen me already while visiting the ruler, said to the ruler, "Give this Zugul to me." After a long conversation, the ruler gave me to the merchant. In return for getting me, the merchant presented gifts and offerings to the ruler. When I went to the house of the merchant, I saw that he, his mother, and two male servants, one of whom was a young Black man and the other white, were there. The merchant and his mother and the others entertained me with total kindness. I was in the house of the merchant for about one week. One day, people in the town were agitated. I went out of the house and saw that the world's condition had changed. I asked, "What has happened?" They replied, "News and a letter from another ruler has arrived to this ruler of Sous Aqsa saying that they are at war with us. The turmoil is for this reason." We said, "Okay, let's go to the ruler's palace and ask what is going on." When I got there, I saw the ruler, the ministers, the chiefs, and the commanders of the army were all gathered inside the tent, and they were busy talking and conversing. In the midst of this, he told one of his ministers, "Go, open the door of the treasury, and prepare whatever is needed for war." The minister got up, bowed, and went to prepare the army. I was there for several hours, then went home. The next day, I came back again and decided to go and watch. I was at the entrance door of the ruler's palace standing and watching a large crowd of people who were coming and going. I saw continuously group after group and crowd after crowd; the well-armed regiments were passing in front of us, moving out to the town's gate. Soon, after seven days, in the morning, while I was standing next to the tent of the ruler, I saw the minister enter and bow. Then, he started reciting prayers and said, "To your endless fortune, during these seven days I marched ten thousand troops, and all have tented outside of the gate because you were in a rush. Otherwise, if you could wait a few more days, I could prepare almost twenty thousand troops." The ruler said, "This is enough." He was very impressed and asked for the robe of honour and gave it to the minister. At the same time, he asked for an animal to ride on. He, himself, other ministers, officials, and commanders got on and left the city and entered the camp. He looked at it and saw the camp was set so that each tent was tight to the next tent. Each community had its own custom. The ruler admired the minister very much. They went all the way until he entered his own tent and throne, then the others entered the tent and sat in their own places. He ordered someone to play the timbal. The cup-bearer served wine. The ruler spent that day and night in the camp. At the crack of dawn, when sunlight illuminated and the embellished the world, I went out of the house to watch and see what would happen. With several of my friends, we went out of the city's gate to watch. We saw they played the drum for the departure. The ruler entrusted the city to one of the ministers and could rest assured that the city was safe. The ruler got on. The troops moved like a wave of the sea and left. After that, we returned home. The city was somehow quiet. After three days, the merchant with whom I was staying went somewhere with one of his servants and I had no news of them. He entrusted the house to his mother and one of his servants. After the merchant departed, the servant and I were out day and night. I had no worries in my heart. I had learned all the quarters, alleys, and bazaars. One day, I was sitting in a corner and started thinking and dreaming about my homeland: "God, for how long will I be separated and suffer from these conditions? I have not been at ease since I left the village of Sousse Azunjan, and in every land where I have arrived, its ruler has started a war. Only You deserve greatness. Oh God, what will my future be? For how long will I run in these cities, deserts, mountains, and wilderness? I said not to see separation, but I saw. Noah saw one storm in one thousand years. I have seen one thousand storms, not even being Noah."

After a week, the merchant returned from the trip. After visiting, he again decided to travel. When he had returned from the trip, he had brought a child *kaniz* and entrusted her to his mother to look after her. This time when he wanted to travel, he took me with him and several merchants and others who, between ten and twelve of them, accompanied us. They were all skilled horse riders. The merchant put me on the back of the horse behind him. We were on the road for two days. On the second day, we arrived in a village that apparently was a harbour in the south of the city of Labyyaz. It was very important and had a large population. They took us to the house of a friend of the merchant and hosted us there for two to three days. They entertained us but, because of too much riding, my thighs were bruised and I could not walk. The skin on my legs had peeled off. During the two to three days that we were there, we had very good times. The tea that I had in that port was a rarity there.

After three days, when the merchant had done his personal work, we went towards the city of Labyyaz with the companions. After two days, we arrived. I was there with the merchant. We were going to the main and back roads in the villages and hamlets to bring and sell grains, and so on, every day. After travelling to all those areas, this time, I did not go with that merchant.

[From El-Obeid to Khartoum]

This time, they decided to depart from the city of Labyyaz to go towards the city of Khartoum, which was then the capital of Nuba. We were at Labyyaz for a week while they did their work. When their personal work was finished, after one week, the merchant went, gave money to a ship that was loaded with goods and food and was about to leave for the city of Khartoum. He made recommendations about us and the merchant came home. It was near the evening; they packed our trip provisions, and we left home. We went all the way until we arrived at the coast of the Nile River. We saw that the ship's crew had put down anchor and were waiting for us. We proceeded towards the ship. They stowed our belongings, then we came. I kissed the merchant's hand and asked forgiveness from him and other friends, and I went on board. Then I saw the merchant's mother kiss his son and come on board with the child *kaniz*. The three of us went on board. Then the merchant said, "Go safely, and I will come after you tomorrow. I will travel by land." There were two ship captains who steered the boat. Near evening, I said goodbye to the city of Labyyaz before the ruler arrived from the war, and I went on board and watched until the ship disappeared from the eyes of the merchant and other friends. The ship sailed sometimes slow and sometimes fast; we were watching the sea and fish. I was sitting on deck and watching.

I will recount a few words. We were three: the merchant's mother, the child *kaniz*, and I. We were travelling for three days and nights on the Nile River. On the third day, I was sitting on deck with the captains and was talking about life. I asked one captain, "Do you know how far away we are from Labyyaz city? How many days will it take to arrive in the city of Khartoum?" He said, "We have not gone further than about fifty to sixty *farsang*s." The captain continued, "If we wanted to sail fast, we would have arrived at Khartoum in five days. Because we sailed three days, seven more days are left. From here to Khartoum all the route is frightening and dangerous. We seldom anchor in the sea unless we know that there is no fear, then we will anchor there." We sailed all the way until we arrived at a big port, two *manzel*s away from Khartoum. One of the captains anchored in the harbour. We disembarked at the port's coast, and we all left the ship and walked a little along the coast; those two captains kept watching us. I kept seeing the inhabitants of the port come group by group; they got water and looked at us.

That day we were in the port until sunset and had no news of the merchant and his companions, nor had he news of our arrival. It was at sunset when the merchant and his companions, and several others of the port's inhabitants, arrived and took us to a house. That night, until the morning, they entertained us very well. With the rising of the sun, the merchant said, "Leave this port quickly today." I said, "I will not go with your mother." He asked, "Why?" I said, "I am scared of the sea. Because last night there was a strong storm, and our ship almost sank. It was God's help that we were not drowned." He said, "Fine, come with us." After an hour, the merchant, the others, and I brought his mother along with the child *kaniz* to the shoreline. We got them aboard and said goodbye to them. The captains sailed the ship to the middle of the sea, and we stood watching until the ship disappeared from our sight; then we returned to the house. That day we were at the port until three hours before sunset. Near dusk, they prepared the animals and brought one donkey for me. We said goodbye to the owner of the house, and we all got on the animals except for a few who had none, so they came on foot. We said goodbye to the port and left for Khartoum.

[Evading British Patrol]

We travelled all the way that day until sunset. Sometimes I walked and the friends got on the animal, and sometimes I got on it. That night, too, we walked in the frightening and dangerous jungle until the morning. We arrived at a small village in the morning and stayed there for several hours, then departed again that day. We were walking until sunset. We came across many cemeteries on our way and walked past them until three hours into the night. While we were going, we saw several horses without an owner in the jungle. I told the friends, "It would be good to get these horses to ride them and after you've rested, leave them." They did so. We arrived at a vast plain field that night and under these conditions, we stayed there until sunrise. Early in the morning, we packed and departed. Several villages were on our way and whenever we arrived at one, they entertained us. We had a good time. On the third day, near dawn, we departed from the last place. Three hours before noon, the palm groves in Baqa' and Khartoum appeared. We went all the way until we arrived at Baqa'. Baqa' is the place of the British factories and machineries. We passed there. We had not yet arrived at the seashore when I saw a mounted British official approaching fast. Once the merchant saw the official, he asked his servant to bring the light white veil from the saddlebag. His servant quickly brought a veil, like the ones used for the night prayer, from the saddlebag. He said, "Put it on Zugul's head, and quickly take him to the seashore. Put him on board the ship, take him to the house, and I will come after you." While he was talking, the official arrived and greeted the merchant. Because the merchant himself was a resident of Khartoum, he had contacts with all the British officials. Then the merchant told his servant, "Hold this child and quickly take him home to keep him away from the sunlight." Now, they had covered my head so that the official could not see me, nor could I see anything. The servant held me and brought me all the way to the shore of the Nile Sea and put me inside the ship and then removed the white veil from my head. When we got to the other side of the sea, we got off the ship. He took me to the house of the merchant, which was next to Mashq Square. He put me by the house and he himself went to the merchant. When I entered the house, I saw his mother had arrived a few days earlier. The child *kaniz*, his wife, two of his daughters, and his son surrounded me. I greeted them and they replied. They said, "Young one, you are very welcome. Your arrival at this house be blessed." They received me very well and with kindness. I was there until the merchant came to the house and, after the visit ended, I was at Khartoum, the capital of Nuba, for two weeks.

During the days I was there, I saw nothing except happiness and joy. All the time, I was walking around, partying, and near the evening would go to the shore of the Nile Sea to walk and watch ships and fish. Every day, in the evening, they would bring sugar cane that we bought and ate. What a nice and populated city! About two hundred and fifty thousand Black and white people and Nasara were in that capital. Perhaps every city has a population, industry, trade, and agriculture. Every day near the morning, we went to watch the British military exercises, and almost all the British soldiers were Black. The city had high civilisation, sciences, urbanisation, railroads, a telegram station, and a post office, which were used throughout the Sudan. Meaning, in the newly civilized territories in the Sudan, everything, such as trees, fruits, booty, and all the wealth in the world can be found there. There is a treasury house that Sultan Mabot Mahdi[7] had built for the people of Sudan during his lifetime. Every day, the Black people would take big drums, kettledrums, bugles, trumpets, reeds, and tambourines and

---

7 Referring to Muhammad ibn ʿAbdullahi, who, in 1881, claimed to be the Mahdi in Sudan.

go to the treasury house to play, beat, and sing the Sudanese songs and verses, respectfully. It is the tradition here that in all the Sudanese territories, from the old times, men and women, young and old, have fun. All homes should have drums and musical instruments of all kinds. It is one of the necessities. There are no poor people and no theft; there are very few. From every point of view, I had very good times. After the one month I spent there, I became familiar with the area. I noticed the merchant packed for travel and planned for a trip. After a couple of days, he travelled somewhere for business. I stayed at the merchant's house in Khartoum. After five to six days, the merchant returned from the trip. On the next trip, he took me with him, and some of his friends also travelled along. The merchant and I walked past roughly a hundred and six villages to buy grains and goods to sell and cash them in Khartoum. All the hundred and six villages we arrived at knew the merchant; they were his friends and he knew all of them. They were kind and entertained us well. For about three months, I was in Khartoum, the capital of Nuba, on the coast of the Nile. I visited the area and the surroundings and became familiar with its inhabitants, and I was not aware of my fate or what would happen.

[From Khartoum to Jedda]

Again, I noticed things changed to a different situation. Once again, the merchant said he planned a trip. I thought to myself that this time I would not return from this trip. I said goodbye to all my friends and acquaintances and asked for their forgiveness. The next day, we left Khartoum, and I said goodbye to Khartoum, Baqa', and that area. It was around evening when we walked past Khartoum and crossed the sea of the Nile River and departed. Some of the merchant's friends became bitter towards the merchant; they were separated from each other and left. The merchant, I, and a group of merchants who were with us moved on. But I was unaware of where they were headed to. We went all the way until we arrived at a village and stayed in the house of a merchant who knew our merchant. They entertained us for two to three days. On the third day, the merchant told me, "You stay here until I return in five to six days." He said so and left the village the same day. That village was the sixtieth and the last one. After the departure of the merchant, I was there for five to six days. Something that happened in that village was that the merchant I was staying with had an old mother. One day I jokingly said, "Oh, the witch." Once the words came out of my mouth, she lashed me and I became unconscious. That was it. During the daytime, I would go out with friends, walk around, and return home. On the sixth day, the merchant returned to the village. After I had entertained him, he called me to the room. When I entered the room, I said my greetings and he replied. The merchant, my master, asked me how I was doing and how the six days had passed for me. I replied, "Thank God. Due to your attention, I am doing well." He showed me kindness and I recited some Sudanese poems. After a few hours, he said, "I am leaving again. You should stay in the house of this merchant." I had realized that if he left, then he would not return. He had come to see if I had been crying or not. When he saw that I hadn't and was fine there, he said, "I will never return to stay and will come to see you only once a week." The merchant was there until the evening, and in the evening, we said goodbye to him. I asked for his forgiveness: "Forgive me if I did anything bad and wrong during the three months when I stayed with you, do forgive me." Then he left. I stayed there for a week. It was in the evening of the following week when five to six *ghulam*s and *kaniz*es, two or three of the merchants of the village, one of whom was lame, and I all left the village, instructed by the merchant, the former master. I said goodbye to the landlord merchant and the village. We left and began walking in the desert.

There is none other than Him [God] in the land

Early in the evening, we began going until we arrived at the first rest stop. We stayed in the first rest stop that night. At the crack of dawn, when the sunlight brightened and decorated the world, we woke up and departed from there. For three days and nights we walked in the desert. At the third rest stop, we spent the night in the desert. Near sunrise, we again continued going. It was dusk when we arrived in a plain land. All that my eyes could see was a desert full of thorny bushes. The merchants helped us off the donkeys and told us, "You should get on the camels, and we should return to the village, and we will entrust you to these merchants." We went. My companions and I were crying and we yelled and begged them not to give us to them, but it was useless. I and the others got on with reluctance. The merchants who had come from the village returned. When the merchants left, I looked and saw five or six other Black *ghulam*s and *kaniz*es, who had been brought together, and the two to three camels that the Hadandawa[8] merchants had brought to carry the larder. While I was riding, I was crying and sobbing like the spring cloud. We were going and one of the Black

---

8 Nomadic pastoralists in eastern Sudan and Nuba.

people was holding the rope of the camel. The two or three merchants were following us on foot.

> Safety should remain in this road
> Stay away from such a long road

I suddenly raised my head to the sky: "God! For how long should I run in these deserts? And there is no way to get out of this. Oh my kind father, it was my fate and kismet to be, at this young age, the slave of the world. There is no judge to help me out. Dear father, there is no way to escape destiny and fate and, whatever the human's karma is, will happen. Whatever kismet wants, it will do; it does not succumb to a wish, but does whatever it wants. Because it was my fate to get this kismet. I have no one to bring my news to you; however, I know there is no hope to return to you, and death will not help me. But my dear father, the breeze that blows now in this dangerous and frightening desert will bring my news to you that your darling child is enslaved in the hands of enemies and has no way to escape. Oh destiny, how loyal are you?"

We did not stop in any place throughout the forty rest stops. We were passing from one place to another and walked past rest stops, roads, and about forty villages. At any rest stops where we arrived, two to three Hadandawa merchants joined us. The number of Black people was increasing and getting greater day by day. I stopped thinking and dreaming. They [the Black people] liked me very much and were kind to me. One of the Black people was telling me, "I am your mother," and one was telling me, "I am your sister," and the other was telling me, "I am your wife," and the other was telling me, "I am your brother." Each of them was kind and a friend in their own way. They did not let me walk on foot. Especially, the Hadandawa merchants and the master liked me very much, more than the others.

We continued going day and night and did not stop anywhere except for a short rest and then we moved on. At nights, we slept in the deserts, mountains, jungles, and plains, which were frightening and full of threats, and, during the daytime, we were walking hungry, thirsty, and tired. If we stopped walking, they would hit us. I could write an endless *Masnavi* book from the unusual things created by God in the deserts. Although separation, distance, and enslavement were difficult, they make one well-experienced and vigilant.

Once we arrived at the second or third rest stop away from the Red Sea, the food was finished. One night, before reaching the Red Sea, we arrived at a large river. Then they carried us in their arms and crossed us over the river. We fed ourselves with the herbs in the desert for three nights and days. On the third day, the merchants realized if food did not reach us, we would die. Imprudently, they arranged a meeting and stood up. Half of them went to the area they were familiar with to bring us food and water, and the rest brought us to the hot poisonous weather that cooks one's flesh. We walked all the way until we arrived at a valley and they left us there. While were waiting for food and water, thinking, "Is it coming now, or in an hour?" the camel riders arrived shortly and brought two to three camels loaded with food, which included dates, rice, and milk. They put the loads down and called us, "Oh community of Black people [Africans], come forward to us and take your share." All of a sudden, we rushed. They gave portions based on an individual's condition. I ate some dates and milk and was full and thanked God.

We were in the narrow valley between the two mountains for ten days because the merchants were waiting for one of the merchants who was behind us to arrive. On the night before the eleventh day, the merchant arrived. It was early in the evening and he came to our camp. The next day, the eleventh, in the afternoon, we saw all ten to twenty merchants become armed and well-equipped. We had no idea what they had in mind. In the afternoon, at half past three, we saw on the top of the mountain a shaykh mounted on a camel and another standing on foot. All of a sudden, the merchants became worried and told us, "All of you gather in one place." We gathered to see what would happen. Then the person riding a camel sent his servant, who said, "My ruler is saying that you should pay the annual tribute." They replied, "Fine." Then, several merchants came and held my hand to give me to them. They said, "This is a child; [give us] one [that] is older than this." I returned and saw all the Black people were crying for me. Once they saw me, they ran, hugged, kissed, and cuddled me. And instead of me, they took a *kaniz* and gave her. Then the ruler's agent left. After that person departed, the merchants came and told us, "We will leave early in the evening. Prepare a dinner." In the evening, after having supper, they packed the loads on the backs of the camels and migrated from that valley.

[British Search Patrol near the Red Sea]

We departed from there and descended the mountain. We said "In the name of God" and started walking in the desert, which was covered with rocks, sand, and thorny bushes. We were going and they were beating us hard as if we were herds of sheep, to the extent that if a thorn went into one's foot, they would not let the person remove it. After walking for about two *farsang*s, the smell of the breeze from the sea started blowing. We realized that we were close to the sea. We arrived at the bottom of a mountain and saw a light shining from afar. They told us, "Do not take a breath at all; wait a little." We waited a little at the bottom of the mountain to see what would happen. Then several merchants ran towards the light to see what that light was. Shortly after, they returned and reported, "It [the light] belongs to the British patrol that is searching around the sea lest Black people are transported and to prevent their transportation." They took us along the back of the mountain. After two more hours, we arrived at a place which had a couple of trees. They ordered us, "Rest there a little." We slept for about two hours on the sand. After two hours, they woke us, and we departed from there. Shortly after, we arrived at the shore of the Red Sea. The camel rider brought the camels down and got the merchants' load. The merchants paid the camel rider his money and apologized to him a lot. The same night, he said goodbye to the merchants and left. After the camel rider departed, I looked at the sea and saw one large ship had anchored at the edge of the sea and a small boat was attached to it. The merchants called the sailor, prepared the boat, and put us on the boat. They put all the Black people on the ship, and the merchants got on the ship with the loads. The boat was moved by the ship. The ship departed towards Jedda the same night. The ship started sailing and the same night I became seasick. I did not know what had happened. I fell down unconscious until the evening of the next day. I felt better after vomiting. They had brought some roasted coffee and divided it among us to eat. We ate and felt better, and the sea turbulence and movement did not bother us. For three nights and days we sailed and looked at the sea, the fish, and the creatures that God, the Greatest, had created in the sea. The food they had brought for us was finished. They consulted. The merchants chose six from among themselves to get off and go at the Jedda port to provide bread for the thousand Black people, and they sent them quickly. Six got off the ship and left towards the Jedda port and the rest stayed on the ship to guard and protect us. The sea water was briny like salt, and bitter. There were only two water containers on the ship, so whenever we needed water, they took a small cup and gave it to us to survive. The ship's crew sometimes cooked rice and gave us two to three bites to stay alive. We had sailed for three days and still had three more days till we would reach a place to get food. We had been waiting for the merchants for six days. On the seventh day, near the morning, we arrived at the coast, which was two to three *farsang*s away from the Jedda port. The merchants decided, when those [six] merchants did not arrive, that we should get off and wait for their arrival. They got us off the ship and we did not board again, because they told us the merchants would arrive that day. We were talking about this when we saw the ship started moving and the merchants yelled, "Wait till we unload our things from the ship!" The ship stopped for the merchants to unload their belongings. It was three hours till the evening. Near the evening, they brought five to six camel loads of bread for us. They put the loads on the ground and we rushed there. They gave us a piece and when we started to eat; it was like a rock, and black. Anyway, we ate some bread. We were there until early in the evening; then we got on and moved towards the Jedda villages.

3 [In Ottoman Arabia[1]]

We walked all the way until we arrived at the Jedda villages. There was a place like a square where they lined us up. Each merchant was calling the name of his own *ghulam* and *kaniz*: "So-and-so, come." It was four and a half hours past night, in the middle of Rajab. The ten to twenty merchants took whatever was their share and went to their own houses and places. We, who were about sixty in number, belonged to a merchant. We went to a house, and they gave us a large external room. After an hour, they brought us several large trays of cooked rice and lentils. I had never eaten rice and lentils before. It was eaten. After having it, we thanked God. That night, with thousands of difficulties, we slept on a straw mat until the morning. At the crack of dawn, when the sunlight illuminated and embellished the world, we awoke, got up, washed, and cleaned our faces and heads from the dust, then returned and sat in the room. After half an hour, they brought us several trays of breakfast and put them before us. It was eaten.

[Slave Trade in Jedda]

From the time that we arrived in the village of Jedda, every day, they were selling two to three of us, to the Nubian, Habashi, and others; *ghulams* and *kanizes*, of all kinds, to the inside and the outside [of the country] and to the bedouin and others, and in return, they were buying goods, cows, and fabric. The residence of the *kanizes* was in the interior and our residence was the exterior. During the ten to fifteen days that we were there, nothing happened to me or the others, except one day when we were playing and one of the playmates broke one of my

---

1 After 1932, Arabia was called Saudi Arabia.

teeth. When the merchant returned home, he noticed that I was playing and my tooth was broken; then he punished them a little. Before this event, I had hit the forehead of one of the Black people with a rock, and they retaliated.

Another incident was that a very beautiful Habashi *kaniz* was with us. Some of the shameless there wanted to assault the *kaniz*. The merchant noticed and punished them. I had nothing to do in the days and nights but to go for walks and have fun. I was unaware what would be my future. We were there until only five or six [Black people] were left out of sixty: three *ghulam*s and three *kaniz*es. We were the special order for the effendis[2] and the others. After ten to fifteen days, near the morning, at the break of day, one of the camel riders, the landlord of the home we were staying in, came. Then, the merchant called me: "Zugul, come." I came and he gave me to that landlord and told him what to do. I said goodbye to the people and was crying a lot that day. I said goodbye to everyone: "Oh my dear brothers and sisters, I am leaving you, but if you saw any troubles from me during these few days, forgive me. Never forget me because I have never seen any good from this world." I said this and came out. The landlord had provided a donkey. He put me on it and got on too. Then we departed from the Jedda village. I said goodbye to that place and then was crying like spring clouds. I had no choice and could do nothing.

I would say more. We walked all the way until we arrived at the Jedda town. We entered the market and went along until we arrived at the door of an effendi merchant's store. I saw an old man with a grey beard. The landlord, who was a middleman, dismounted and got me off. He said hello and the old man replied. The middleman said, "This is the slave whom I had recommended and brought." He said, "Take him to my house." He took me to the house and knocked on the door. A slave woman came to the door. He entrusted me to the slave woman and left. I entered the house and followed the slave woman. From one floor to the next, she took me up to the seventh floor. The seventh floor was the living room. I entered the room. The wife of the merchant was sitting with her children and *kaniz*es. I greeted them and they replied. They pointed at me to sit. I sat in a corner. They started asking me questions: "Oh young one, you are very welcome. Your arrival to this place be blessed. When did you come? Where are you coming from? From what region are you? Tell us about yourself." I started telling them everything about my past, from the time I was enslaved in the

---

2 Effendi is an Ottoman Turkish term meaning master or sir.

town village of Sousse Azunjan, near the Futenjalun mountain, near Qerqiat Island, near the sea, when they took me from there to the Saljmattyah town and to the ruler of Dez castle, and from there to the Sous Aqsa town where I was [with] its ruler, and from there to the town of Labyyaz and Khartoum, and about all the difficulties and sufferings that descended on me until I entered the town of Jedda. They became very surprised to hear this and told me, "Indeed, you, young one, have suffered a lot." They entertained me a lot. That day I was there until noon when they prepared lunch and it was eaten. Then the lady told me, "You should not feel homesick here. Go play with the effendi's daughters and sons," and she ordered them to look after me. I was in the town of Jedda for three nights and days and was unaware what would happen next.

[From Jedda to Mecca]

On the fourth day, with the crack of dawn and when sunlight illuminated and embellished the world, they said that they planned to depart from there to the Great Mecca and from there to Ta'if. They brought several camels, packed their belongings, and everyone, the women, children, the *kaniz*, one *ghulam*, and I and the others moved on. We said goodbye to the Jedda town and left. Many residents of Jedda left in lots of caravans and all were on the camel litter that is called *hawdaj*.[3] From Jedda to Mecca was a distance of three rest stops. We passed from one rest stop to another. On the fourth day, two hours before the evening, we arrived at the land of Mecca, where the Abu Qays Mountain appeared. We came all the way until we entered Mecca. There was no incident on our way, except on the road, at every point-to-point security post, soldiers were guarding and walking back and forth. When we arrived at one of the Meccan mountains, the effendi merchant told the camel rider, "Lay the female camel down and get this Zugul and take him to the house of the Jangali Effendi and return quickly." The camel rider laid the female camel down and got me off and took me and rode the camel. We came all the way until we arrived at the door of the effendi, who was the owner of the first group. He [the camel rider] laid the female camel down and got me down. He knocked on the door. A *kaniz* came to the door and he entrusted me to her, as instructed by the effendi merchant. The camel rider returned. I followed the *kaniz* and

---

3 *Hawdaj al-jamal* (camel litter) was a large basket with a canopy attached to the back of camels in which usually women would sit.

went to the upper floors and reached the third floor. She directed me to a salon and said to me, "In the name of God, please sit." I sat in a corner, but there was no one at home except the Habashi *kaniz* who was trained in the Hijazi manner.

[New Identity]

I was very tired and slept. Two hours after nightfall, the *kaniz* came and woke me up. "Wake up, eat your dinner." I woke up and saw the electric lights were on and two respectful women were sitting next to me. Once I saw them, I stood up and greeted them. They said, "Please, sit." I sat in a corner. They brought me dinner. It was milk and bread. They had put sugared jam on it. I sliced the bread and said "In the name of God" and ate. After having dinner, the women ordered, "bring one pillow," and they brought it for me. They said to me, "You must be tired, have a rest." I slept that night under these conditions. At the crack of dawn, when the sunlight illuminated and embellished the world, I woke up and saw the sun had come up to half a *zar*'. The women were sitting and drinking tea. I said hello and they replied. The elder woman got up, held my hand, and put me inside a bath. She took off my cloths, sat me on the frame of the bath, and washed me very well with a washcloth and soap. After finishing, she called, "*kaniz*, bring the cloths pack." She brought it and it was an elegant cloth. We said "In the name of God" and put it on. We came out of the bath. I looked like a human being who had come out of that monstrous look with the rag. Then they started teaching me how to do the service and other things. It did not take long. On the third day, I learned all the service, sayings, and manners to the extent that I was loved by the great sir, his son-in-law, his wife, his daughter, and the others. Friends and enemies liked me a lot. They changed my name to Almas.

It did not take more than a month before the rental payment of the west house became due, and we moved to the east house and settled there. I was having fun and enjoyed my days and nights there too. The people of the effendi, group after group of men, were coming every day. There was not a day that no one came. The daughters of the effendi, who was my master, were coming group by group, day and night, playing music, and leaving. I did not notice the passing of time [for having a good time] until at the end of the month of Ramadan, when we went for the prayer of Eid al-Fitr. What a prayer! No eyes have seen and no ear has heard the like of it! After the prayer ended, we went home for festivity. They had such a celebration; no other countries celebrate like this!

[From Mecca to Ta'if]

After Eid al-Fitr, the master packed for the trip to Ta'if. After one week, near evening, we got on the camels and left from the Great Mecca for Ta'if. They entrusted the house to their friends, and we left. They could rest assured about the house. It was also the summer season, when all the people of Jedda and Mecca go to the countryside. We too left. It was half an hour before the evening when we departed. After half an hour, we arrived at the Jabal al-Noor mountain. Apparently, the Prophet was on this mountain, and the mountain rose and elevated itself when they wanted to kill the Prophet Muhammad, may God bless him and his family/household and may God honour him and grant him peace. From that time, it was called Jabal al-Noor. We walked past there and came all the way until we entered the first rest stop. That night we camped and spent the night with thousands of difficulties at the first rest stop. The first rest stop was a good place and had good weather with lots of fruit trees and many citrus fruits. At the crack of dawn, when the sunlight illuminated and embellished the world, we again departed from the first rest stop. We continued going until we arrived at the second rest stop. We spent the night there and the next day, an hour before the evening, we left the second rest stop. We were half a *farsang* away when I saw a camel with an injured foot carrying a tent and food. It could not move. Its master and his servant tried so hard to move the animal and make it get up, but it did not. When this was happening, ten to twenty of the military bedouin, who had several camels, came to us. Once they arrived, my master said, "Come on and raise this camel." Whatever they tried, they could not get it up. They became disappointed, said goodbye, and left. Then our master told one of his servants, Ibrahim Beyk Effendi, "You go slowly, and I will come behind you later." He sent one horse rider to the front to go ahead and find the camel rider.

The horse rider went fast, and the poor master was left alone with his horse and that camel load in the desert, and it became night and dark. On the one hand, I was thinking of our master that, Oh God, he is left alone in the dangerous and frightening desert, and on the other hand, I was scared and thought that, Oh God, all the caravans have left. There was only a camel load of food, whose rider was Ibrahim, the servant; another camel, which the old lady, her daughter, her little baby grandchild, and her *kaniz* were on; and I was riding the other camel in the back with the load of food. The child was crying, and we were going, and the moon had just come up. Shortly after, the rider whom the master had sent, returned, and I asked him, "Didn't you see the camel rider?" He replied, "No, I didn't," and walked past us. After an hour, the master and the rider joined us. They had put the camel load in the desert and returned. We were happy that the master had returned safely.

We got to the caravan under the circumstances. We arrived at the sandy ground. I was sleeping on the camel when, all of a sudden, I fell off the camel in the dark. Nothing happened to me, and then a young person came in the dark, hugged me, and put me back on the camel. This time, they tied me firmly on the camel. We soon arrived at the third rest stop. When the camel fell, the cage with a very cute furry cat in it fell on the ground and broke, and the cat fled that night. The master liked the cat very much and became very sad. That night we spent at the third rest stop under these conditions. In the morning, we packed. The servants had found the camel rider and brought him to the master. After punishing the camel rider, the master told him, "From this third *manzel*, you should return and bring the camel back with its load by tomorrow and, if there is even a little wrongdoing, I will punish you severely." He said that and we left the third rest stop going towards Ta'if.

Soon, before noon, we arrived safe and sound in the town of Ta'if. They prepared a house for us, and we settled there. We sought relief from the dangerous and frightening deserts and mountains. For several days, friends would come to visit us. Then it was our turn to go to visit. Every day we were going somewhere. Such a city! Such buildings, valleys, bazaars, and quarters! Such people! Good and rich! Such weather! Such citrus fruit! There were always seven to eight army camps. The city was very nice, with polite people, liberty, and order that makes one surprised. All the poor received their livelihood from the treasury. I used to visit the shrine of Hamza, the uncle of the Prophet [Muhammad], the Messenger of God, blessings of God be upon him and his progeny. We had gatherings for women and men every day and night. We had such a good time! Day and night we had musicians. I was at their service until, one day, we were partying outside in the garden. It was the garden of the effendi merchant from Jedda. It was near the morning; we came to the garden and walked until we arrived at the door of the garden. We knocked on the door, and the gardener came and opened the door. We said "In the name of God" and entered the garden.

> There is a garden like heaven
> Wherein all kinds of colourful flowers have bloomed
> We saw a very pleasant green garden. It looked like the Shaddad earthly heaven.

Sandalwood, aloeswood, and ivory were in that garden
Its beauty stolen from the tribute of the whole world

Water was running from all the canals like Salsabil [the fountain of paradise] near the trees. Flower, basil, the beautiful song of birds, the song of the nightingale and the turtle-dove all made me unconscious.

Is it the paradise breeze that is running in the brooks?
It smells musky in the air of the meadow
The green field grown on the soil and clay
It looks not like a plantation, but heavens, not ten but hundreds
The turtle-dove created two hundred melodies out of its throat
It has played the songs with low and high pitches
They have tossed, buzzed, and whispered
On the branches of cedars and bushes, both partridges and starlings
From the rainfalls bubbles are on the water
Like a silver stream running water from the waterfalls[4]

Such a garden! It was like heaven, amber in character! Wherever I looked was grassland, and the song of nightingales, animals, martins, canaries, and parrots. We picked fruits from trees and ate. We were walking in the garden when we arrived at a very large pond surrounded by flower vases, basil, hyacinth, and others. A variety of colourful fish were inside the pond. We strolled a little and arrived near a palace building. We went up and I saw the effendi's ladies were sitting on aloeswood and sandalwood chairs. We went inside, said hello, and they replied. I sat a little then came out to the garden and strolled around. That day, until the evening, we were there and we had a very good time. At dusk, we said goodbye and came out of the garden and went towards the house. Another day, the family of the effendi merchant of Jedda was invited to our house until the evening and then they left. After several days, the camel rider arrived with the load safe and sound without there being any problem. We were in Ta'if for five to six months. We spent all the time having fun. One thing that happened in Ta'if was that the granddaughter of the master passed away. They mourned for three days. One day, at the mourning, I was laughing with the kids when the wife of the master got up, brought a rope, tied my shoulders tight, and locked me up in the storage room for one day. I was released

---

4 The poem is the sixteenth *qasida* of Qa'ni in praise of Amir Kabir, the prime minister of Iran during the Qajar period.

through the intervention of her daughter, Sayemah, who took off the ropes. After one week, the master, his wife, and his son-in-law all left for an invitation. No one was at the house except the master's daughter, me, and one servant. The servant was talking in the Istanbul Turkish language with the daughter. In the midst of this, the master's son-in-law arrived and I had heard the servant talking to the lady. That day he called me and said, "Tell the truth. Did the lady talk with the servant?" Out of fear, I said, "Yes." Then he whirled a rope around his head and whipped his wife several times until she was unconscious. That was it. I saw what I should not have seen in Ta'if.

[From Ta'if to Mecca: Education]

After five to six [months], we packed for travel and left Ta'if to go to the Great Mecca. I was in the Great Mecca for five months. I was doing both service and going to the *maktab* to read the Qur'an. The teaching tradition in the schools there was that, until the child had not completed the Qur'an, it [the Qur'an] should be on a plaque. Once the child delivered [completed] the Qur'an, they give the Qur'an to the child. Mecca was like my homeland. I had contact with all the dignitaries and nobles there. I was there until the season of pilgrimage, when the pilgrims came to Mecca. The master wanted to take me to Mina and Arafat, but because there was no male at home, he left me and went. Almost all the Meccan residents went to Mina and Arafat. The city of Mecca became to some extent vacant. The women took tambourines in their hands and played in alleys and markets until the morning. I had so much fun until all the Hajjis[5] returned from Mina and Arafat to Mecca. I kept seeing the world had changed. When the master returned from the trip of the illuminated and pure Medina, he brought some gifts, presents, and honorary cloths. These things happened at that time.

I kept seeing the lady ask for property money from the master. We had no relief, day or night, from these two people, so our times were always bitter. When the *kaniz*, the servant of the master, got sick and died, life became so difficult for me. Every day, the lady was unjustly complaining about me and the others and her mood changed. She and the master were bothering me and beating me so much. Still under this condition, I was going to the *maktab* to read the honourable Qur'an. One day, the family of the effendi master were guests at the house of another effendi, but I did not know they were guests there. They were

---

5 Pilgrims.

sitting on a wooden balcony near a latticed window, and that balcony was facing the *maktab khana*. While I was playing with the kids, they saw me. In the evening, when I returned home, they told me, "You play; there is no need for you to go to the *maktab*." I did not go anymore to the *maktab*. I was beaten a lot at the *maktab* and was beaten a lot by the master and his wife. Even with all these mistreatments, their behaviour was good. But I was, day and night, at their service. I had good times. I was having such fun that I did not know if it was day or night.

[Circumcision]

This was when I slowly noticed the conditions changed. They circumcised me at the Great Mecca. They liked me so much. Day and night I had nightmares in my sleep. Some nights, I dreamed that lots of dogs surrounded me and wanted to tear me into pieces. Then a young person came to my rescue. That was what I saw one night in an arid desert. I was talking to two people, and we had our hands around our necks and were walking. During this, I saw one person with a black turban, who was of medium height and wore black woollen cloths. He had a weapon in his hand and was coming fast towards us from the desert. Once I saw him, I left the two people and escaped. I saw he followed the two and left. I woke up and interpreted that it meant soon there would be a separation between me and my master. To some extent this happened. When Hajjis were shopping and wanted to return, every clan went towards its own land.

[Slave Market in Mecca: Reselling]

One of my friends, who was very polite and educated, used to come to our house every night. He was a very good friend of mine, coming every night and consoling me that God had given me a livelihood, and so on and so forth, [reassuring me] of what had happened and what had not. He was advising me to not get homesick and that he hoped I would reach high positions. After several days, someone came near the morning whom the master instructed, "You take Almas to the slave shop for sale." He took me. I was in the slave shop until noon. At noon, he returned me to the house. I stayed in the house until the next day. Next day, in the morning, I put on the Hijaza cloth. The same [slave] dealer came to take me. I told him to wait a minute so I could say goodbye to the master, the ladies, and friends and ask for forgiveness before I came. I kissed the hands and feet of the master and the ladies and asked for their forgiveness. I told them, "During the period that I was at your service, forgive me if I troubled you. Because I am certain I will not come back again, and I did not see any good from this world. But do not forget to pray for me." I said goodbye to everyone and walked down the building. The dealer of the [slave] shop was standing, waiting for me. He held my hand, and we left to go towards the shop, which was a special place for the sale of *ghulam*s and *kaniz*es. We arrived at the door of the [slave] shop. They brought me a chair, and I sat. I saw slaves; the female slaves were placed in rows: best, intermediate, inferior. After half an hour, I saw the [slave] dealer, whose name was Hajj Sa'idi. He came and took me with him to walk to the court of God's house [the Ka'ba] for sale. He walked me around to get me to be quiet, but I did not. I was crying like the spring cloud and was asking him to return me to the house of the first master. He was buying me presents such as fruits and sweets to calm me down, but it was impossible. Then he took me to a house where all the Black people were for sale. I watched and saw two Habashi *kaniz*es who were trained in the Hijazi tradition and had been brought along with me for sale. They saw I was crying. They were crying too and were saying, "Child, why are you crying so much? We feel sorry for your loneliness. We look like you too. Stop crying." Minute by minute, my cries became worse.

That day, until three hours before dusk, I was at the [slave] shop and strolling. Near the evening, the [slave] dealer came, held my hand, and we went together. But I did not know where he was taking me. We came all the way until we arrived at the door of a house. We entered the house. We walked up the stairs towards the exterior. We entered a room. I saw there was no one there except a few people, such as camel loaders, a female servant, and the house owner. He sat me down and entrusted me to the camel loaders and said, "I leave this Almas here and I must go. Either I myself or his master, who is the effendi, will come and decide whatever he thinks is appropriate for him." Then the dealer went. I stayed there and was crying like the spring cloud. The camel loaders and the landlord surrounded me and comforted me, saying, "Oh young one, why you are crying so much? Be calm for an hour. We feel for you. We have some compassion for your loneliness."

[At the House of the 'Ulama': New Identity]

After a short time, as it did not last long, I saw His Highness, Excellency, and Eminence Mr. Hajj Shaykh 'Abdullah Mazandarani, pure be his soil, and His Excellency, the Great Mr. Hajj Shaykh Ishaq Ayatullahzadeh [Rashti] Gilani, long may he live, come in and, after half an hour, the effendi master came in. I said hello and they replied. After [exchanging] greetings and the conversation about my purchase, they counted the amount of a hundred and fifty tomans and gave it to Mr. Effendi, the master. He said goodbye and left. I could not stand still. I ran quickly and held his cloth and said, "Take me with you. I do not want to be here." He said, "You should be here. I will check on you two or three times." He said this and left. I was disappointed and could not do anything. Again, I sat. The men showed compassion and kindness towards me and said, "Why are you crying? We are your fathers. Don't be sad." But whatever they were saying to each other, I did not understand because my language was Sudani and Hijazi, and I could not understand the Iraqi Arab language.

After half an hour, they started speaking Farsi with each other and said they would take me to the interior to the women and perhaps I would calm down. They took me to the interior, to the women. When I saw the women, I became quiet. Because the women kept me busy, I did not cry. But they assigned several of the servants and camel loaders to guard and protect me day and night, lest I be kidnapped or escape without their knowledge. When they were going out, half of them would stay and half would go. After several nights, two hours past nightfall, they changed my name over dinner. After *istikhara*[6] with the Great Qur'an, they named me Mahboob. I was there until I left the Great Mecca. I had interpreted my dream the same way. It happened that I fell into the hands of the Shi'i Ithna 'Ashari and the religion of Ja'far, God's blessings and peace upon him. In the Great Mecca, when I wanted to pray with folded hands, they prohibited it and said, "Do not pray like this." Gradually, I diverted from the aberration to the right way, and I said, "Thanks be to God, who took me out of the darkness and into the light and guided me to the straight path, with the sovereign power of Muhammad and his pure family." And I said, "If only my people could know of how my Lord has forgiven me and placed me among the honoured."

They were educating me day and night. But I was not eating food out of fear. They kept telling me, "Why don't you eat anything?" I was telling them, "I do not need to." And they were waiting for me to say something or that I wanted something. One day, I told someone I wanted watermelon, which in the Hijazi language is called *habhab*.[7] All of a sudden, I saw a watermelon as big as his head! I ate two pieces then the camel loaders took it and ate it.

---

6 Seeking guidance from God by consulting the Qur'an.
7 A watermelon in Saudi Arabia, according to the Hijazi dialect.

I was there until the Hajjis wanted to return from Mecca. Each clan returned to its own land: the inhabitants of Medina to Medina, the inhabitants of Sham to Sham,[8] the inhabitants of Iraq to Iraq, and the rest to their own cities. Soon, they packed to travel and chose a good time to leave the next day. The tenth day, near dusk, three hours before the evening, they brought the camels from the Great Mecca and tied the carriage to the camels. They assigned about five to six camel loaders to safeguard and look after me. The ʿAlawi ladies and gentlemen[9] had gone to circumambulate in the Great Mecca. They had told the camel loaders, "Move ahead, and we will arrive after you but take good care of Mahboob."

> A heart made of stone can tolerate
> When the carriage bids farewell and departs[10]

We got on and departed from the Great Mecca two to three hours before dusk. My feelings that day were that I was riding and was surrounded, then all of a sudden I cried uncontrollably and raised my head and said, "Oh ill-behaved destiny, for how long will you enslave and imprison me, taking me from mountain to mountain, city to city, country to country? I am not at peace for a moment!" That day, near evening, we got on and travelled until we arrived at and passed the graves of our Sayyid ʿAbdul Mottaleb and our Sayyida Khadija, peace be upon them. I was expressing my heart's feelings and confabulated, "Oh my master and oh my Bibi,[11] goodbye. Oh Mecca, my dear homeland, goodbye. What did I do for this to be heavenly predetermined and God's wish? Whatever is one's destiny will happen, and no one can escape kismet." We said goodbye to Mecca and left.

[From Mecca to Medina]

I will say a few words. We departed from the Great Mecca to the radiant Medina. We proceeded until sunset that day. At dusk, we arrived at Wadi al-Maymon,[12] where the Hajji had encamped. I looked around and saw the tents were tightly set up. We slept at Wadi al-Maymon

---

8 Damascus, Syria.
9 Mahboob's reference to the ʿulamaʾ.
10 Saʿdi, *Qazaliyat*, 263.
11 Referring to ʿAbdul Mottaleb, the paternal grandfather of the Prophet Muhammad, and Khadija, the wife of the Prophet.
12 A valley between Mecca and Medina.

that night. The first drum was beaten to collect the tents and loads at the crack of dawn, when the sunlight illuminated and embellished the world. The second drum was beaten to place and tighten up the carriages and loads. When the third drum was beaten, we got on, and the caravan of the Hajji departed. It started moving like a sea wave. They kept going from one valley to another valley, from one rest stop to the next and moved past the roads and did not stop anywhere. Whatever they were doing, I was following, in practising the religion and their teaching of the rules and prayers. They were guiding me and said, "If you act well, Almighty God will send you to the beautiful heaven, and if you act poorly, then God will send you to hell." I chose the right path and stayed away from wrongdoings and did right things. I thanked God and said, "Thanks be to God, who took me out of the darkness and guided me onto the straight path," meaning, it was for the path of Islam, kindness, and the custodian of the infallible family of the Prophet Muhammad that I converted to Islam. But I was illiterate when in the Great Mecca. I was going to the *maktab*, where they taught me "What is the striking calamity?"[13] and I knew parts of the honourable Qur'an.

Something happened on our way between Mecca and Medina – I am not sure where Najd is between the illuminated Medina and Jabal – before arriving to the illuminated Medina. We had five or six days left to get to the city when we entered the strait. When entering the strait,

> The killer arrow became paired with the snake
> Destiny both smiled and said, "Well done!"

The bedouin had a tribute the previous day but, that year, Hajj Akbar had reduced their tribute. For this reason, they arrived at the strait at the crack of dawn and, like hail and flocks from above, the mountains and valleys fell over the head of the Meccan pilgrims. God forbid such things for any Muslim! Once Amir Hajj saw this event, he ordered the pilgrims to move fast but oh, how they sped! He saw from their fear that the loads had dropped from the camels, the carriages had fallen, and some had been killed. They were fleeing. Then, the camel loaders and other servants started fighting with the Arab bedouin. Amid the war, the caravan, which was assigned to move the carriage of Zeynab, peace be upon her, from Mecca to Sham [Syria], arrived and started helping the pilgrims. The enemy was defeated. They attacked the Arab

---

13 Referring to Qur'an 101:2.

army and the fighters were separated like the stars and returned with victory in less than two hours. But it was useless, and they did not stop.

That day we walked in the deserts, mountains, and plains covered with thorny spikes. It was half an hour to dusk when the Arab fighters approached like ants and grasshoppers, group by group, from behind the poor pilgrims. When the caravan of pilgrims arrived at the rest stop and set up the tents, they surrounded the pilgrims, like a gemstone ring, all around, so if pilgrims wanted to escape, no one would be left alive. Then then they started shooting and throwing bullets. From early dusk to the crack of dawn, the noise of shooting lessened. That night, several of the pilgrims, sayyids and others, were killed. We could not sleep well in the barren arid desert with stormy weather that night.

We were there until day-spring, when sunlight illuminated and embellished the world. Amir Hajj, the camel loaders, and the elders gathered and collected some money for the fighters and gave it to them. Then they made peace and left. After they were gone, the departure drum was beaten and the caravan of pilgrims started moving like the sea waves. We departed from there towards the illuminated Medina and did not stop anywhere. We kept going from rest stop to rest stop and walked past them all.

[In Medina]

After five to six days, we entered the illuminated Medina. The servants rented the house of an effendi in the new place and we stayed there. It was a very large and pleasant house with trees, fruit trees, running water, canals, drinking water, baths, and other things. It was a very good house.

We stayed there during the several days we were in the illuminated Medina. We would visit the shrine of the honourable Prophet, Fatema Zahra, peace be upon her, and that of other Imams, peace be upon all of them, the grave of Khadija, the daughter of Khovaylid,[14] and the mosques that were there, such as the Fadak[15] garden and the mosque of Qoba, where the camel of the honourable Messenger of God had descended at that time, and the spring which was the miracle of the Prophet. We would visit the beautiful gardens and the cave where the Prophet had taken refuge. We went to all the honourable places

---

14 Khovaylid ibn Nofayl, or Khovaylid ibn Asad, was the father of Khadija, the Prophet's wife.
15 A vibrant village 140 kilometres from northern Medina.

and visited them. There was no place left for us to see for we visited them all.

We were there until they brought back the carriage of Zeynab, peace be upon her, which they had taken from Medina to Sham [Syria]. It was brought with so much glorification and magnification by an army of three to four thousand. We had gone out to watch that day and no one was left to come out to see. But the carriage of ʿAʾisha, peace be upon her, had been taken by the Egyptians by sea to Egypt and had not been brought from Medina. But Lady Zeynab's was something different.

One day, they got me to wash the dirt off myself to get clean. When they put my head under water, I suffocated and screamed, "Oh people, come here. These ʿAjamis[16] want to eat me!" I said that and ran outside naked out of fear. The gentlemen were sitting in line and were surprised by my action. They said something among themselves and took me with encouragement, and they laughed and poured water over my head, and I became clean.

I saw everything in the illuminated Medina. We were there until the Hajj finished, purchasing souvenirs, goods, and other things. Then news came from Medina that they would depart the next day. But in the house where I was, the son of the landlord was coming and telling me every day to pray like they did, and I was not listening at all.

[In Najd: Chants and *Khayzaran*[17]]

We left from the illuminated Medina and moved towards Jabal Najd and said goodbye to the illuminated Medina. We passed rest stop after rest stop and walked past valleys and the scary deserts, mountains, and barren plains where no drinking water could be found except for a little in some strange places. We did not stop anywhere. After eleven to twelve days, we arrived at a house. That day the Hajj left late because they wanted to get the tribute from the pilgrims. They got up late that day at the order of Amir Hajj. ʿAnbar Ghulam took the tribute from all the pilgrims and the others who walked past one by one. We all departed and arrived at Jabal Najd. The camp of the Hajj was set up in the vast plain facing the palace of the ruler. After five to six days, I was sitting behind the tent and was playing. At every location where we arrived I had toys, like monkeys, donkeys, goats, and others, so did

---

16 Non-Arabs or Persians.
17 A long wooden stick used during special ceremonies such as by the *zar* spirit possession cults.

not get homesick. I saw that two of the servants of Amir Jabal had been assigned by the ruler to take me to the ruler. I was scared of them and escaped and went to the tent of harem.

After several minutes, one of the camel loaders, Ojan Qasim Kermani, who was travelling with us and had travelled at least forty times to Mecca, came behind the women's tent and called me. He said to come and walk around. He held my hand with the two servants of the ruler and we all went together to the palace of the ruler. We ascended the palace and entered and saw the ruler himself with some of the Arab shaykhs, and others were sitting and talking. The ruler himself was sitting next to the window that oversaw the entire plain where the Hajj had set up camp. Under the palace of the ruler there were about five hundred people sitting and they had the *khayzaran* cane in their hands and were chanting something in their own language. To honour the ruler, they were tapping the *khayzaran* on the ground.

When I entered the palace, the camel loader who had taken me there told me to sit and kiss the hand of the ruler. I sat and kissed it. When I kissed him, the ruler caressed my head with kindness and asked, "Are you *kairh* or *antalo*?" This was an idiom used by the Arabs to mean, "Are you a eunuch or not a eunuch?" The camel loader replied, "No, he is not eunuch." Then he asked, "Who does he belong to?" He replied, "His master is Mr. Shaykh ʿAbdullah Mazandarani, who is the resident of the noble Najaf." He said "great" and shortly after I asked permission to leave. We came out of the palace and went to our tent. I should compliment the palace of the ruler; everything was available there. The next day, his eldest son, along with some companions, invited us to a feast. They went after having tea and coffee and smoking cigarettes. They were riding a coastal donkey. The day after next, he himself, with a large group of the Arab shaykhs and the others, hosted us and left. But I cannot say enough of the bravery, generosity, kindness, hospitality, and goodness of the ruler. When he was riding, all surrounded him like a gemstone ring. He was a competent man.

[From Najd to Najaf]

We stayed ten to twelve days in Jabal Najd. On the twelfth day, early in the morning, they took down the tents with the first drum. With the second drum, they loaded everything. With the third drum, we got on and said goodbye to the Jabal in the land of Najd and left. The camp of the Hajj started moving like the stars; each clan went the way they wanted. After a while, the same day, we arrived at a two-way junction.

One, on the right side, was going to Yanbu'[18] or Iran, and the other, on the left side, was going to the Arab Iraq.[19] We went towards the illuminated Najaf, but the rest went the other way. We walked in the deserts filled with thorns, with no greenery or vegetation, and with harsh weather that day until sunset. At dusk, we arrived at a land with reeds. They set up the tents. After some rest and tea and the hookah, we performed the evening prayer. That night we were there with thousands of difficulties and at dawn, when the sunlight illuminated and embellished the world, they beat the departure drum. The caravan of the Hajj departed from there and we did not stop anywhere. We walked past three rest stops, and had two rest stops only for prayer, cooking and eating, and resting, then we moved on. At night, we were moving with a large torch, and during the days and nights we were eating meals on the camels.

We came all the way and walked past rest stops, roads, deserts, wilderness, mountains, and thorns. The weather was warm, and we were drinking salty water and moving. After eleven days since our departure from the mountain of Najd, near noon, the dome of the guardian, custodian, our master, the commander of the faithful,[20] became visible. We thanked God. It took twelve days from Jabal Najd to the illuminated Najaf. That day we entered a large green land that was the property of the honourable Amir al-Mu'minin, peace be upon him. The land was fertile and green with a very pleasant running water canal. The camp of the Hajj was set up there and the tents were pitched tightly together.

We were there until dusk. At sunset, we performed the prayer. Shortly after, supper, hookah, and coffee were taken. Three hours later, an Arab with several donkeys carrying citrus fruits and others arrived. He greeted me and placed the loads on the ground. I asked, "Who did this?" He replied, "Brother, your own master has sent it and he himself will come by wagon to welcome you tomorrow." Soon we slept until the sunrise illuminated the world. After morning prayers, they beat the drum of departure. All the caravan of the Hajj got up like the sea waves and moved on towards the honourable Najaf. It was the twelfth day. After half a *farsang*, we saw the residents of the town were moving and coming with so much glory to welcome their own family and relatives. Some were riding, some were on foot, and some were on wagons. I saw one wagon brought for us. They took me off the donkey and we got

---

18 A port in the Hijaz, on the Red Sea coast of western Saudi Arabia.
19 The Arab Iraq is in western Iran; to its north is Turkey, to its west Syria and Jordan, to its south Saudi Arabia, Kuwait, and the Persian Gulf, and to its east Iran.
20 Referring to 'Ali, the first Imam of the Shi'ites.

on the wagon, but the camels, the loads, the women, the servants, and the camel riders came from a different road, meaning from a different gate, and entered the town. We came from a different gate and entered the honourable Najaf. Prior to entering the gate, the gentlemen in the wagon told me not to give a slave tribute to the effendis. We entered the town and got off the wagon. The gentlemen went to the harem and entrusted me to Mr. Sayyid Muhammad ʿAbdulnabi Shushtari, long may he live. We came all the way until we arrived at the large market square. I was a stranger and became worried and scared. Once, I released my hand from the hand of the sayyid and asked, "Where did the gentlemen go and why did they leave me alone?" The sayyid told me, "Don't be scared. They have gone to the harem and will come back to the house." We came all the way until we entered the house. They sacrificed a large, castrated rooster near my feet for the protection of the journey. That day I was scared a lot. I had not seen such people, strange women and men who were jubilating and yelling for us. They took me above the sash and entertained me in their own tradition, but I did not know their language, only the Hijazi language.

For the period of one month, people, group after group and crowd after crowd, were coming to see Mr. Hajj Shaykh Ishaq Ayatullahzadeh Rashti. During this one month, my sleep, behaviour, speech, and deeds were foreign, and I was not at all familiar with the people and did not know them. Gradually, I became close to the household and their kids. It was then that I became acquainted with all the people. All great people, nobles, old and young, all loved me from the bottom of their hearts. I learned all the alleys, quarters, markets, houses, and meetings. I became skilled in doing housework, and so on. After one year had passed, I saw that the kids of the gentleman's aunt were going to the women's *maktab*. When the servants or the concubines were going to bring the kids home, they would hold my hands, take me with them, and bring the kids back. I would go and watch their *maktab khana*s but did not understand what they were saying. They would take me every day to stroll in the promenade; perhaps, I would gradually become familiar with the people and stop being wild. They entrusted me to a *lala*, a well-experienced old man, to be with me wherever I would go and to not let anyone bother me.

After a year had elapsed, in 1319,[21] I entered the honourable Najaf. It was the year of the Great Hajj. I was interested in going to the *maktab* to study. After much insistence, they took me to the *maktab* that was near

---

21 Mahboob has made a mistake in the year here, which does not correspond with the timeline of the narrative. It is mostly likely 1321 (1903).

the small mosque of Indians. The name of the teacher was Shaykh Asadullah Shushtari. For a short time, I studied with him, God be praised. When they took me to the *maktab*, Sayyid Husayn Bahr al-'Ulum was our neighbour. He had brought a *ghulam* with us from Mecca. That year many *ghulam*s and *kanize*s had been brought. To keep up with the times, he decided to study, but it did not happen, and he died. But I remained determined and busy to study and be educated, to become a tool to help my spiritual and material life. One day the teacher noticed my hand was broken. Later, they took me to Shaykh Mirza Ibrahim Hamadani, because almost more than half of the honourable Najaf studied under him, and they became professors and teachers. The shaykh was a very nice person and liked me very much. I studied Qur'an and about ten to twelve or more of the Persian books, including mathematics, studying under him for five to six years. Then I got several students. I was taking presents, gifts, tributes, souvenirs, and other things to him. God damn it! Because of jealousy and envy, they did not let me complete my education there because I became far more advanced than the nephew of the sir who had started going to the *maktab* several years before me. They felt ashamed. For this reason, they asked them to expel me from the *maktab* and for me to be at the service of the household. They said they brought me to work, not to be educated! Thus, they took me out of the *maktab*.

I had nothing to do for a while. After one more year, I studied new lessons, including geography, mathematics, and French in the 'Alawi school in Najaf for a year. Shortly after, I left. The events that happened to me during these ten years that I moved out of the Hijaz to here are that, in 1321 [1903], we moved to Karbala', from there to Baghdad, Kazemiyah,[22] and 'Askarin.[23] What do I write?! The pen cannot and is unable to write these events! What illnesses had been inflicted on me! First, during the ten years I was there, whatever sicknesses were in this world were inflicted on my body. What extraordinary bad things! I was trapped! I was also ignorant. My teeth at the age of seven fell out there. What misbehaviour I did! What travels I undertook! What fun I had! What days passed on me with men and the others! I did work before puberty! What else is there to say! I strolled all around Najaf. There was nowhere I had not gone! What misbehaviour I had not done during childhood!

---

22 A northern neighbourhood of Baghdad.
23 'Askarin refers to the shrines of 'Ali ibn Muhammad, the tenth Imam of the Shi'ites, and his son, Hasan 'Askari, the eleventh Imam, located in Samarra. 'Askar is another name for Samarra, a city in Iraq.

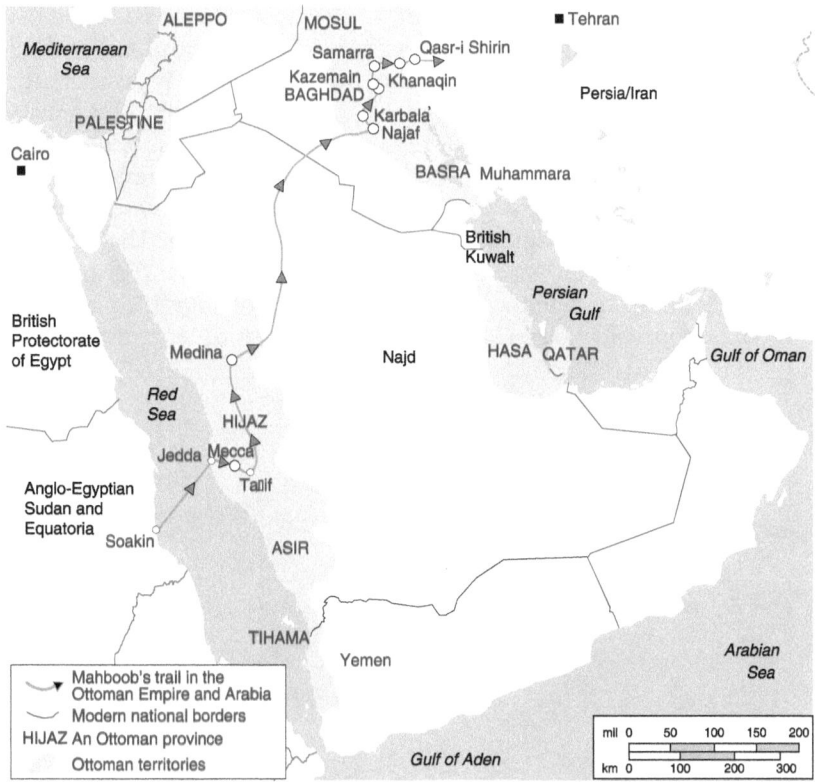

Map 6. Mahboob's trail in the Ottoman Empire and Arabia

[Constitutions and the Political Events]

I was there until the Iranian Constitution and after the Ottoman Constitution, and all the events and their impact on Najaf, the people, and the 'ulama', and the damage to Najaf, its surroundings, and some of the regions of the honourable Najaf: the destruction resulting from the Iranian Constitution; the arrival of Sayyid 'Abdullah Behbehani to Iran; the construction of the railroad of Kufa; the death of sixteen of the 'ulama' of Najaf; the departure of Mr. Hajj Shaykh Isma'il and I with them to Karbala', Baghdad, Kazemiyah, and Samarra; the news of the bombardment of the Iranian Parliament; the arrival of the telegraph; taking me to the telegraph to Ayatullahzadeh Mirza-yi Shirazi, after one week of moving to Samarra towards Kazemiyah, staying there for several days; and from there along with Sayyid 'Abdullah Behbehani, who was not coming, the departure of Hajj Shaykh Isma'il with a group of dignitaries to India; asking me by a telegraph that forced me to say farewell to the honourables, and my return with 'Abdul Karim Kermani to Najaf; until Sayyid 'Abdullah arrived and his welcome; then after, the arrival of the Friday Imam of Tehran; and after, the events of Khurasan; the emigration of all the 'ulama' and Muslims for jihad; the return of the great 'ulama' of the honourable Najaf; the emigration of the Iranian people; the arrival of the telegraph from Hajj Shaykh Isma'il from Tehran; and the departure of the caravan to Iran. The remarks were enough for Noah, who saw one storm in one thousand years! I am not Noah, but I saw one thousand storms in the honourable Najaf! We left the honourable Najaf, said farewell to those lands, and moved out.

4 The Departure of Hajj Mahboob to Iran

Hear these few words. This is a short travelogue of the year 1329 [1911]. When I moved to Iran from the honourable Najaf, for the record, on Friday, 10 Jumada al-Thani 1329 [8 June 1911], at seven o'clock, we departed from the honourable Najaf. We said farewell to all the friends and dignitaries and asked for forgiveness. We moved towards the Great Karbala'. The distance from the honourable Najaf to the Great Karbala' is three to four rest stops. From Najaf to the first rest stop, which is the prayer stop, is three to four *farsang*s. From the prayer stop to the second rest stop is three to four *farsang*s, and from the second rest stop to the third rest stop, in Nukhayla,[1] is four *farsang*s. From Nukhalya to the Great Karbala' is three *farsang*s.

We were on our way that night. On the morning of Saturday 11 Jumada al-Thani [9 June], three hours past the day, we arrived at the Great Karbala'. We spent the nights of 12 and 13 Jumada al-Thani [10 and 11 June] in Karbala' and went for a pilgrimage. We brought whatever we could. The next day, Monday 13 Jumada al-Thani, we departed from the Great Karbala' to go to Kazemiyah. At six o'clock in the daytime, we entered Musayyib.[2] From the Great Karbala' to Musayyib is five *farsang*s. We waited until sunset to perform the evening prayers. We crossed the bridge to the other side of the water going towards Baghdad. At two o'clock at night we entered Mahmudiya.[3] From Musayyib to Mahmudiya is four *farsang*s. We departed from Mahmudiya to Iskandariya.[4] It was six o'clock at night when we arrived at Iskandariya. We

---

1 A region near Kufa.
2 A district in Babil Province in Iraq.
3 A rural city south of Baghdad.
4 An ancient city in central Iraq.

stopped there while they changed the horses of the carriages. From Mahmudiya to Iskandariya was three *farsangs*. We got on from Iskandariya towards Baghdad. From Iskandariya to Baghdad was seven *farsangs*. At eleven o'clock in the morning, on Tuesday 14 Jumada al-Thani [12 June], we entered Baghdad. We stopped for one hour near the centre for the metal carriages. We loaded the stuff in the carriages and moved towards Kazemiyah. From Baghdad to Kazemiyah was one *farsang*. At four o'clock in the daytime we arrived at Kazemiyah. We stayed there for one day and night and brought everything we needed for travel. We made the pilgrimage in Kazemiyah. It was my third time going to Kazemiyah, but I had visited Samarra twice. The next day was Wednesday 15 Jumada al-Thani [13 June]. Since I did not have a passport, the dignitaries mentioned that Mr. Mirza Muhammad Hindi should send Mirza Ahmad Salmasi to the British embassy, meaning to the consulate, to get a passport for me. After returning, they said that I should wait two to three days for them to give it to me. Then we did not stop there. At six o'clock in the daytime, we departed from Kazemiyah towards Baghdad and from there to Iran. We took whatever stuff was in the carriages and left. We said farewell to the friends, Mr. Shaykh ʿAbdul Karim, the wife of the uncle, and the other friends. We departed from there and crossed using the Moʿazzam[5] bridge, which was like hell and trouble. They took the carriages on the bridge to the other side of the water and delayed for a while at Moʿazzam, may it be cursed, for two hours or more. Then we moved on from Moʿazzam towards Iran. We came all the way until near sunset and arrived at one of the coffee houses, which was near the road to Baghdad, more than two *farsangs'* distance. We got off. There was a lot of water in front of us and flooding. The water had risen and created a big canal. They had brought a boat for the pedestrians. They were taking something, and everyone was paying what they could afford. They put the stuff on the boat, and we sat and crossed to the other side of the water. We got off with the stuff and put it near the canal. We performed the prayers, then had supper, coffee, hookah, and freshened up. They put the stuff into the carriages. We were twenty people. They rented three carriages and got on them. It was two o'clock at night and we moved on towards Iran. At eight o'clock at night we arrived at Khan Bani Saʿad.[6] From Baghdad to the caravanserai of Bani Saʿad was nine *farsangs*. We passed there and it was near dawn. In the morning, at the crack of dawn, in a coffee house,

---

5 A bridge over the Tigris River in Baghdad.
6 A city in Diyala Province in Iraq.

we performed the morning prayers. We had tea there and stopped for a while until the carriage of the dignitaries arrived from the back. After half an hour, the carriages arrived, and we moved on towards Baʿquba.[7] From Khan Bani Saʿd to Baʿquba was three *farsang*s. We entered Baʿquba. They passed the carriages from the bridge to Baʿquba. That night we slept at Baʿquba and in the morning, at six o'clock, we said goodbye to Mr. Hajj Shaykh Ishaq, Mr. Sayyid Hasan Bastam, his uncle, and the other dignitaries who had come with us to say farewell and to send us off. We departed from there. Mr. Hajj Shaykh Ishaq had asked Mr. Hajji Mirza Ahmad to look after me and take good care of me.

We arrived at Jasmiya[8] from Baʿquba, which was three *farsang*s. We arrived at Khan Abu Hamrin from Jasmiya. From Baʿquba to Khan Abu Hamrin was six *farsang*s. We stayed there one night and early in the morning, the next day, we departed to Shareban,[9] which was Friday 17 Jumada al-Thani [15 June]. When we passed half a *farsang* from that rest stop, we arrived at a green and lush meadow. We looked at it and saw about several thousand storks there. I passed there for about two *maydan-i asb* because the wheel of our carriage came off. We all got off until the wheel was fixed and then got on. We arrived at Shareban. From Khan Abu Hamrin to Shareban is six *farsang*s. From two o'clock daytime, we were there until five hours past night. We departed from Shareban to Qazal Rabat.[10] While we were going, we arrived at exotic places where all we could see were mountains surrounding us. From there we entered a coffee house. From there we arrived at a very large bridge. That road was very difficult because it was full of rocks and clods. We passed from there and entered Qazal Rabat. From Shareban to Qazal Rabat was five *farsang*s. On Saturday 18 Jumada al-Thani [16 June] we entered Qazal Rabat. The morning prayers were performed there and tea and hookah were taken. Once the ruler of Qazal Rabat heard that Ayatullahzadeh Mr. Hajji Mirza Ahmad, the son of Mr. Hujjatul Islam Akhund Mulla Muhammad Kazem Khurasani, had entered Qazal Rabat, they came as a group to welcome and visit him. But we did not stop there and after one hour we departed to the Arab

---

7 In the original text it is Yaʿqobiya, but the correct form is Baʿquba, in Diyala Province, Iraq, fifty kilometres to the northeast of Baghdad.
8 A region in Diyala Province, Iraq.
9 In the original text it is Shahrban, which refers to Shareban in Kurdish, or Al-Meqdadiya, which in Arabic is a city in Diyala Province, Iraq.
10 In the original text it is Qazar Robat, a reference to Jabal Qazal Rabat, Diyala Province, Iraq. Jabal in Arabic means mountain, and the reference here is the mountainous area of Qazal Rabat.

and 'Ajam[11] Khanaqin.[12] We went all the way and wherever we looked were mountains, valleys, and bridges. We had not arrived at Khanaqin yet, because two to three times, the wheel of our carriage came off on our way. We were delayed on the road for a while, before we arrived at the Arab and 'Ajam Khanaqin. It was four hours into the daytime that we entered and settled in the caravanserai of the customs [office]. From Qazal Rabat to Khanaqin was five *farsang*s. I got one of the rooms in the upper level of the customs caravanserai. The friends each got a place and residence for themselves.

The honourables and we paid the rent of the carriages and they left. We were there for six days. On Sunday 19 Jumada al-Thani [17 June], the government of Khanaqin came to welcome Mr. Hajj Mirza Ahmad and brought one sheep and some other presents for Mr. Hajji Mirza Ahmad as tributes and gifts. He divided them among all the friends and shared out the meat of the sheep. After that, the border guards came for the passports. They saw ours and the others' passports and left. We stayed in Khanaqin for three days and nights to get a wagon. Since the wagon did not come from Iran, Mr. Hajji Mirza Ahmad ordered that, since there was no wagon to rent, he would instead rent several carriages and pack animals for our departure. They set the departure date as Wednesday 22 Jumada al-Thani [20 June]. During the three days we were there, I had so much fun. We would go somewhere for a stroll every day; to the markets, near the water canals, and to watch people. One day in Khanaqin, several pilgrims arrived and stayed at the same customs caravanserai. Several masters, servants, and women settled near our rooms. The next day, the servant of the master said to me, "Are you planning on going to Iran?" I replied, "Yes, we intend to depart for Tehran tomorrow. Do you need anything?" He said, "Yes. I will write a request in French and give it to you. When you arrive in Tehran, give it to the Alliance[13] school." I waited until he wrote the letter, took it from him, said goodbye, and left.

[In Iran: Kurdistan]

Hear these few words. On Wednesday 22 Jumada al-Thani [20 June], early in the morning, we departed from Khanaqin to go to Qasr-i

---

11 'Ajam is an Arabic word referring to the Iranians.
12 A Kurdish city in Diyala Province, Iraq, near the Iranian border.
13 The French Alliance school was founded in Tehran and Shiraz in 1889, and the Alliance Israélite Universelle was founded in 1898 in Tehran.

Shirin.¹⁴ We performed the morning prayers and at dawn, when the sunlight illuminated and embellished the world, we arrived at the bottom of a huge mountain. On the mountain was a very large tower. They said, "From Khanaqin up to there is the border of the great Ottoman government, and from there to Qasr-i Shirin, itself, belongs to the great government of Iran." Anyhow, we ascended the mountain and passed from there. We saw that near the tower was a large caravanserai where the Kurdish people were staying and strolling, and their horses were there. We entered the coffee house and had tea. There was no one in the coffee house except a Kurdish man and a very tall strong *kaniz*. We rested there for a while and got on our way. That castle is called Sabzish. We departed from there to go to Qasr-i Shirin.

We came all the way until we arrived at Qasr-i Shirin. I saw several Kurdish riders who passed us. One of them asked me, "Where is the gentleman?" I said, "He is behind us." Here they wanted to get close to the front when they understood it was Ayatullahzadeh. They rode fast, arrived at the gentleman, got off, and kissed his hand. They were riding along with us and were riding the horses fast. They were unloading their guns,¹⁵ not for danger and not like soldiers, but they were playing. The government itself came to welcome us and with so much respect brought us into Qasr-i Shirin. At three o'clock in the daytime, we entered Qasr-i Shirin, and all of us with difficulty settled in a caravanserai. Once we entered, Mr. Shaykh ʿAli mujtahid invited all the gentlemen to his house and Mr. Davood Khan Kalhor¹⁶ with his group came to visit Mr. Hajj Mirza Ahmad Ayatullahzadeh and brought many sheep as presents and gifts as tributes for him. The gentleman¹⁷ did not accept them, but returned them and said, "They all belong to the Muslims. They are stolen and looted. They are haram.¹⁸ I do not want them. I do not need them."

In the evening, we went for a stroll and looked around. What a pleasant place it was! The customs office that Farhad had built for Shirin in Qasr-i Shirin was there. We were watching the riders of Davood Khan riding with horses on the mountain. The weather, water, and trees

---

14 A Kurdish city in Kermanshah Province, in western Iran, near the Iraqi border.
15 Unloading rounds into the air is a customary sign of celebration during weddings, religious ceremonies, and other important occasions among some local communities.
16 An important political figure and head of the Kurdish Kalhor clan appointed by Mozaffar al-Din Shah Qajar in 1902. He was killed during a war with Reza Khan.
17 The term "gentleman" or "gentlemen" appears throughout in lieu of *aqa* or *aqayan*, which Mahboob has used in the original text. The title refers to the ʿulama'.
18 Haram means forbidden. It refers to acts that are illegal according to Islamic law.

made Qasr-i Shirin a very pleasant place. We spent that night there. From Khanaqin to Qasr-i Shirin was six *farsang*s. We departed from Qasr-i Shirin to go to Pol-i Zahab[19] at seven hours past the night on Thursday 23 Jumada al-Thani [21 June]. They sent several of his riders along with us for our safety on the road. We came all the way and watched the mountains and the creek that Farhad had built for Shirin and at the end of the creek was Qasr-i Shirin, which stretches up to the Bisotoun mountain.[20] From there we arrived at a coffee house and the riders returned and entrusted us to several other riders of Davood Khan. They were with us from the coffee house to Pol-i Zahab. We saw three towers built to protect the road. I asked the friends and the Kurds, "What are these towers for?" They said, "To protect the road. If something happens to the guards, they light a fire and the tower will notice and will come to protect, guard, and help each other." The Kurdish riders were in front of us. I sent my donkey and caught up with the donkey riders. The gentlemen were a little behind. I asked the riders how they were doing, and they also asked me how I was doing: "You can come with us, and we will take you and give you a horse, a gun, money, and a woman, if you want." They were teasing and joking with me. They were chatting together. They were singing and playing on the horses. We were talking with the Kurdish riders as we rode. Then they told me that there were beautiful local women and, "If you like, we will go get one for you." I said, "I do not need one; I am a eunuch." We arrived two *maydan-i asb* near Pol-i Zahab and I saw that its government with many riders were coming to greet us. They had a small drum on a horse and were beating it until they reached me and asked, "Where is Mr. Ayatullahzadeh?" I said, "They are coming behind us." I passed them and arrived at Pol-i Zahab. From Qasr-i Shirin to Pol-i Zahab was five *farsang*s. I got off and waited for the arrival of Ayatullahzadeh and the others. Shortly after, the gentlemen arrived. They got a house for us and changed the horses. Then the government took us near a stream inside a tent that the government had set up. All the gentlemen and the others, with total respect, went inside the government's tent. After bread, tea, coffee, hookah, music, and rest, we all went to purchase some groceries and things we needed. The government had brought some presents and gifts, including sheep, ice, cucumbers, and

---

19 A Kurdish city in Kermanshah Province, Iran, near Qasr-i Shirin and the Iraqi border.
20 Mount Bisotoun is located among the Zagros Mountains in Kermanshah Province, Iran.

rice for Ayatullahzadeh as tributes. The gentleman did not accept them and returned them.

That day and night we stayed there. At seven thirty at night we departed and moved to Mian Taq, and several of the government's riders accompanied us to guard us on the road because all those roads were dangerous. On Friday 24 Jumada al-Thani [22 June] we departed to go to Mian Taq. After almost one and a half hours, in the daytime, we arrived at Mian Taq. We arrived at Mian Taq on Saturday and the governor himself with a group of its people came to greet us on foot. After half an hour, they brought a horse as a gift for Hajj Mirza Ayatullahzadeh. We did not stop there. They took the gentleman off the carriage and got him on the horse, and we moved from the bottom of Taq to Mian Taq. The riders who had brought us turned around and went away. In their stead, the governor came to say farewell and goodbye and then returned. But the horse which the gentleman was riding went up the mountain and then the gentleman got off and the horse was returned to Mian Taq. [...][21]

That day, until five o'clock night-time, we were in Harun Abad.[22] After five hours had passed on Monday 27 Jumada al-Thani [25 June], we departed from there at night to go to Maydasht.[23] We did not stop anywhere. We kept passing rest stop after rest stop and roads, and we saw deserts, mountains, valleys, plains, jungles, villages, and hamlets until we arrived at Maydasht. On our way between Harun Abad and Maydasht, we arrived at a coffee house. Again, there they got two qirans and *qarasoon*[24] from the *charvadars*.[25] We entered Maydasht. It was past three in the daytime. From Harun Abad to Maydasht was six *farsangs*. We were there until six o'clock night-time on Monday 27 Jumada al-Thani [25 June]. We did not sleep or rest. We got ready and moved that night and departed to go to Kermanshah. That night we walked until the morning. At sunrise, we got off, performed ablution and the prayers, and got on our way. It was twelve o'clock when we entered Kermanshah. From Maydasht to Kermanshah was four *farsangs*. On Tuesday 28 Jumada al-Thani [26 June], we entered Kermanshah. Several of the

---

21 Two pages of the original text are missing here.
22 A Kurdish city in Kermanshah Province, Iran. It was part of the Kalhor district. In 1314, Reza Shah changed its name to Shah Abad, and after the Islamic Revolution its name changed to Islam Abad Gharb.
23 A plain near Kermanshah Province, Iran.
24 *Qarasoon* or *qorosoon* means "protection."
25 *Charvadar* refers to someone who lends pack animals for hire and himself accompanies the passenger.

honourable gentlemen who heard Mr. Ayatullahzadeh had entered Kermanshah and were his friends came to greet him. They took us with so much respect to the house of Mr. Sayyid Habib, the merchant of Kermanshah. We stayed in his house. It had *biruni* and *andaruni*, two sets of backyards, one outside for men and one inside for women.

After unloading and giving the stuff to them, we came and sat. After having tea, bread, hookah, coffee, and cigarettes, I went to take a shower. After taking a shower, I came back and saw a group of nobles, dignitaries, local rulers, and honourable 'ulama' sitting in rows to see Ayatullahzadeh. We were in Kermanshah for eight days and, every day, people, crowd after crowd, from Najaf were coming and going to visit and, sometimes, we were going with them. During the days I was there, every day I would go for a stroll. What a city! It was full of blessings, people, and an abundance of resources! May God preserve it! During the few days I was there, I learned where the market, alleys, quarters, offices, and the squares of Toopkhana and Mashq, police headquarters, and the other places were. One day we were going out of the city gate with Mr. Shaykh Isma'il and Mr. Shaykh Ibrahim Turk, the preacher. Another day I was going to the caravanserai of Mustufi al-Mamalik to visit Mr. Sayyid Husayn Lari, one of our honourable friends from Najaf who had come with his relatives, wife, and child to live there for a while. He said he was the son-in-law of Mr. Shaykh 'Abbas Lari Karbala'i. After some entertainment, lunch was eaten there that day. He advised me to not forget them when we went to Tehran and to write them letters. Then we went to his house, and there, he and his wife, who was our friend, entertained us with so much respect and honour. I was there until the evening and at sunset I returned home. I had lots of fun that day.

The events during our few days' stay there were that first, from sunset to sunrise, no one could rest because of the noise from the shooting from the fights among the local people who were killing each other. One of the cases was that, on the first night of the month of Rajab, they killed and beheaded one great and honourable sayyid. The fact is that they are religious, perform prayers, fast, call for the prayers, and read litanies and Qur'an. This is good. But their wrongdoing is the fighting. One day, we argued with the wife of my uncle for nothing. After two to three days, they made peace with us.

[From Kermanshah to Qom]

We were in Kermanshah for nine days. We waited for the wagon to come. When the wagon came, we left. We rented one wagon and one carriage to go the next day to Tehran. We got whatever we needed for the travel and made ready to depart from Kermanshah in the morning. In the afternoon, I went to see all the friends, buddies, dears, acquaintances, and associates and kissed them one by one and said goodbye and left. There was a *dalandar*[26] who, from the first day we arrived, helped me so much. I had a jacket and a cloak. Since I had no money, I gave them to him instead, as a gift or tip, and asked him for forgiveness and left. We were there on the night of Tuesday 7 Rajab [4 July]. On the morning of Tuesday 10 Rajab, we performed the prayers, and after having tea, bread, hookah, coffee, and cigarettes, we gave all the stuff to the porters at the wagon house. Askar and we all departed. Askar was the boss of the wagon house. He was a tall, broad-shouldered, and robust man. He was very strong. There was no one as stoutly built as him in Kermanshah. We put the stuff in the wagon and carriages and got on our way. It was twelve hours in the daytime when we departed from Kermanshah to Bisotoun.[27]

Anyhow, hear these few words. We arrived at a coffee house in the centre of Sar Zanjar. Here they verified our passports. We went all the way and arrived at Bisotoun. From Kermanshah to Bisotoun was six *farsang*s. We remained at Bisotoun until the evening. We visited the balcony and the rock that Farhad had carved for Shirin. In the evening, we departed from Bisotoun. While we were going to Sahna,[28] we saw villages, coffee houses, gardens, mountains, plains, jungles, and deserts. In the evening, we entered Sahna. From Bisotoun to Sahna was three *farsang*s. We stayed there at night with so many difficulties. On Wednesday 8 Rajab [5 July], we departed from Sahna to Kangavar.[29] The same night, before our departure, we heard from Sahna that a sayyid was killed and then cut into pieces by thieves on the way to Kangavar. The road from Sahna to Kangavar was very dangerous and I was fearful. We were so concerned that when we arrived at a coffee house, we got off and stayed there for a while. We had some tea there, then left. After only going half a quarter of an *asb*, we saw that several Iranian Qazaq[30] were coming from Tehran and going to Kermanshah. We passed them and arrived at the bottom of the Bid Sorkh mountain pass. The wagon rider said there was always the smell of blood! I was really scared of

---

26 A guard of the caravansaries and the bazaars.
27 A Kurdish city in Kermanshah Province, Iran, and the location of an important historical site.
28 A Kurdish city in Kermanshah Province, Iran.
29 A city in Kermanshah Province, Iran.
30 A military division in Iran built with the assistance of the Russians in 1879.

the mountain pass and its greatness because people were always killed and robbed there. We entrusted ourselves to God. The wagon was very heavy and could not go up the mountain. We got off. Women and men helped push the wagon up the mountain. We arrived at a coffee house at the top of the mountain pass. We saw that several of the Kurdish guards were staying there. Once they saw us with the wagon, they came close and said: "You should pay us for protection on the road." We gave them four qirans. We looked at the top of the mountain and saw, in the distance, thieves carrying some merchandise that they had stolen the night before. We passed there while chanting one thousand times "Allah." We descended from the top of the Bid Sorkh mountain pass and went to the centre of the wagon house where we had to change the horses. We were there for about half an hour, so they could change the pack animals. I do not know for what reason it was that Mr. Hajji Mirza Ahmad Ayatullahzadeh changed his mood towards me a little.

We left there and kept going until we arrived at Kangavar. There was a plain where the thieves had killed about fifty to sixty camels the night before our arrival. About two thousand pack animals, donkeys, horses, and camels were grazing. They had brought merchandise to the desert and packed goods from one to another. For fear of the thieves, we entered and stopped in Kangavar. From Sahna to Kangavar was five *farsang*s. We stopped for one hour in Kangavar to have lunch, tea, hookah, listen to music, and perform the noon and evening prayers. We departed from Kangavar to go to Farsiya.[31] We saw two to three villages and coffee houses and passed from there. We were on our way and the sun had set. What a bad road! It was a serpentine road that was scary and frightening. It was two hours past the night-time when we arrived at Farsiya. From Sahna to Farsiya was nine *farsang*s. We stayed there that night. The next day was Thursday 9 Rajab [6 July], and we were in Farsiya. That day we went to the garden and stayed there. What a garden! It had very good weather and was a pleasant place. We were in the garden until the evening. In the evening, we came to the caravanserai that was at the wagon centre and stayed there. For two nights and days we were in Farsiya. I asked the friends, "Why did we stay there for two nights and two days?" They said, "For Mr. Shaykh 'Ali Hamadani, who had heard that Mr. Hajj Mirzai Ahmad was going to this region. They had prepared to come to welcome him. Tomorrow we will depart from here. Our stay here is useless, and these two nights days we stayed here were because of him. We should depart tomorrow."

---

31 Refers to the village of Farsinj or Parsinah in Kermanshah Province, Iran.

Mr. Shaykh ʿAli Hamadani did not come, and that night Mr. Shaykh ʿAbdul ʿAli Dashti[32] and Mr. Hajj ʿAbdul Rasul, the servant of Ayatullahzadeh, had a fight. I did not know for what reason. We made reconciliation between them.

On the ninth or tenth day of Rajab, we were in Farsiya. On the morning of Saturday 11 Rajab [8 July], we performed the morning prayers. On 11 Rajab we departed from Farsiya to go to Jamil Abad. After passing about two *maydan-i asb*, the women said that one of our pillows was lost. One said, "It will not be found." The other said, "It is lost." I said, "Now, I will go to find it for you." I got off the wagon and walked almost one *maydan-i asb*. There, under a tree, several dervishes were sitting next to each other. I reached them and said hello. The dervishes returned my greeting. I asked if the gentlemen had seen a small pillow fall when the wagon was going past. They said yes, they had seen a pillow fall from the wagon, and they had taken it. But they said I could get it only if I gave something to the sayyid child. I gave several shahis to the sayyid child and retrieved the pillow from them, said goodbye, and returned. I ran and arrived at the wagon. I got on and they were surprised at how I had found the pillow as I explained to them everything that had happened.

We moved on and, while we were proceeding, about one *farsang* away from Farsiya, I saw one of the residents of the village approach the wagon. He greeted us and we replied. Then he asked whose wagon it was. I said, "It is belongs to Mr. Hajj Mirza Ahmad Ayatullahzadeh." He said, "I am a messenger from Mr. Shaykh ʿAli Hamadani, who has given me a letter to bring to Mr. Ayatullahzadeh." We took the letter from him and gave it to the gentleman. After seeing the letter, the gentleman said, "Bring the messenger onto the wagon." We took the messenger and departed from there to go to Jamil Abad. We entered a coffee house. We passed the coffee house. We entered Jamil Abad. From Farsiya to Jamil Abad was two *farsang*s. We stopped there and had lunch, tea, hookah, and listened to music. After one and a half hours we proceeded to Husayn Abad. We passed Jamil Abad while we were going. We entered the wagon centre that was between Jamil Abad and Husayn Abad. We waited there until they changed the horses. Then we got on and arrived at a coffee house. We passed from there. We came all the way and arrived at Husayn Abad. We saw there was a water canal. The wagon and carriage with the gentlemen crossed, but when our wagon was crossing, the wheel of the wagon got stuck in the mud.

---

32 The son of ʿAbdulnabi Dashti, a prominent Shiʿite scholar.

Amid this, we saw a group of gentlemen on foot and riders who had come to welcome us. Mr. Shaykh ʿAli Hamadani approached us. They asked us, "Where is the gentleman?" We said, "They went ahead with the wagon." They told us, "Stay here a bit so that we can send our servants to dislodge the wheel of your wagon." We stayed there for a while. They got on the horses. What horses! It makes one wonder! They pulled the ropes and wires with the horses and then they quickly disappeared from our sight, and we could not see the riders or those on foot. We were left there until the servants returned with a shovel and a pickaxe and got the wheel of the wagon out. We got on and entered Husayn Abad. The wagon went to the centre. All the women and men got off. They took us to a very large garden. We walked in the garden. What a garden! The trees were tall, near the sky, and there were colourful flowers, the scent of basil, water canals, the twittering of nightingales and pigeons, animals, evergreens, ailanthus, poplars, pines, and elm trees. It would take one's breath away. It was a very pleasant place. I wished all my friends were there! They set up a place for us, servants and helpers, and set up a place for the gentlemen. They entertained us with so much kindness, respect, and greatness – I swear it is the truth![33] Mr. Shaykh ʿAli Hamadani entertained us. He took the women to his house and entertained them well. In the evening, a large group of the residents of the same village and who were honourable got ready for the evening prayers. They lined up behind the gentleman. After finishing the evening prayers, the people scattered, and everyone went to their own houses. But Mr. Shaykh ʿAli himself and several others remained with the gentleman. We were busy talking until three hours past night-time. We saw they spread the cloth and prepared dinner. After having dinner, coffee, hookah, and listening to music, they set up our beds. They prepared a place for us and the gentlemen. That night we spent under these conditions. On Sunday 12 Rajab [9 July], we performed the morning prayers. After having bread, tea, hookah, listening to music, and drinking coffee, we saw that group after group of gentlemen and dignitaries were coming there to see Mr. Hajji Mirzai Ahmad Ayatullahzadeh. Mr. Hajji Mirza Ahmad thanked them and respected all the gentlemen and showed kindness. The gentleman said, "It is noon. Why do they not pack the wagon?" The gentlemen there said, "They have gone to bring pack animals. Since there are a few animals for the wagon, it takes a bit longer. This is why they are late. Please relax a little until they bring the horses." We were in the garden. After

---

33 Literally, "between me and my God!"

one hour, they brought the wagon and carriage horses. We went and brought the women from the house of Mr. Shaykh ʿAli Hamadani, put them on the wagon, said farewell to the gentlemen there, and got on our way. We departed from Husayn Abad to go to Dolat Abad. From Dolat Abad we went to Baris Abad, then to Husayn Abad, to Qelija Tapa, to Muhammad Abad, to Saroq, to Navazin, and to Dolat Abad. We kept going and did not stop anywhere. We passed a rest stop and moved along the roads, centre to centre, coffee house to coffee house, mountain to mountain, desert to desert, valley to valley, plain to plain, jungle to jungle. We went on until noon when we entered Dolat Abad. Some of us went and bought something for lunch. We had lunch. After lunch, we performed the prayers. After the prayers, we had tea, hookah, and listened to music. We were there until three hours before evening. From Dolat Abad there are two roads, and one goes to Borujerd. One man from the Siaf of Borujerd was with us. He said goodbye and went to Borujerd. We moved on from Dolat Abad to Sultan Abad. From Hasan Abad to Dolat Abad was nineteen *farsang*s.

We were going to go all the way. But what a road it was between Dolat Abad and Sultan! It was terrifying and scary, with a narrow mountain pass. At three o'clock in the night-time we arrived at a coffee house. There was a wagon house. We got off. We washed our hands and performed ablution and the prayers. After the prayers, we had dinner. We moved on to Sultan Abad. At night, on Monday 13 Rajab [10 July], we were on the road until a little after daytime. We kept going from rest stop to rest stop until half past eleven. It was almost sunset when we arrived at Sultan Abad. From Dolat Abad to Sultan Abad was twenty *farsang*s. That night we spent there under these conditions. On Tuesday 14 Rajab [11 July], after performing the prayers and having bread, tea, hookah, and listening to music, several officers came from the government of Sultan Abad and invited the gentlemen and the women to their house and gave a present to the daughter of the gentleman from the women of the government. They all went except one of the servants and I, who stayed at the wagon house guarding the stuff, and six other servants of the gentleman who stayed to look after their own stuff. At noon, one of us went to the bazaar to get some bread. We ate lunch with the guys in the wagon centre. After lunch, at four o'clock, the women returned to the centre and, after having tea, we put the stuff in the wagon and carriage and waited for the gentlemen. During this time, someone came from the government to the wagon house centre and said, "The gentlemen said that you should all get on the wagon and go out. The gentlemen are waiting near the gate." They had brought us food for our travels. We put it in the wagon and filled the pots and put them in the carriage and wagon. I saw one of my friends whom I knew in Najaf, whose name was Muhammad Turk. Once he saw me, he greeted me and kissed me. He said, "When did you come from the Great Najaf?" I said, "We came near the evening with the gentlemen." He expressed so much kindness and said, "I am in the house of the government. If I was not there, I would have come with you. But it is useless because I cannot come." I said, "It has been kismet." He said, "Now that you have packed all the stuff, do you need any help to go near the gate until the wagon and carriage arrive?" I said, "Sure." He and I moved on to the bazaar and entered. What a nice bazaar! So many compliments! Once I had seen [the bazaar], he turned to me and asked, "Friend, what do you want to eat? What do you need?" I replied, "I do not need anything." He insisted. I said, "Get me some sour cherries." He took my handkerchief and got me half a kilo of sour cherries and offered them to me. I took them from him, and we came to the end of the bazaar. He suggested we go to the coffee house to have two cups of tea, then to leave. I did not refuse. He and I sat for a while and had cups of tea then moved on towards the gate of the town in Sultan Abad. The government offered a lot of things as gifts to the gentleman.

We proceeded until we arrived near the city gate. We looked and saw that Mr. Ayatullahzadeh, the government, and the honourable gentlemen of elders, dignitaries, and nobles had lined up sitting on the other side of the city and were waiting for the wagon and carriage. It was not long before the wagon and carriage arrived. The gentlemen got up and kissed Mr. Ayatullahzadeh and said goodbye. I also kissed my friend and said goodbye. We got on the wagon. The honourable gentlemen stood until we departed from Sultan Abad. We left near sunset to go to Sava. We had gone about one *farsang* from Sultan Abad when we saw a black lamb wandering along the road. It had no owner. It probably had been left behind by its shepherd and herd. The wagon rider got off and grabbed it and placed it in the front of the wagon and we moved on. While we were going, we would sometimes recite the *Mathnavi* and sometimes talk. We arrived at a centre that was between Iraq Sultan Abad[34] and Sava. We got off and we remained there for a while. After half an hour we got on and travelled until four o'clock night-time. We arrived at Sava. We got off and performed the evening and night prayers. After dinner and hookah, we waited until the horses, wagons, and carriages were changed. We got on and departed from Sava to Ibrahim Abad. It was the night of Wednesday 15 Rajab [12 July]. We

---

34 Iraq Sultan Abad or Iraq was the old name for Arak.

were on our way and performed the morning prayers. From Iraq Sultan Abad to Sava is three *farsangs*; from Sava to Ibrahim Abad is three *farsangs*; from Ibrahim Abad to Sorkha[35] is three *farsangs*; from Sorkha to Banaviz is three *farsangs*; from Banaviz to Salafchegan is two *farsangs*; and from there it is two *farsangs* to Shurab.[36] We were going from rest stop to rest stop and did not stop anywhere until we arrived at Shurab. There, we walked a bit and waited until they attached the horses to the wagons and carriages. We got on from there on Wednesday 15 Rajab. We departed from Shurab to go to Ma'someh, peace be upon her, Qom. That road was all mountains and valleys with rocks and clods, up and down. The mountain pass was scary and full of thieves. We went until we arrived at a coffee house, and we passed from there until we arrived near Ma'someh, peace be upon her, Qom. It had been twelve days. Here, the wheel of our wagon broke, and we all got off and did not get back on. We arrived at a wagon house centre in Qom. We entered the centre and waited for the wagon to arrive. From Shurab to Ma'someh, Qom, it had been four *farsangs*.

We remained at the centre for about an hour until they went and got a house for us and came to take us. Mr. Shaykh 'Abdul 'Ali Dashti was a servant of Ayatullahzadeh. We gave all the stuff to several porters and left to go to the house of the gentleman, the custodian of the holy shrine of Lady Ma'someh in Qom. From the passengers with us, one man and one woman and several others who were on the road with us left us at the Dolat Abad Road and went to Borujerd. We had no news about what happened to them.

[In Qom]

We went to the house. The house had *biruni* and *andaruni*. The *biruni* was set up for men and the *andaruni* for women. For three nights and days we stayed in Ma'someh, Qom. During this period, the several days we were there, every day in the morning, evening, and at night we went on pilgrimages and visited the [shrines of] all the Imams' descendants there. I watched and strolled through all the bazaars, alleys, quarters, streets, courts, and rooms. On Thursday 16 Rajab [13 July], I wrote a letter to the Great Najaf, sent it, and came back home. I gave them any cloths I needed washed. I rested and was relieved from the travel exhaustion of the days on the road. The gentlemen who knew Mr. Hajji

---

35 Refers to Sorkheh Deh, a village in Kermanshah Province, Iran.
36 A village in Qom Province, Iran.

Mirza Ahmad, such as the guardian of the shrine and the others, came every day to visit Mr. Hajji Mirza Ahmad Ayatullahzadeh. The several days we were there were not bad and I had a good time. On Friday 17 Rajab [14 July], Mr. Hajji Mirza Ahmad said, "Tomorrow we should get a stagecoach for you, the women, and children, and you will depart to Tehran." We said, "Sure." Near the evening, I went out and bought a pair of *ersi* [shoes] and a pair of socks for myself and returned. We spent the night there.

On Saturday 18 Rajab [15 July], we performed the morning prayers, and after having bread, tea, coffee, hookah, and listening to music, we got some of the necessary stuff, packed it, put it in the saddlebag, and closed it. We were there until noon. At noon we had lunch and tea. The women went to the shrine for pilgrimage and returned. Then I, along with the children, went and made the pilgrimage. The women had given me three qirans to give to the shoe keeper in the shrine, and I gave it. We said goodbye and returned home. Then they brought the porters and took the stuff to the wagon centre. We also said goodbye to Mr. Ayatullahzadeh and the others and came to the wagon centre. They placed the stuff in the stagecoach and brought the stuff and attached it. We got on. It was one hour to the evening. We departed from the honourable Ma'someh, Qom, to go to Tehran.

[From Qom to Tehran]

Hear these few words. While we were travelling, we arrived at Zanjireh. We had to show our passports. They verified the passports in Zanjireh and there we filled the pots with water and attached them to the stagecoach. We got on and moved to Manzarieh. We got off at Kosh Nosrat[37] and performed the prayers of evening and night. We had dinner and several cups of tea. We did not have water. We filled the pots, came back, and attached them to the stagecoach. We were there about one and a half hours while the pack animals ate barley and straw and rested. I saw in the coffee house they were playing the *ney*,[38] which would make one unconscious [it was so good]. We listened a while. After an hour, we departed from there to go to the castle of Mamdali Khan.[39]

---

37 It refers to Koshk Nosrat, a village in Qom Province, Iran.
38 A flute.
39 Muhammad Ali Khan Castle is in Qom Province, Iran.

We were on the road that night and arrived at a coffee house near the morning. We performed the morning prayers. On Sunday 19 Rajab [16 July], we departed from there. We went away about half a *farsang* from the coffee house and saw a stagecoach coming in the distance and going towards Ma'someh, Qom. When we got close, the rider got off and changed the horses. He went to Qom but we came towards the Mamadali castle. I asked the carriage driver why he was changing the horses at every station. The carriage driver said, "It is a custom on Iranian roads. For example, if the horses of that centre arrive to this centre, the next time, the carriage driver should go to the first centre." But there was a lake between Qom and Tehran and it was foggy so it was as if it was a dark night.

We proceeded until we arrived at a centre between Kosh Nosrat and Mamdali castle. We got off there to change the wagon horses. Here we washed our hands and had several cups of tea. Then, I saw a stagecoach coming from Tehran to Qom, peace be upon it. They got off at the same coffee house. I stayed and watched. I saw a pregnant woman enter the wagon centre with grace, beauty, and honour, accompanied by several riders and others whose stagecoach and horses were staying outside. They spread a rug for her, and brought samovar, hookah, and cold water to her. They put everything in front of her. The servants all lined up in front of her, group by group like *ghulam*s. I entered the centre to drink water and saw the woman, the wife of the Hajji, who said to me, "Come here. Where are you from?" I went, greeted her, and said, "Lady, I am from the Great Najaf." She said, "Who are the women in the stagecoach?" I said, "They are the relatives of Mr. Hajji Muhammad Taher mujtahid Najafi." I was scared to say they were the family of Akhund Mulla Muhammad Kazem Khurasani because from the time we departed from Najaf to Tehran, whenever anyone would ask, I would reply that they belonged to that [other] family because this family has so many enemies. She said, "Go and convey my greetings to them and ask them how they are, and tell them to come here to rest a bit to have tea, water, and hookah, then they can depart." I went and told them what she had said. The women's reply was, "We are so thankful for the kindness of Her Excellency, may your mercy and protection be eternal. We would not otherwise have come. Please accept our apologies." I went, said exactly that, bid farewell, came out, and got on. We left to go to the Mamdali Khan castle and passed a coffee house. We entered the Mamdali Khan castle at noon. We got off and had lunch. We needed water. It was noon and a good time to wash our hands and perform ablution and the prayers.

[Customs and Beliefs]

I got the pitcher and asked, "Where is the water?" They said, "Go to this village. There is water." The distance was about one *maydan-i asb* from the wagon centre to the village. I walked and arrived at a running water canal. I sat near the water canal to fill the pitcher. I saw several men and women were sitting under a tree. I called and asked them, "Where is the washroom?" A woman came out of a house and said, "Come to my house." I went to the house of the woman and used the washroom. I came out of the house of the woman and went near the water canal to perform ablution. I saw three women and two men under the tree. One woman, who was holding a water jar, got up and came towards me. Once near, she greeted me, and I greeted her. She said, "Hajji, take this water jar from me and say prayers. I have someone who is ill and coughs a lot. Perhaps out of your blessings, this ill person will recover and be healthy." I took the jar from her and started the prayers; then I gave the jar back to her. Then she said, "Put some water in your mouth and return it to the jar." I put some water to my mouth and returned it to the jar and said, "God willing, the sick will be well. Do not be sad." The woman appreciated my help a lot and left. I sat and performed ablution, filled the pitcher, and went back towards the wagon house.

While I was walking, a girl with grace and beauty, about seventeen or eighteen years old, and a boy, who was thirteen or fourteen years old, approached me. The girl said, "Hajji, where are you from?" I said, "I am from the Great Karbala'." She said, "When did you come here?" I said, "It has been half an hour since I arrived." She asked, "Have you come alone?" I said, "No." The girl was surprised at seeing me as if she had not seen anyone for a while.

She looked at me then said, "What are these scars on your face?" I said, "It is a custom in my land, and they have a rule that they cut the face of all men and women with a blade." She held my hand and said, "What are these rings on your hand?" I said, "They are *dorr*,[40] agate, and turquoise." She asked, "Do you sell them?" I said, "No. I do not sell them." I saw the girl and boy leave, and I went to the wagon house centre. They got the pitcher to perform the ablution. I started performing the prayers. After the prayers, they said, "There is no more water. We do not have water." I took the pots. For the second time I went to the village. I asked someone who was Lur, "Uncle, where can I find drinkable

---

40 *Dorr* is a smooth and transparent stone. *Dorr* from Najaf has special religious value since the graves of many important religious historical figures are found there.

water?" He said, "The canal ahead of you." I said, "The water from that canal is salty and not drinkable." He said, "Go near the tents you see there. There is a road where the drinkable water canal is." The man said that and left. I arrived at the road and entered there. It was like a scary cave. I filled the pots with water, drank some, and washed my face. The water was cool like tears. After that I went to the water canal that they had dug underground and came back up. While I was leaving, I saw the same girl standing at the same spot where I had seen her the first time. She said hello. I replied. She held my hand and said, "I swear by God, I have nothing to give you to buy this one ring from you, but if you can wait, I will go bring some sugar cubes, tea, and some fruit from my house to get this one ring from your hand." Then she said, "By God, I was a little girl of ten years old when they kidnapped and enslaved me from my country and brought me here. They bother me a lot and beat me." Then she pulled up one leg of her trousers and said, "See my ankle. All these blisters are burns where the woman has burned me with metal. I have no one here – no father, no mother. I am having a hard time here." I felt for her from the bottom of my heart. Then I told the girl, "Tell me which of the rings do you want?" She said, "I want the turquoise one." I took it off my finger and gave it to her. I said, "I give this to you for the sake of God." The girl became so happy, prayed for me, said farewell, and left. I walked until I arrived at the wagon house centre. I gave them the water and after one hour we departed for Mamdali Khan. We proceeded until sunset. After dusk, we arrived at a very large bridge. They said, "This is the Rud Khan bridge." I saw there was a large coffee house. I bought some ice. About twenty to thirty small and big pigs were in the coffee house. We watched them. We departed from there after a quarter of an hour and arrived at a coffee house near a mountain pass. We stopped at that coffee house for a while. I saw someone come out of the coffee house and get on the stagecoach with us, in the front, next to the rider. I saw his mouth was like the mouth of someone wretched, since he had drunk the venomous snake – alcohol.

We passed from there and arrived at the centre of Hasan Abad. They changed the pack animals. We departed from there to go to Kahrizak. I fell asleep and did not know what had happened. Suddenly, I opened my eyes and saw it was four o'clock in the night. We arrived at Kahrizak. We stayed there under these conditions. In the morning, we performed the prayers. After the morning prayers, I got several cups of tea from the coffee house and had them with bread. We moved on and changed the horses. On Monday 20 Rajab [17 July], we departed from Kahrizak to go to Shahzadeh 'Abdul 'Azim, peace be upon him. It was half past twelve when we departed from there. While travelling, we came to two coffee houses on the road. We got off near a water canal and had some water. We proceeded until we arrived at the gate of Shahzadeh ʿAbdul ʿAzim, peace be upon him. We saw the holy dome. We thanked God. Near the gate of Shahzadeh ʿAbdul ʿAzim, while we were on the stagecoach, I saw a young person with a hat on come in front of the stagecoach and say, "Oh sir." I did not respond to him because the women and children had told me, "If anyone on the way asks who these passengers are, tell them you do not know." One of the attendants replied and introduced himself. The young man said, "So, wait a bit for the khan to come." We waited. They changed the horses. Then we did not wait any longer.

[In Tehran]

We departed from Shahzadeh ʿAbdul ʿAzim to go towards Tehran, the state centre, the capital. We arrived at the gate. They gave them our passports at the gate. Then we moved on and entered the house of the centre, which was the wagon house for the army and related to the Najaf of Iraq. We got off there and said, "There is no need to get the women off." Then I saw the nephew of my master and the servant go to the house to find the house of the master and come back. I waited in the wagon house centre with the women and the children until they returned and took us. From Qom to Shahzadeh ʿAbdul ʿAzim was nineteen *farsang*s, and from Shahzadeh ʿAbdul ʿAzim, peace be upon him, to Tehran, the state centre, was about one *farsang*.

When they went, I saw a person wearing a tie[41] phoning someone from the office at the centre. I did not know who he was calling or with whom he was talking. After he finished his call, he asked one of the servants who was one of the cleaners of that place, "Go sweep up and wash one of the lower rooms." After sweeping and washing, he came to me and said, "Get the women off and take them to the room that I cleaned up and wait until your servants come back." I got the women and children off and took them to the room to have some rest. Shortly after, one stagecoach arrived, and our servants and several other servants of the master arrived and got the women and children off and took them home. One of our own servants and I gave the stuff to the porters and went towards the house in the alley of Hajji Mirza ʿAli Harir Forosh, Pamenar, across from the mosque and the *ab anbar* of

---

41 Mahboob uses the term *fokoli*. During the Qajar period the term was used to refer to those who dressed like Europeans.

Bahram Khan, the late eunuch, to the alley known as the Kashiha. At four o'clock in the daytime, we entered the house and delivered all the stuff to the *andaruni* and came to the *biruni*. When we came to the *biruni*, my master was not there. They had gone to Shahzadeh ʿAbdul ʿAzim for us since they had heard that we would enter. In short, only a sayyid, his son, and two to three other servants were in the *biruni*. I greeted them and we kissed each other. With the sayyid and the others, we sat and started chatting. They brought tea and sharbat and we drank them. Soon they prepared lunch, and we ate it. After lunch, we had some rest. At four o'clock before dusk, I went and performed ablution and the prayers. I had heard about the squares of Toopkhana[42] and Mashq.[43] So I was interested in seeing them. I went there alone to look. They were playing music. I remained there for a while, watched the street, and returned home at dusk. I saw that the master had come. I greeted him and kissed his hand. We asked how he was. Then, the master told me, "You are crazy; you have not yet rested after the trip! Who taught you?" I replied, "I learned myself." Then he said, "Go to the *biruni* to see who is there. Entertain them and give them whatever they need until I come." I went to the *biruni* and saw that some of the honourable gentlemen were sitting there. I gave them whatever they needed: sharbat, tea, water, hookah, cigarettes, and other things. Then the master came to the *biruni* and began a conversation with the gentlemen. At three o'clock night-time, the meeting ended and everyone went to their own houses. Dinner was ready. After having dinner, coffee, hookah, and listening to music, the bedding was spread, and we rested.

Hear these few words about Mr. Hajj Mirza Ahmad Ayatullahzadeh, who came along with other friends when we left Qom and travelled until they arrived at Shah ʿAbdul ʿAzim, peace be upon him. The gentlemen went to welcome them. After two to three days, they arrived at Tehran. Mr. Hajj Shaykh, my own uncle, entertained them greatly for ten to twelve days and I was always at their service. All the men and women were in the same place. But Mr. Shaykh Ahmad Shah with his brother, mother, and son had a separate house. Before long, we were divided into five groups, and each went to a different place. First, Mr. Hajj Mirza Ahmad, Mr. Mirza Ibrahim, his paternal cousin, and two of the servants, and Mr. Shaykh ʿAbdul ʿAli Dashti, the son

---

42 Toopkhana Square (literally, "artillery square") was built in 1831 during the Qajar period.
43 Mashq Square was one of the largest military squares in Tehran built in the Qajar period.

of Mr. Shaykh Muhammad Dashti, and his companion, Hajji 'Abdul Rasul – these four went towards Shemiran. Second, Mr. Muhammad, Mr. Bazaz the merchant, and Hajj 'Ali, our companion, and Mr. Shaykh 'Imad al-Din, the son of Mr. Shaykh Muhammad Rashti Ayatullahzadeh, the brother of my uncle – these four returned to the Great Najaf. Third, the daughter of Mr. Hajj Aqa Bozorg and her servant and the helper – these three went to Rasht. Fourth, Mr. Shaykh Ahmad Shahrudi, his brother, mother, and son went to Shahrud. Fifth, I and my uncle's wife, with her two sons and one servant, remained in Tehran, in the state centre.

After this, several events happened in Tehran. First, among the family of my uncle and me, a great hostility broke out, with fights, skirmishes, quarrels, and animosity. They accused me falsely of vulgarity, scandals, beatings, defamation, lies, and made other allegations against me. I heard and saw things I should not have heard or seen from any of them, whether right or wrong, from the gentlemen, the servants, the women, the helpers, and so on. I kept quiet and tolerated it.

> Khaja, blessings be upon him,[44] spoke rightly:
> "I never complain about the strangers –
> Anything that happened to me by the acquaintance."[45]

I said in my heart, "Hajji Mahboob, you have suffered so much in the world; this is not worse than slavery in those deserts, and will not be. We want an end to the issues." I said, "From the time I came here, I have not cared about myself."

In the first house, the conversation of the gentlemen, men, and women was about whether I should get married. Some agreed that I should and others disagreed.

There was also the murder of Arshad al-Daula[46] by Yafar Khan,[47] the arrival of Salar al-Daula to Kurdistan, Luristan, and the forming of an army with the intention of capturing Tehran, and the departure of Yafram Khan Armani[48] to fight with him, and after the war so many

---

44 Khaja Shams al-Din Muhammad Shirazi, also known as Hafez, the famous Iranian poet.
45 Hafez, *ghazal* no. 130.
46 He was in the military during the Qajar period and against the Constitution in Iran. He was killed in battle by Yapram Khan.
47 The original text is Yafar Khan, but the correct name is Yapram Khan, also known as Yapram Khan Armani.
48 Mahboob writes a different form of the name (see previous note), referring to Yafar (Yapram) Khan.

were killed. Shu'a al-Saltana intended to capture the capital but was defeated. Rashid al-Sultan arrived from Mazandaran but was murdered by the Mujahedin. News spread that Muhammad 'Ali Shah intended to capture the capital, but he was unsuccessful, according to the news from the provinces, surroundings, foreign countries, and so on.

We departed from the first house. At the second house, news arrived from the Great Najaf that Mr. Akhund Mulla Muhammad Kazem Khurasani, great be his place, had died in the month of Dhu al-Hijja, and there were discussions about my marriage. In the year 1330, on the night of Friday 11 Rajab [26 June 1912], I got married. God bestowed upon me three children; two of them died, they were girls, and one son survived, [born] on Tuesday 24 Dhu al-Hijja al-Haram [...] [4 December].

After these events was the ultimatum of the Russians, who said that people should not use Russian goods, and the animosity of the gentlemen. Every day I went to the Majles Parliament to discuss security, and after that, we discussed the murder of the Qafqazi Mujahedin. The Mujahedin with the gentlemen, Samsam al-Saltana, wanted many Bakhtiyaris to be at the door of the house of the Mujahed gentlemen to protect and safeguard them. There was a bread shortage and Russian food shortages, and a boycott of sugar and tea; however, people were using these secretly! Before long, it became peaceful, when the fighting stopped between the Bakhtiyaris and the Ajans.[49] Peace was established between them, then the Bakhtiyaris departed from Tehran. After that was the event of Kashan, Naib Husayn, and the departure of the army from Tehran. After so much fighting, peace was established, which meant the parties got frustrated. After that, the shah ordered for the army to be equipped in the surroundings of Shiraz, Kurdistan, Lurestan, and so on, for security. For two days, the army was marching and performing. The shah came three times to see the army. A Russian plane came from Russia for show, and again the shah came. It did not last long. The events related to Majles Parliament had to begin. I wish it was not that the Muslims' blood was shed unjustly. They imposed tariffs on the people who did not deserve them in each quarter, and in the alleys, markets, and mosques. After removing the tariffs, they entered Parliament, and the coronation took place in the year 1333[50] [1915]. [There was also] the war of European countries, and so on; the war of Russia and the Ottomans; the coming of the two[51] to Iran; the departure

---

49 Police.
50 The correct year of the coronation is 1332 (21 July 1914).
51 Refers to the occupation of Iran by Russia and Britain.

of the crown prince along with Muvasiq al-Daula[52] to Tabriz and his settling there; the events of the wars of Tabriz and Ardabil regarding the Russians and the Armenians and whatever they should not have done but did to the Muslims and the blood which was shed and the injustices that they committed. From there, they came to Khurasan and bombed the dome of the holy shrine [of Imam Reza], peace be upon him. I wrote to all my friends and they replied to me. The war of the Ottoman Empire before the event of the European wars lasted for three years; after that, was the arrival of the Russians to Iran. Then, in the third house, was the departure of the gentlemen to Shemiran and after the arrival, emigration, along with the Mujahedin lawyers.[53] The lawyers signed their names saying that the shah should go to Isfahan, but the shah did not go. There was the departure of the gentlemen to Qom, and from there to Isfahan, and after that, the death of many of the gentlemen and the 'ulama', like the late Sadr al-'Ulama', and so on. There was the issue of Robat Karim and the arrival of the Russians to Iran, the pursuing of the Mujahedin and the Ottomans, and after that, the pursuing of the Russians by the Ottomans. There was the departure of the Armenians and the Russians and the ambassadors, out of fear of the Ottomans and being captured. Before this, the Russians were hunting for the great ambassador of the Ottomans in the capital. After that, the event of the murder of the 'ulama', dignitaries, nobles, and others, like Mr. Mirza Mohsen and others, and again the issue of bread that became bad and nothing could be found. [Then there was] the arrival of the Mujahedin and Muhajerin after the withdrawal to Kermanshahan, and so on. After the arrival of the Mujahedin to Tehran came the famine and people died, and something was distributed to the doors of the houses of the poor; and the escape of the gentlemen to Shemiran, away from the poor and needy. There was also the issue of not giving the New Year's gift. After that, I was infected with typhoid and [witnessed] the deaths of people and the death of my own little daughter, and my friends and buddies, and the sickness of my uncle who, after a year, still did not recover. After so much suffering, while I was badly infected with typhoid, he passed away on the night of the twenty-second of the month of *siyam*[54] [3 August]. I had pain in my eye, but it did not last long. The purveyance changed and there was more killing, one by one, and two to three hangings. Shortly after, there was the event of Eid

---

52 The minister of Ahmad Shah.
53 The original text uses *vukala* (lawyers), a reference to parliamentary representatives.
54 *Siyam* (literally, "fasting") refers to the month of Ramadan.

Ghadir Khom, when people went to Shah 'Abdul 'Azim and carried out debauchery, and then God's rage descended upon them like the wind and people died like the autumn leaves on the peasants' land, until 1 Muharram al-Haram 1337 [7 October 1918]. All these catastrophes and miseries kept happening constantly. I accrued a debt of 2,500 tomans in Dar al-Khilafa,[55] and I gave all for the sake of God.

[Leaving Tehran for Mashhad]

I was hurt both physically and financially, but I was well and added to my knowledge, as every loss adds to one's intelligence. From Thursday, 2 Rajab 1329 [29 June 1911], until Muharram 1337 [October 1918], for seven years, six months, and several days, we were in Tehran. After seeing Tehran, its surroundings, alleys, quarters, and markets, and, for example, Tehran's outskirts, I visited all the Imamzadas,[56] and so on. We were there until the new year, Muharram 1337, when a letter arrived from the sons of the 'ulama', peace be upon them, from the honourable Najaf, which said, "Certainly, you should depart from Tehran to go to the Holy Land. Shortly, we will send several people to Tehran to help you depart." And several times letters arrived from Mr. Ayatullahzadeh from Khurasan which said, "Certainly, you should depart." From here they replied both by sending telegraph messages and mailing letters. They waited for the arrival of the response. In Muharram 1337, the response arrived from Khurasan both by letter and telegraph.

Hear these few words. After we received the answer from Khurasan and the Holy Land, the sanctuary of [Imam Reza in] Mashhad, peace be upon him, we were determined to move to the Holy Land. Any items belonging to the house, I wrote down and listed and gave to the legal guardian of the late Hajj Shaykh Isma'il Rashti Gilani, may his dust be fragrant. We planned to leave with all the family of the deceased from Tehran to go to the state centre on the night of Tuesday 7 Safar al-Khayr [12 November]. It was near dusk and we left from there, and said goodbye to the friends, men and women, who had come to bid us farewell. When I moved out of Tehran, I had with me about two tomans.

We departed from there and went all the way until we arrived at the first rest stop, which was Khatun Abad. From Tehran to Khatun Abad is four *farsang*s. We got off for prayers and had dinner and tea. They brought pack animals and attached them to the stagecoach.

---

55 Refers to Tehran, the capital.
56 Refers to the descendants of the Imams.

We departed to go towards Sharif Abad. We arrived at Sharif Abad. From Khatun Abad to Sharif Abad is four *farsang*s. From Sharif Abad to Ali Abad, known as Kalle-yi Umar,[57] is three *farsang*s. From Ali Abad to Iyvan Kayf is seven *farsang*s. From here we went to a coffee house. From Iyvan Kayf to Qeshlaq is seven *farsang*s. From Qeshlaq to Ali Abad is four *farsang*s. From Ali Abad to Deh Namak is seven *farsang*s. From there we went to Ab Barik, and from Ab Barik to Las Gerd. The distance from Ab Barik to Las Gerd is one *farsang*. From Las Gerd to Deh Sorkh is two *farsang*s. From Deh Sorkh to Semnan is two *farsang*s. From Semnan to Ahoovan is six *farsang*s, minus two. From Ahoovan to Ghoshah is three *farsang*s, and with Semnan together is six *farsang*s. From Ghoshah to Dolat Abad is three *farsang*s. From Dolat Abad to Amir Abad is three *farsang*s. From Amir Abad to Damghan is three *farsang*s. From Damghan to Mehmandust is three *farsang*s. From Mehmandust to Dehmolla is three *farsang*s. From Dehmolla to Shahrud is four *farsang*s. On Thursday 16 Safar al-Khayr [21 November], we arrived at Shahrud and stayed two nights and two days at the house of Mr. Shaykh Ahmad Shahrudi, the mujtahid. After that, they prepared food for our journey, and we departed to go to Meyami, which is twelve *farsang*s. From Meyami to Meyandasht is seven *farsang*s. From Meyandasht to Alhak[58] and from there to Abbas Abad is six *farsang*s. From Abbas Abad to Kahak[59] is six *farsang*s. From Kahak to Mazinan[60] is five *farsang*s. From Mazinan to Sadkharve[61] is four *farsang*s. From Sadkharve to Rivand[62] is four *farsang*s. From Rivand to Sabzvar is four *farsang*s. From Sabzvar to Sar Push[63] is four *farsang*s. From Sar Push to Za'faraniya[64] is six *farsang*s. From Za'faraniya to Shuryab[65] is four *farsang*s. From Shuryab to Neyshabor is five *farsang*s. From Neyshabor to Fakhre Davud[66] is six *farsang*s (between Fakhre Davud and Sharif

---

57 Ali Abad, Kalle-yi Umar (head of Umar), refers to the ancient village of Ali Abad Abulqasim Khani, Tehran Province, between Tehran and Semnan.
58 Alhak is Semnan Province, Iran.
59 In the original text it is written as Kahar, but the correct name is Kahak.
60 A village in Razavi Khurasan Province, Iran.
61 A village in Razavi Khurasan Province, Iran.
62 A village in Razavi Khurasan Pdrovince, Iran.
63 Robate Sar Push is a village in Razavi Khurasan Province, Iran. In the original text Mahboob refers to it as Sar Push.
64 A village in the Robat Rural district, Razavi Khurasan Province, Iran.
65 In the original text it is Shurab, but the correct form is Shuryab, a village in Taghenkoh district, Razabi Khurasan Province, Iran.
66 A village near the Silk Road in Neyshabor, Razavi Khurasan Province, Iran. In the past, its caravanserai had been one of the stop locations for the caravans travelling between Mashhad and Neyshabor.

Abad⁶⁷ is Qadamgah⁶⁸). From Fakhre Davud to Sharif Abad is three *farsangs*. From Sharif Abad to Toroq⁶⁹ is four *farsangs*. Between the two is a place called Hoze Ramazan, where there are several coffee houses. From Toroq to the holy Mashhad is two *farsangs*.

[In Mashhad]

On the night of Thursday 23 Safar al-Khayr [28 November], we arrived at the Holy Land safely. We were travelling all the way, night and day, but many of the places were scary, dangerous, and unsafe. What scary roads there are! All mountains, plains, deserts, steppes, and jungles are filled with danger and horror. Wherever we arrived on our way, houses, places, cities, villages, and settlements, we had very good times. But we were surprised that this road was full of blessings like running water and nice weather. May God protect it. "Praise be to God, the best of creators."⁷⁰ It cannot be expressed how God has bestowed His blessing upon the people of Iran and the people of Khurasan, but alas! They do not know the value of God's blessing.

The point is this: When we arrived at Toroq, Mr. Mirza Muhammad, the son of the late Mr. Mulla Muhammad Kazem Heravi Khurasani, the mujtahid, may his dust be fragrant, came with servants and relatives to the stagecoach to welcome his sister and the children of his sister. But we were in the stagecoach, which we had rented. They got on the stagecoach and moved on in front, then we followed behind them. We entered the city of the Holy Land and our eyes were brightened by seeing the dome of our Imam, His Excellency, the eighth Imam, praise be to God, the best of creators. We arrived at the house of the son of the honourable. After ten to fifteen days of hosting us, they got a private house for us. We all went and moved in there and the honourable provided us with everything from black to white!

After settling here, we stayed about eight months in Khurasan. I spent the days, nights, weeks, and months praying, going on pilgrimages on behalf of the friends of my master Amir al-Mu'minin and the other Imams, peace be upon them. I was busy working, doing my own duties and service in interior and exterior jobs. I had very good times during these eight months, from the perspective of making a living, and so on, and being in contact with the residents, the gentlemen, and

---

67 A village in the district of Neyshabor, Razavi Khurasan Province, Iran.
68 A city in the district of Zeberkhan County, Razavi Khurasan Province, Iran.
69 A village in Razavi Khurasan Province, Iran.
70 Quoting Qur'an 23:14.

young men of that region and that land. From the perspective of finding friendship, they liked me very much. They respected and honoured me and showed kindness. The benefit of this trip for me was that from interior and exterior work, I collected about two hundred tomans and several more. But alas, people in places where I had borrowed were disturbing my peace. I was a bit depressed there and, since the world is a place for sorrow and sadness with jealous, revengeful, envious, and torturous people, I sought refuge in God, the great God.

After a while, we and the companions who were together separated; some went towards Qochan, and others moved out of the house. It was my turn. Since the past was changed, some people were jealous and envied me, and every day and every night, various and different reports and lies from the interior, exterior, and surroundings were sent to the family of the deceased, saying, "I saw Hajj Mahboob do this and that." And when these false reports and rumours that were nonsense were told about me, my soul was suffering a lot. Any advice and explanation I offered was useless and had no effect. It was as if I had animosity with the family!

[Expelling Mahboob: Moving from Mashhad to Tehran]

My work and services lasted until the family and I had a bitter fight, with enmity and hostility. Thus, they made their minds up that I would move out of Khurasan. After I proved to the family and to everyone that I was right, it was entirely obvious.[71] The son of the gentleman said, "Tomorrow you and your family should move out of here and go to Tehran." In response, I said, "I will depart tomorrow." For a week, he was giving me promises and delays until, between me and one of the friends and intimates of the son of the gentleman, who was my close friend, we wrote several letters, and intermediaries, talks, obligations, and conversations were exchanged. Then, they arranged my departure. When it was clear, I prepared for the journey. After making pilgrimages and visiting friends, one by one in that beloved honourable place, I saw my dear friends; I said my goodbyes and left. On Wednesday, 2 Dhu al-Qaʿda al-Haram 1337 [30 July 1919], half an hour before sunset, we departed from Mashhad. We stayed three nights at Toroq.

Near Ibtidaʾ, a young person, whose name was Sadegh, bothered me so much in buying and renting the carriage that the cane became lost. The carriage could not go forward; it was four tomans for the damage

---

71 Literally, "clearer than the sun."

that I had to give for the stagecoach until we got to Toroq and near Ibtidaʾ. I negotiated with the first creditor of the carriage and gave him five tomans. During the several days we were in Toroq, many times fights broke out, and I saw various strange things. From Mashhad to Toroq is two *farsang*s. From Toroq to Shairf Abad is four *farsang*s. From Sharif Abad to Fakhre Davud is three *farsang*s.

To make a long story short, hear these few words. From Fakhre Davud to Neyshabor including Qadamgah is six *farsang*s. From Neyshabor to Shurab is five *farsang*s. From Shurab to Zaʿfaraniyeh is five *farsang*s. From Zaʿfaraniyeh to Sabzvar is six *farsang*s. From Sabzvar to Rivand is four *farsang*s. From Rivand to Sadkharve is four *farsang*s. From Sadkharve to Mazinan is five *farsang*s.

Here I wrote this couplet:

Oh Mazinan, the tavern temple, we went towards Tehran
I wander in the desert like Layla and Majnun

I wrote it since the rhyme corresponded to my condition.

From Mazinan to Kahar is three *farsang*s. From Kahar to Abbas Abad is three *farsang*s. From Abbas Abad to Meyandasht is six *farsang*s. From Meyandasht to Meyami is seven *farsang*s. I wrote these verses here too. I mean, some of the versed people wrote poems about these three rest stops, Alhak, Meyandasht, and Meyami, and I am completing the rhyme here:

We will pass through this road
Like Esfandyar, Bahman,[72] and Dey[73]
The bird sings, "Hey, hey,
Sit, relax, and have some wine
Friends desire to be with him
May not this world be without wine."

From Meyami to Shahrud is twelve *farsang*s. I left from here to go to Bastam, which is one *farsang*. I visited one of the gentlemen and friends. From here to Bagh Zendan is two *maydan-i asb*. We stayed there two nights and one of the friends was not visited. In brief, after doing some work, we left the company of the friends and departed from here. From Shahrud we went to Sar Push, which is a very pleasant place with a

---

72 A winter month of the Persian calendar corresponding to February.
73 A winter month of the Persian calendar corresponding to January.

famous descendant of an Imam. From there to Zaʿfaraniyeh is four *farsang*s. From Shahrud to Dehmolla is four *farsang*s. From Dehmolla to Mehmandust is three *farsang*s. From Mehmandust to Damghan is three *farsang*s. Here we were guests for lunch. From Damghan to Amir Abad is three *farsang*s. From there to Dolat Abad is three *farsang*s. From Dolat Abad to Goshah is three *farsang*s. From Ghoshah to Ahoovan is three *farsang*s. From Ahoovan to Chasht Khoran and from there to Attar Abad is three *farsang*s. There was no bread in these two rest stops and the weather was so cold. From Attar Abad to Semnan is three *farsang*s, which is in total six *farsang*s. From Semnan to Deh Sorkh is two *farsang*s. From Deh Sorkh to Las Gerd is two *farsang*s. From Las Gerd to Ab Barik is one *farsang*. Here, there was a very sweet melon. From here to Deh Namak is seven *farsang*s. From Deh Namak to Ali Abad is four *farsang*s. From Ali Abad to Qeshlaq is seven *farsang*s. From Qeshlaq to Iyvan Kayf is five *farsang*s. Before Qeshlaq is the coffee house of Mr. Qoreishi. Ali Abad is known as Kalle-yi Umar, which is three *farsang*s away. We stayed there at night. The rest of Ab Barik leads to the guardhouse tower to Sepool. From Sepool we went to ʿAbdul Abad. On Monday, 28 Dhu al-Qaʿda 1337 [25 August 1919], at noon, we were there. In the afternoon, we went to Deh Namak. From Iyvan Kayf to Sharif Abad is two *farsang*s. From Sharif Abad to Khatun Abad is three *farsang*s. From Khatun Abas to Tehran is four *farsang*s.

[In Tehran]

We entered. That day was a day when they were not allowing anyone to enter from the city's gate. They were inspecting. Whatever it took, we entered the city. We and the friends and companions, including men and women, were separated from each other and said farewell. Everyone went to his or her own house and residence. We also went to our house, but our belongings were left in the wagon house because of the debt of the road. I did not have enough money and could not cover the cost. It remained there for several days. For ten to twelve days [I hoped] maybe something would happen so that we could take our belongings out of the wagon house. It did not happen until I explained the situation to one of my friends. He borrowed money from his own family to let us take our belongings out of the wagon house. After I entered Tehran and had visited for three days, I became severely sick. The Almighty and blessed God saved me. I ran out of money. If I want to explain it, the pen cannot write it! Only now will a reminder suffice.

I stayed in Tehran for two months and seventeen days. In what conditions and how! I had written before that we had a quarrel in Mashhad and sufferings on the road, of not having enough money, becoming ill, the belongings being left in the wagon house, having nothing, looking after my wife and child, and the talks and conversations of friends and enemies, but the enemies were many. The friends, especially those with whom I did service with kindness and generosity, were more hostile. My brothers, the lawyer of that house, and the person whom I had served previously more than the others while he was ill were saying, "Throw him to ruin." What should I write to my brother of my condition!

I was there until Muharram 1338 [September 1919]. After three days, meaning 3 Muharram [28 September], the family of the first master arrived. But I was in the same first house. When they had passed two to three rest stops, that family sent a messenger in advance and a message that if I had been exiled for enjoining good and forbidding wrong by the order of their brothers, family, and relatives from Khurasan and that region, then here too I, along with my wife and child, should not be in this house. Thus, I was grumpy and angry. I took my wife and child and left that house and went to another house which was nearby and belonged to my wife; we stayed for several days until my situation in staying or leaving became clear. But they brought us dinner, lunch, and everything to eat. After sixty-five days passed, the family stopped. So, I had to write a letter to them explaining what had happened in Khurasan, the road and the sufferings, which I already had said. He responded, "Do you have any business with them? Tell me whatever you need." In short, the issue ended.

But after eight to nine years of having journeyed to Iran, Khurasan, and its districts, it did not take long before I had had enough and, for me, moving towards the holy shrines[74] was the priority instead of staying in Iran. For this reason, I made up my mind to leave to go towards the holy shrines. I say those quarrels, disputes, disagreements, feuds, miseries, sufferings, sorrows, and talks were between the creditors and the others and I got delayed, and everything was explained to them but had no effect.

[Imprisonment]

The legal executor to whom they had written said, "With the arrival of this letter, send him to the holy shrines and give him whatever belongings are his." I prepared little by little for the journey and provided

---

74 The holy shrines in Iraq.

anything needed for the trip. Another thing for me was that, close to the last journey, before the passing of the deceased, I had some debts. I paid off some of them, but others remained. It was written in the will, but they had not executed the will when it was near to my trip, which was after one year and several months had passed. In this recent journey, one person who had lent me money told a creditor, "Why are you delaying? That person wants to go to the holy shrines. If he leaves, then you will lose your money." That creditor and a government officer came to the door of the house for his debt. After two or three days, I had done all the work and had said goodbye to my friends; it was 17 Muharram al-Haram 1337[75] [23 October 1918]. The same day, in the evening, I had sent the family to Shah ʿAbdul ʿAzim to be there when I arrived. The house belongings went first with the wagon and then the family followed from behind. No one was left at home except me, the legal executor, the creditor, and the government officer. I discussed a lot about the debt and explained it to the legal executor, but he did not accept it. To all the friends, meaning the people to whom I had done kindness, the officer and the creditor asked them to bail me out. I said, "There is no one to bail me out." I asked one person to whom I had done kindness the most to come and bail me out. He replied, "I will not." Thus, based on the government law and the government pursuit, it was determined that I had to be imprisoned in the same place until I paid the debt of the creditors. There were many discussions, but the questions were rejected and had no effect.

[Release from Prison]

I stayed to see how my situation would end; I remained there for three days and three nights. On the night of 20 Muharram al-Haram [15 October], I was released from prison. The reason for my release was that I took refuge in God and the twelfth Imam and the Fourteen Infallibles, God's blessing be upon him and all of them. When I was in prison, I was sad and crying, "God, what did I do to deserve this misery?" I was wanting my death from God every second. God was kind, and this passed. They released me from prison. I had some friends who became sad to hear of my situation. One of those friends, with whom I was close for several years, heard about me and became very sad. He came and said, "I did not know about your situation. Now I will go and inform the honourables." He went and informed the honourable

---

75 The correct year is 1338 (12 October 1919).

Mr. Mir Sayyid Muhammad Behbehani that I was in prison and for him to go and bring me out. Mr. Mir Sayyid Muhammad received all the information and sent his attendant and said, "Go and give this ten tomans." He himself gave five tomans. The creditor waived five out of the twenty tomans. After the enormous damages, the family understood their own humiliation. The overseer of the legal executor felt for me and gave twelve tomans out of his own pocket to the person who had informed the creditor in advance to go and make peace. We reduced twenty to twelve tomans.

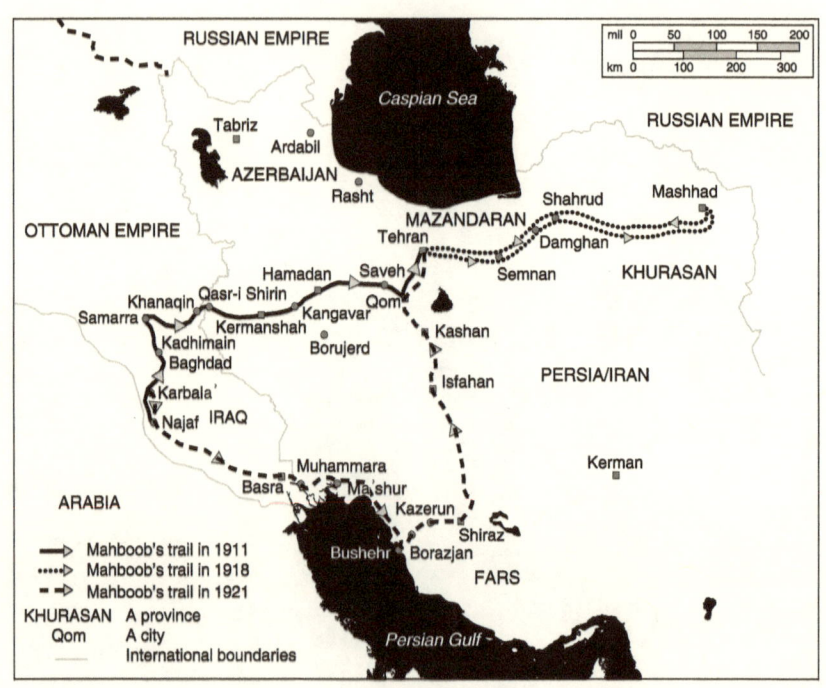

Map 7. Mahboob's trails in Iran and Ottoman Iraq

5 [Leaving Iran for Iraq]

[The Departure of Mahboob from Tehran to Shah ʿAbdul ʿAzim, Peace Be upon Him]

That night, 20 Muharram al-Haram [15 October], I came out and said farewell to some of the government officers and the others and left. The person who was hostile to me said, "I will come with you to Shah ʿAbdul ʿAzim." I was afraid that he might take revenge and harm me on the road in the darkness of night. God did not ordain it. So it happened that I went alone until I was near the gate. It was closed. I spent the night at the coffee house until the morning. I got up with the call for prayers in the morning and performed the prayers. I picked up some stuff, including the cloth wrapper in which were my socks, and came to the gate. I saw people were standing and waiting for them to open the door of the gate. Shortly after, they opened the door. I moved out. It was still dark and twilight but there was moonlight. I said "In the name of God" and walked fast. I said goodbye to that damn ruined Tehran and left.

Hear a few words from me. We departed from Tehran. It was 20 Muharram. I departed from there and went with no stops to Shah ʿAbdul ʿAzim. I arrived there at sunrise. Then I went home and found my children.[1] How they were! They were crying and lamenting. They were worried and thinking about me. I went immediately to the holy shrine and performed the Fear prayer (*salat al-khawf*). I said farewell to my master.[2] I took whatever was needed, like bread, and got the road map and came to the caravanserai. We immediately took the belongings

---

1 "Children" here includes both his wife and children.
2 Referring to the honourable ʿAbdul ʿAzim Hasani, whose grave is there.

and got the children on and said goodbye and farewell to the family, community, friends, and supporters, and left.

What was the condition? It was that all the caravans and pilgrims had moved out and were two or three rest stops ahead of us. But we stopped every second rest stop to reach them. What season was it? It was winter. The beginning of winter. We departed in the state of weeping, sorrow, sadness, and grief, on Wednesday, 20 Muharram al-Haram 1338 [15 October 1919]. From Tehran to the honourable Shah 'Abdul 'Azim, peace be upon him, is one *farsang*. From Shah 'Abdul 'Azim to Kahrizak is three *farsang*s. From Kahrizak to Hasan Abad is three *farsang*s. From Hasan Abad to Ali Abad is nine *farsang*s. From Ali Abad to Manzariyeh is five *farsang*s. From Manzariyeh to Ma'someh, Qom, peace be upon her, is five *farsang*s. On the third day we arrived safely and stayed there for three days for prayers and a pilgrimage on behalf of all our friends. On the fifth day we departed from Ma'someh, Qom, by the Taj Khatoun Road. From Ma'someh, Qom, to Taj Khatoun is six *farsang*s. From Taj Khatoun to Jahroud is four *farsang*s. From Jahroud to Siyah Shoon is five *farsang*s. From Siyah Shoon to Lavash Kerd is four *farsang*s. From Lavash Kerd to Sarooq is three *farsang*s. From Sarooq to Diz Abad is five *farsang*s. From Diz Abad to Qazan is four *farsang*s. From Qazan to Jamil Abad is six *farsang*s. From Jamil Abad to Farsiya is three *farsang*s. From Farsiya to Kangavar is five *farsang*s. From Kangavar to Sahneh is four *farsang*s. From Sahneh to Bisotoun is four *farsang*s. From Bisotoun to Kermanshahan is six *farsang*s. We stayed there five or six days. After buying souvenirs, visiting friends, and delivering the letters of friends, we departed from Kermanshahan. It was near the morning. To May Dasht is four *farsang*s. From May Dasht to Harun Abad is eight *farsang*s. From Harun Abad to Karand is five *farsang*s. From Karand to Paeen Taq is three *farsang*s. From Paeen Taq to Pol-i Zahab is one *farsang*. From Pol-i Zahab to Qasr-i Shirin is five *farsang*s.

Things that happened on the way were illness and flu, falling and whipping, and hostility among some of the passengers. I also fell into the hands of the British. Since we arrived at Ba'quba[3] at night, we, along with the pilgrims, went near the Euphrates and moved on in the morning towards Baghdad; we arrived at Baghdad in the evening. Early in the morning, with pack animals we departed from Baghdad towards Kazemain, peace be upon him. On 20 Arba'in, or 5 Safar al-Khayr [30 October], we stayed for eight days there. I sent the children to Samarra and after returning several days later we did some work and business

---

3 It is Buqa' in the original text, but the correct form is Ba'quba.

in Kazemain and Baghdad. On the first night of Rabi' al-Mulud 1338 [24 November 1919], we, along with some pilgrims, departed from Kazemain to go to the Great Karbala'. On the first day when we arrived at Karbala' it was dusk. We went to the house of Mr. Mirza Hasan Nuri, near the door of the tomb of Sayyid al-Shuhada', peace be upon him. But we had no news about the family of Mr. Hajj [Ishaq] Rashti Ayatullahzadeh. After they heard of our arrival, they took us to their house and all the friends went on with their own business. We stayed for two whole months in the Great Karbala'. In the winter, the first of the month of the eminent Rajab, we departed from Karbala' towards the honourable Najaf. But I rode with the belongings with the horse and pack animals. I stayed one night on the way and the next day at noon, after ten years of being away from Iraq, my eyes fell upon the brilliant dome of our master of the masters.[4] I offered my thanks.

---

4 Refers to 'Ali, the first Imam of the Shi'ites.

6 [Returning to Iran]

We remained for twelve months in the honourable Najaf. During this period, we were at the service of the family, doing the work of the interior and exterior, whether the *biruni* or the *andaruni*, and whatever was related to small tasks, like services. We spent some time in Kofa and in the honourable Najaf, for days, nights, and months until after the month of Ramadan, the same year, 1338 [May 1920].

The second recent fight that happened was when we were there from the beginning of Saturday 29 Rabi' al-Mulud [11 December], until Tuesday, 6 Jumada al-Thani 1339 [15 February 1921], when we departed from the honourable Najaf. Again, as a group we decided to go towards the port of Ma'shoor[1] with the grandchildren of the mujtahid Mr. Hajj Shaykh Javad Behbehani, may God bless him, to take their wives and children and to send them.

After this period, again I left the family and wife in Najaf and left in the year 1339 [1921] to go towards Karbala'. We stayed there for one week, then moved on towards Kazemain and stayed there two days. We bought some things and boarded a ship. We were on our way for five days towards Basra. Hajj Shaykh Ishaq Ayatullahzadeh remained in the building for twenty-two days. We took the family towards Basra. We arrived at Basra at night. The next day, we took the road towards Muhammara, the house of Mr. Hajj Shaykh 'Ali mujtahid, the uncle of Mr. Hajj Shaykh Javad Behbehani. We stayed there two nights. We left on the night of Friday to go towards Fallahiyah and at night arrived at Fallahiyah; in the morning we departed from there to go towards the port of [...]. We stayed on the road that night. The morning of the

---

1 The port of Ma'shoor is located on the coast of the Persian Gulf, Khuzestan Province, Iran. Its name was changed to Mahshahr in 1947.

next day, we arrived at the port of [...]. At noon we were the guests of Mr. Hajj Mahdi, the brother of Hajj Reza, who was in Fallahiyah. They brought a pack animal in the afternoon and we moved on towards the port of Ma'shoor. We arrived at the Ma'shoor port in the evening. That was three *farsang*s. We stayed there for four days and nights. We had a very good time when we were there in Nowruz. Since Mr. Hajj Shaykh Javad heard that Mr. Hajj Shaykh Ishaq planned to arrive there, we again together returned from that road towards Muhammara. We stayed in Muhammara. The next day in the evening we went towards Basra. Mr. Ayatullah Gilani and some of the honourables and companions were together. We stayed there for two or three nights. Again, we returned with the honourables to go towards Muhammara and stayed there for ten or twelve days. From there we prepared to journey to the port of Bushehr. On Saturday, 14 Sha'ban al-Mukarram 1339 [23 April 1921], we boarded a ship. We moved on towards Bushehr port on Saturday 14 [Sha'ban] and arrived there on the morning of Monday, 16 Sha'ban 1339 [25 April 1921]. A day before our arrival, the sea was stormy and several ships with groups of people had drowned in the scary and dangerous sea. With several sailboats from the ship, we arrived at the wharf, meaning the harbour. We arrived at the house of Mr. Shaykh mujtahid Muhammad [...] Dashtestani, may God bless him, and stayed there for fourteen days until the end of the Great Sha'ban, 1339 [May 1921]. Here, for the whole fourteen days we were invited by nobles, honourables, merchants, and others, and I earned five to six tomans[2] for allowance, and I had cloth sent through someone to the honourable Najaf. Mr. Mulla 'Ali Ruzekhan Khauja and the other honourable gentlemen were kind and good people. God bless them. The gentlemen of Bushehr were Mr. Shaykh Muhammad Dashtestani and his children, Shaykh 'Abdul 'Ali, Isma'il, Ahmad, and Mahmoud, and the grandchild was Sediqa. Also, there were Mr. Sayyid Muhammad, Shaykh Mahdi, Sayyid 'Abdullah, Karbala'i 'Ali Borazjani, the official of Mu'ayn al-Mamalek, Mr. Hajj Muhammad Baqir, the merchant of Bushehr, and Mr. Reza Khan, another Bushehr merchant.

Several days before the end of the month, we planned to go towards Shiraz. We prepared the pack animals, carriage, and the trip stuff and left with a group of pilgrims who had arrived from Karbala' and the holy shrines. On Thursday, the first of the month of the new moon, Ramadan, we departed from Bushehr towards Shiraz. From Bushehr to Shiraz is eleven rest stops. It was evening when we departed from

---

2 About 8 to 9.6 dollars.

there. The first rest stop, Ahmadia, from Bushehr is six *farsang*s. From Ahmadia to Borazjan is five *farsang*s. We stayed in the caravanserai at night and were the guests of the governor of Dashtestan, Mr. Asif al-Mulk, who had so much respect and dignity. From there to Dalaki is two *farsang*s. From there to the bridge of the late Mushir al-Daula, may God bless him, is three *farsang*s. That bridge is so important, and it is said that, in the past, whenever they fixed it, it got damaged. The latest repair fixed it by putting four Qur'ans over the pedestals at the beginning of the bridge and at the end of the bridge. From the blessing of the Great Qur'an, the water never damaged it.

From there to Konartakhta[3] is five *farsang*s. From Konartakhta to Kamaraj[4] is three *farsang*s. From Kamaraj to Kazerun is five *farsang*s. The environment was not yet spiritual in Kazerun. The governor of Fars, Mr. Nusrat al-Saltana,[5] had sent a telegraph to that region saying, "Mr. Ayatullahzadeh Gilani is on his way to that region. Prepare a military welcoming reception for him." The honourable asked my opinion, and I replied, "Your position is spiritual; it is good to let them go." It was not accepted. The honourable was taken on a donkey which had been sent by the gentlemen, and we brought him with so much ostentation to Kazerun, to the government house. After arriving, I, along with the passengers, went to the caravanserai and stayed there at night. In the morning again we departed from there to go towards Miyan Kotal. From Kazerun to Miyan Kotal is five *farsang*s. There was a water reservoir which was apparently built by Mr. Mushir, who had died. The water was very refreshing and the climate was spiritual. Before we got there, I saw a pigeon. I pointed out, "I am from Bushehr, the house of Mr. Reza Baqer, the Bushehr merchant. I want to go to Shiraz. The heaven is above me. I will be your servant." I liked the pigeon, and I entertained it wherever we went. We had too much stuff with us. But the pigeon was with us, and I liked it. I asked the other people to be kind to the pigeon and not to bother it along our way.

In Miyan Kotal, the sister of Mr. Amanullah Khan, the prince, was with us. One day she had beaten the servants there. She called to me and said, "I need some water and some stuff. Prepare them for me." I obeyed the order. It caused her to respect me. In any rest stop and place where we arrived, the companions, friends, and acquaintances would gather around me. It was a good time on this road. From there to

---

3 A city and the capital of Kamaraj, Kazerun County, Fars Province, Iran.
4 A district in Kazerun County, Fars Province, Iran.
5 The son of Mozaffar al-Din Shah.

Dasht-i Arjan,⁶ and from Bushehr, on the left and right side were flowers that the Almighty God has created, which the mind cannot describe.

From Miyan Kotal to Dasht-i Arjan is three *farsang*s. We stayed there at night. On Thursday, 11 Ramadan 1339 [19 May 1921], we arrived at Fars. Before arriving, from the government of Fars, Mr. Nusrat al-Saltana and Mr. Sulat al-Daula and a group of gentlemen had arranged a reception to welcome us. We had seen so many strange things on the way. They took us to the house of Mr. Shaykh Murtaza Mahallati, may his grave be sanctified. The honourables went to the government house until the evening when they returned to the house of the mentioned gentleman, the father of the gentleman. To Khana-yi Zenyan⁷ is three *farsang*s and from there to Shiraz is eight *farsang*s.

[In Shiraz]

Anyhow, we get back to the main point again. We stayed there for three and a half months. During this period, we accepted invitations, we went for strolls, and had fun. One day, we were going on a pilgrimage of holy graves in Shah Cheragh, those of Mir Sayyid Muhammad⁸ and Mir Sayyid 'Ala' al-Din,⁹ the brothers of the eighth Imam, peace be upon him, and Hafezia, Sa'dia, and Delgosha Garden. For three days, we were the guests of Qavam al-Mulk Shirazi. In the mornings, we would have milk and tea in the Eram Garden of Mushir al-Saltana, God bless him, and would be in the presence of the honourables and others. Among the famous places there, which are from the works of the old Iranian kings, are Vakil Mosque, Bazaar Vakil, Hammam Vakil, the water reservoir of Vakil, and Joma Mosque, whose history goes back fifteen hundred years and its pilgrimage has been from the time of the caliphate. This mosque has so many stories with the honourable Imam, peace be upon him. When he entered Shiraz, he performed prayers there. The mosque has a pulpit that has about 1,210 steps to reach the top. Then, on it, they have built a dome of the pulpit. People donate lights here. One of the buildings there is Bagh-i Takht-i Muhammad Khajou, which is half a *farsang* away from Shiraz. No mosque, [copy of

---

6 A village in Shiraz County, Fars Province, Iran.
7 A city in Shiraz County, Fars Province, Iran.
8 Muhammad ibn Musa Kazem, also known as Sayyid Mir Muhammad, was the son of Musa ibn Ja'far, the seventh Imam of the Shi'ites. He is known to have written many copies of the Qur'an and freed numerous slaves from the earnings.
9 Husayn ibn Musa, also known as Sayyid 'Ala' al-Din Husayn, was the son of Musa ibn Ja'far.

the] Qur'an, [shrine of] Khaja Naser Tusi, or other old monuments are like these, of which there are many here. And the Ark Vakil, and so on. Among them, in the building of Qavam, there is a rug with this poem: [...].

After three months, we decided to move towards Isfahan with a stagecoach. Two days before the departure, the gentlemen one night prepared for us a garden near a river and we had a very good time there. In the morning of 19 Dhu al-Qa'da al-Haram 1339 [25 July 1921], we bid farewell to all the friends and departed from Shiraz to go to Isfahan. From Shiraz to Baj Kah (Malek Majd Turk)[10] is two *farsang*s. From Baj Kah ('Abbas) to Zarghan (Ghulamhusayn Bazaz) is three *farsang*s. From there (Ahmad) to Pool Khan (Muhammad) is two *farsang*s. From there (Husayn) to Bagh Kordi (Jafar Qoli) is two and a half *farsang*s. From there to Sivand (Husayn) is two *farsang*s. From there (Muhammad) to Saadat Abad (Qamar) is six *farsang*s. We stayed there during the day. From there to Qader Abad (11 Hasan) is six *farsang*s. We stayed there at night (12 Mahmoud). From there (13 'Ali Akbar) to Bedid Kah (14 Ghulam Husayn) is four *farsang*s. At noon we were here (15 Ghulam Husayn). From there (16 Hormoz) to Fal Marje (17 Ghulam Husayn) is four *farsang*s. From there to the Deh Bid (18 Abul Qasim) is four *farsang*s. We stayed there overnight until Nusrat al-Saltana sent a rider and pursued Yar Muhammad Khan, the brother of Sulat al-Daula, and the road was opened. From there to Kole Kesh (19 Mahdi Khan) is three *farsang*s. From there to Khan Haram (20 'Azizullah) is three *farsang*s. From there to Morche Khar is three *farsang*s. From there to Sormekah is three *farsang*s. From there to Shorjestan is three *farsang*s. From there to Yazd Khas is three *farsang*s. From there to Navdaniye Amin Abad, the border of Fars, is three *farsang*s. From there to Maqsod Beyk is three *farsang*s. From there to Qamshe is four *farsang*s. From there we arrived at [...] 1:05, which is three *farsang*s. From there to the village of Shaban [...] to Chah is two *farsang*s. To Isma'il Khan is three *farsang*s. To Marghzar is three *farsang*s. We stopped there. From there to Isfahan is three *farsang*s.

---

10 In the original text, the names in parentheses were given under the names of the places. It is not clear what they refer to. They may be the names of people they met and stayed with on the road. Some also include numbers, which again are inexplicable.

[In Isfahan]

Anyway, we saw all the suffering and strange things on the way. On Wednesday, 26 Dhu al-Hijja al-Haram 1339 [31 August 1921], in the evening, we arrived at Isfahan. First, we went to the house of Hujjat al-Islam Mr. Hajj Nour al-Din. After that, we went to the house of Hujjat al-Islam Mr. Sayyid 'Abdul Husayn Sayyid al-'Araqain. On the way, there were welcoming receptions, and so on, wherever we arrived.

We stayed in Isfahan for three and a half months. During this period, we received many invitations and spent the days having fun and going to the religious gatherings,[11] mosques, and sanctuaries for the months of Muharram and Safar 1340 [September and October 1921]. We were invited to the old monuments several times, such as Shah 'Abbas Mosque, Shah Mosque of Sultan Husain, Chahar Bagh, and Chehel Sotoon. We were invited by the government of Sardar Heshmat Bakhtiyari. We saw Monar Jonban, one *farsang* outside of Isfahan, which the late Shaykh Baha al-Din al-'Amuli, may he rest in peace, had built, and Takht-i Folad,[12] which is a spiritual cemetery that is a burial place of scholars and pious souls such as Mir Fendereski[13] and Mirdamad. The grave of the late Majlesi, may his position be great, is in Isfahan. We visited the building of Pol-i Khaujo, where the stream of the water of the Zayandeh Rud dam passed under. I was there in 1340, the year that the deceased Mr. [...] passed away.

[Departing from Kashan]

It was fun there. After our arrival at Isfahan, on 7 Muharram al-Haram 1340 [10 September 1921], we saw the pilgrims who had been killed because of Yar Muhammad Khan, the brother of Sulat al-Daula. After all these observations, we decided to move towards Kashan. On the same day we were the guests of Mr. Qavam al-Daula. He had arranged a great reception outside his own garden. After having lunch and hookah and tea, we headed towards Kashan. From Isfahan to Kashan is six rest stops. After passing the rest stops, we entered Kashan. Mr. Hajj Mirza Shahab al-Din mujtahid and the other honourables of Kashan had prepared a great welcoming reception. We stayed in Kashan for fourteen days. Because of the suffering on the way and the difficulties of

---

11 The commemoration of the martyrdom of Husayn, the third Imam of the Shi'ites.
12 A historic cemetery built in the fourth/eleventh century.
13 A Persian philosopher, poet, and mystic of the Safavid era (d. 1640).

the road, I became ill, and could not eat anything for twenty-five days. After fourteen days, we bid farewell to the honourables and friends in Kashan and moved on towards the honourable Ma'someh, Qom, peace be upon her. From Kashan to Ma'someh, Qom, is six rest stops, or more, I cannot remember. Over there, too, we went to the government house of the gentleman, the deputy of justice. I went for a pilgrimage to Bibi for the third time. Every day I would go for a pilgrimage, and on behalf of friends, and I resorted to the honourable Ma'someh and the soil of the grave of Bibi, peace be upon her.

Bibliography

Archival Sources

British Library (BL), London.
Gulestan Palace, Albumkhana-yi Kakh-i Gulestan [The Photo Collection Centre of the Gulestan Palace], Tehran, Iran.
The National Archives of the United Kingdom (NAUK), Kew, London, UK.
Sazman-i Asnad va Kitabkhana-yi Milli-yi Jomhuri-yi Islami-yi Iran (SAM) [The National Archive and Library of the Islamic Republic of Iran], Tehran, Iran.
Vezarat-i Umur-i Khareja-yi Iran (VUK) [Ministry of Foreign Affairs of Iran], Markaz-i Asnad [Centre of Documents], Tehran, Iran.

Published Sources

Abushouk, Ahmed Ibrahim. "Ideology versus Pragmatism: The Case of the Mahdist Public Treasury in the Sudan (1881–1898)." *Die Welt Des Islams* 46, no. 2 (2006): 148–67. https://doi.org/10.1163/157006006777896849.
Adamiyat, Fereydun. *Fekr-i azadi*. 1340. Reprint, Tehran: Sukhan, 1961.
Afary, Janet. *The Iranian Constitutional Revolution, 1906–1911: Grassroots Democracy, Social Democracy & the Origins of Feminism*. New York: Columbia University Press, 1996. https://catalogue.nla.gov.au/catalog/3661616.
Algar, Hamid. *Mīrzā Malkum Khān*. Berkeley: University of California Press, 1973. https://doi.org/10.1525/9780520327863.
Al-Janabi, Abdul Sattar. "The Administrative Situation of the Holy City of Najaf and Its Impact on the Political Activity of the Scientific Seminary 1917–1924: A Historical and Documentary Study." *Kufa Journal of Arts* 1, no. 11 (March 2012): 283–330. https://doi.org/10.36317/kaj/2012/v1.i11.6531.
Allen, Richard B. *European Slave Trading in the Indian Ocean, 1500–1850*. Athens: Ohio University Press, 2014.

Alpers, Edward A., and Matthew S. Hopper. "Speaking for Themselves? Understanding African Freed Slave Testimonies from the Western Indian Ocean, 1850s–1930s." *Journal of Indian Ocean World Studies* 1, no. 1 (2017): 60–89. https://doi.org/10.26443/jiows.v1i1.20.

Amin, Camron Michael, Benjamin C. Fortna, and Elizabeth B. Frierson. *The Modern Middle East: A Sourcebook for History*. Oxford: Oxford University Press, 2006.

Arfa, Hassan. *Under Five Shahs*. New York: William Morrow, 1965.

Assaad, Marie Bassili. "Female Circumcision in Egypt: Social Implications, Current Research, and Prospects for Change." *Studies in Family Planning* 11, no. 1 (January 1980): 3–16. https://doi.org/10.2307/1965892.

Atamaz, Serpil. "Constitutionalism as a Solution to Despotism and Imperialism: The Iranian Constitutional Revolution in the Ottoman-Turkish Press." *Middle Eastern Studies* 55, no. 4 (2019): 557–69. https://doi.org/10.1080/00263206.2019.1566123.

Barz, Gregory. *Music in East Africa: Experiencing Music, Expressing Culture*. New York: Oxford University Press, 2004.

Bassett, James. *Persia, the Land of the Imams: A Narrative of Travel and Residence, 1871–1885*. London: Blackie & Son, 1887.

Bayat, Mangol. *Iran's First Revolution: Shi'ism and the Constitutional Revolution of 1905–1909*. New York: Oxford University Press, 1991. https://doi.org/10.1093/oso/9780195068221.001.0001.

Berberian, Houri. *Armenians and the Iranian Constitutional Revolution of 1905–1911*. Boulder, CO: Westview Press, 2001.

Binning, Robert B.M. *A Journal of Two Years' Travel in Persia, Ceylon, etc.* 2 vols. London: Wm. H. Allen, 1857.

Blassingame, John W. *Slave Testimony: Two Centuries of Letters, Speeches, Interviews, and Autobiographies*. Baton Rouge: Louisiana State University Press, 2002.

Bozdağlioğlu, Yucel. *Turkish Foreign Policy and Turkish Identity: A Constructivist Approach*. New York: Routledge, 2003. https://doi.org/10.4324/9780203502037.

Browne, Edward Granville. *The Persian Revolution of 1905–1909*. Washington, DC: Mage Publishers, 2006.

Burton, Richard F. *Personal Narrative of a Pilgrimage to Al-Madinah & Meccah*. 2 vols. 1893. Reprint, New York: Dover Publications, 1964. https://archive.org/details/personalnarrati01burt/page/n19/mode/2up.

Caldwell, John C., I.O. Orubuloye, and Pat Caldwell. "Male and Female Circumcision in Africa from a Regional to a Specific Nigerian Examination." *Social Science & Medicine* 44, no. 8 (April 1997): 1181–93. https://doi.org/10.1016/S0277-9536(96)00253-5.

Campbell, Gwyn. "Female Bondage and Agency in the Indian Ocean World." In Toledano, *African Communities in Asia and the Mediterranean*, 37–61.

Cetinsaya, Gokhan. *The Ottoman Administration of Iraq, 1890–1908*. Abingdon, Oxon: Taylor & Francis, 2006. https://doi.org/10.4324/9780203332467.

Chehabi, H.E. *Onomastic Reforms: Family Names and State Building in Iran*. Boston: Ilex Foundation, 2020.

Clancy-Smith, Julia Ann. *Rebel and Saint: Muslim Notables, Populist Protest, Colonial Encounters (Algeria and Tunisia, 1800–1904)*. Berkeley: University of California Press, 1994. https://doi.org/10.1525/9780520920378.

Conermann, Stephan, Youval Rotman, Ehud R. Toledano, and Rachel Zelnick-Abramovitz, eds. *Comparative and Global Framing of Enslavement*. Berlin: De Gruyter, 2023. https://doi.org/10.1515/9783111296913.

– "Introduction: What Is Global about Global Enslavement?" In Conermann et al., *Comparative and Global Framing of Enslavement*, 1–6.

Costanzo, Angelo. "The Narrative of Archibald Monteith, a Jamaican Slave." *Callaloo* 13, no. 1 (Winter 1990): 115–30. https://doi.org/10.2307/2931614.

Dehkhoda, Aliakbar. *Lughatnama-yi Dehkhoda*. 14 vols. 1373. Reprint, Tehran: Daneshgah-i Tehran, 1995.

Deutschmann, Moritz. *Iran and Russian Imperialism: The Ideal Anarchists, 1800–1914*. London: Routledge, Taylor & Francis Group, 2016. https://doi.org/10.4324/9781315676487.

De Wolf, Jan Jacob. "Circumcision and Initiation in Western Kenya and Eastern Uganda: Historical Reconstructions and Ethnographic Evidence." *Anthropos* 78, nos. 3–4 (1983): 369–410.

Diouf, Sylviane A. *Servants of Allah: African Muslims Enslaved in the Americas*. New York: New York University Press, 1998.

Doughty, Charles M. *Travels in Arabia Deserta*. 2 vols. 1888. Reprint, London: Jonathan Cape and the Medici Society Limited, 1923.

Douglass, Frederick. *Life and Times of Frederick Douglass*. 1881. Reprint, Hartford, CT: Park Publishing Co., 1892.

– *My Bondage and My Freedom*. London: Partridge and Oakey, 1855.

– *Narrative of the Life of Frederick Douglass, an American Slave*. Boston: The Anti-Slavery Office, 1845.

Drescher, Seymour. *Capitalism and Antislavery: British Mobilization in Comparative Perspective*. London: Macmillan Press, 1986. https://doi.org/10.1007/978-1-349-07000-8.

Durugönül, Esma. "Construction of Identity and Integration of African-Turks." In Toledano, *African Communities in Asia and the Mediterranean*, 285–95.

– "The Invisibility of Turks of African Origin and the Construction of Turkish Cultural Identity: The Need for a New Historiography." *Journal of Black Studies* 33, no. 3 (2003): 281–94. https://doi.org/10.1177/0021934702238632.

Ebrahim Khan, Mirza Husayn ibn Muhammad. *Jughrafiya-yi Isfahan*. 1342. Reprint, Tehran: Daneshgah-i Tehran, 1963.

El Hamel, Chouki. *Black Morocco: A History of Slavery, Race, and Islam*. New York: Cambridge University Press, 2013. https://doi.org/10.1017/CBO9781139198783.

Eppel, Michael. "The Elite, the Effendiyya, and the Growth of Nationalism and Pan-Arabism in Hashemite Iraq, 1921–1958." *International Journal of Middle East Studies* 30, no. 2 (May 1998): 227–50. https://doi.org/10.1017/S0020743800065880.

Erdem, Y. Hakan. *Slavery in the Ottoman Empire and Its Demise, 1800–1909*. Houndmills, Hampshire: Macmillan Press, 1996. https://doi.org/10.1057/9780230372979.

E'temad al-Saltana, Muhammad Hasan Khan. *Yaddashtha-yi E'temad al-Saltana Marbut be Sal-i 1300 H. Q.* 1350. Reprint, Tehran: Vahid, 1971.

Ettehadieh, Mansureh. "The Social Condition of Women in Qajar Society." In *Society and Culture in Qajar Iran*, edited by Elton L. Daniel, 69–97. Costa Mesa, CA: Mazda Publishers, 2002.

Farzaneh, Mateo Muhammad. *The Iranian Constitutional Revolution and the Clerical Leadership of Khurasani*. Syracuse, NY: Syracuse University Press, 2015.

Frith, Nicola, and Kate Hodgson, eds. *At the Limits of Memory: Legacies of Slavery in the Francophone World*. Liverpool: Liverpool University Press, 2014. https://doi.org/10.5949/liverpool/9781781381595.001.0001.

— "Slavery and Its Legacies: Remembering Labour Exploitation in the Francophone World." In Frith and Hodgson, *At the Limits of Memory*, 1–22.

Glassman, Jonathon. *Feasts and Riot: Revelry, Rebellion, and Popular Consciousness on the Swahili Coast, 1856–1888*. Portsmouth, NH: Northwestern University Press, 1995.

Gordon, Murray. *Slavery in the Arab World*. New York: New Amsterdam, 1989.

Green, Arnold H. *The Tunisian Ulama 1873–1915: Social Structure and Response to Ideological Currents*. Leiden: Brill, 1978. https://doi.org/10.1163/9789004491816.

Hairi, Abdul-Hadi. *Shī'ism and Constitutionalism in Iran: A Study of the Role Played by the Persian Residents of Iraq in Iranian Politics*. Leiden: Brill, 1977. https://doi.org/10.1163/9789004659797.

— "Why Did the 'Ulamā Participate in the Persian Constitutional Revolution of 1905–1909?" *Die Welt Des Islams* 17, nos. 1–4 (1976): 127–54. https://doi.org/10.1163/157006076X00080.

Hamidullah, Muhammad. *Introduction to Islam*. Paris: Centre Culturel Islamique, 1957.

Hamli, Mohsen. "The 1890 Legal Wrangles over Sudanese Slaves in Tunisia." *The Journal of North African Studies* 16, no. 3 (2011): 421–9. https://doi.org/10.1080/13629387.2010.504536.

Harms, Robert, Bernard K. Freamon, and David W. Blight, eds. *Indian Ocean Slavery in the Age of Abolition*. New Haven, CT: Yale University Press, 2013. https://doi.org/10.12987/yale/9780300163872.001.0001.

Hasan, Yusuf Fadl. "Some Aspects of the Arab Slave Trade from the Sudan 7th–19th Century." *Sudan Notes and Records* 58 (1977): 85–106.

Hassim, Eeqbal. *Elementary Education and Motivation in Islam: Perspectives of Medieval Muslim Scholars, 750–1400 CE*. Amherst, NY: Cambria Press, 2010.

Heern, Zackery M. "One Thousand Years of Islamic Education in Najaf: Myth and History of the Shi'i Ḥawza." *Iranian Studies* 50, no. 3 (May 2017): 415–38. https://doi.org/10.1080/00210862.2017.1285486.

Hooper, Jane, and David Eltis. "The Indian Ocean in Transatlantic Slavery." *Slavery and Abolition* 34, no. 3 (2013): 353–75. https://doi.org/10.1080/0144039X.2012.734112.

Hopper, Matthew S. *Slaves of One Master: Globalization and Slavery in Arabia in the Age of Empire*. New Haven, CT: Yale University Press, 2015. https://doi.org/10.12987/yale/9780300192018.001.0001.

Huber, Valeska. *Channelling Mobilities: Migration and Globalisation in the Suez Canal Region and Beyond, 1869–1914*. Cambridge: Cambridge University Press, 2013. https://doi.org/10.1017/CBO9781139344159.

Husayni, Mustafa. *Bardegi az didgah-i Islam*. 1372. Reprint, Tehran: Bunyad-i Da'rat al-Ma'aref-i Islami, 1993.

Ibn Abi Diyaf, Ahmad. *Ithaf Ahl al-Zaman bi-Akhbar Muluk Tunis wa-'Ahd al-Aman*. 8 vols. Tunis: Secrétariat d'Etat à l'Information et à la Culture, 1963–6.

Issawi, Charles. *The Economic History of Iran, 1800–1914*. Chicago: University of Chicago Press, 1971.

Kasravi Tabrizi, Ahmad. *Tarikh-i mashruta-yi Iran*. 1370. Reprint, Tehran: Amir Kabir, 1991.

Katouzian, Homa. "Liberty and Licence in the Constitutional Revolution of Iran." *Journal of the Royal Asiatic Society* 8, no. 2 (July 1998): 159–80. https://doi.org/10.1017/S1356186300009962.

Keddie, Nikki R. "Iranian Politics 1900–1905: Background to Revolution-II." *Middle Eastern Studies* 5, no. 2 (1969): 151–67. https://doi.org/10.1080/00263206908700125.

–, ed. *Religion and Politics in Iran: Shi'ism from Quietism to Revolution*. New Haven, CT: Yale University Press, 1983.

Keefer, Katrina H.B. "Scarification and Identity in the Liberated Africans Department Register, 1814–1815." *Canadian Journal of African Studies / Revue canadienne des études africaines* 47, no. 3 (2013): 537–53. https://doi.org/10.1080/00083968.2013.832337.

Keita, Maghan, ed. *Conceptualizing/Re-conceptualizing Africa: The Construction of African Historical Identity*. Leiden: Brill, 2002. https://doi.org/10.1163/9789004474758.

Kermani, Nazem al-Islam. *Tarikh-i Bidari-yi Iranian*. 3 vols. 1371. Reprint, Tehran: Amir Kabir, 1992.

Kouba, Leonard J., and Judith Muasher. "Female Circumcision in Africa: An Overview." *African Studies Review* 28, no. 1 (March 1985): 95–110. https://doi.org/10.2307/524569.

Kramer, Martin S. *Shi'ism, Resistance, and Revolution*. Boulder, CO: Westview Press, 1987.

Kresse, Kai. "The Uses of History: Rhetorics of Muslim Unity and Difference on the Kenyan Swahili Coast." In *Struggling with History*, edited by Edward Simpson and Kai Kresse, 223–60. Oxford: Oxford University Press, 2008.

Landor, Henry Savage. *Across Coveted Lands*. 2 vols. New York: Charles Scribner's Sons, 1903.

La Rue, G. Michael. "Khabir 'Ali at Home in Kubayh: A Brief Biography of a Dar Fur Caravan Leader." *African Economic History* 13 (1984): 56–83.

Law, Robin, and Paul E. Lovejoy, eds. *The Biography of Mahommah Gardo Baquaqua: His Passage from Slavery to Freedom in Africa and America*. Princeton, NJ: Markus Wiener Publishers, 2001.

Lee, Anthony A. "Half the Household Was African: Recovering the Histories of Two African Slaves in Iran." *UCLA Historical Journal* 26, no. 1 (2015): 17–38.

Lindsay, Lisa A., and John Wood Sweet. *Biography and the Black Atlantic*. Philadelphia: University of Pennsylvania Press, 2014. https://doi.org/10.9783/9780812208702.

Lorimer, J.G. *Gazetteer of the Persian Gulf and Central Arabia*. 6 vols. Calcutta: Superintendent Government, 1915.

Lovejoy, Paul E., and Nielson R. Bezerra. *Mahommah Gardo Baquaqua: An Enslaved Muslim of the Black Atlantic*. Chapel Hill: University of North Carolina Press, 2025.

Majd, Mohammad Gholi. *The Great Famine & Genocide in Iran, 1917–1919*. 2nd ed. Lanham, MA: University Press of America, Inc., 2013.

Malcolm, John. *Sketches of Persia*. 2 vols. London: John Murray, Albemarle Street, 1827.

Malekzada, Mehdi. *Tarikh-i Enqelab-i Mashrutiyat-i Iran*. 7 vols. 1333. Reprint, Tehran: Ibn Sina, 1956.

Manning, Patrick. *Slavery and African Life: Occidental, Oriental, and African Slave Trades*. Cambridge: Cambridge University Press, 1995.

Marck, Jeff. "Aspects of Male Circumcision in Subequatorial African Culture History." *Health Transition Review* 7 (1997): 337–60.

Mbaegbu, Celestine Chukwuemeka. "The Effective Power of Music in Africa." *Open Journal of Philosophy* 5, no. 3 (March 2015): 176–83. https://doi.org/10.4236/ojpp.2015.53021.

Mbiti, John S. *Introduction to African Religion*. 2nd revised ed. Oxford: Heinemann Educational, 1992.

McDow, Thomas F. "Deeds of Freed Slaves: Manumission and Economic and Social Mobility in Pre-abolition Zanzibar." In *Indian Ocean Slavery in the Age of Abolition*, edited by Robert W. Harms, Bernard K. Freamon, and David W. Blight, 160–79. New Haven, CT: Yale University Press, 2013. https://doi.org/10.12987/yale/9780300163872.003.0009.

McMahon, Elisabeth. *Slavery and Emancipation in Islamic East Africa: From Honor to Respectability*. New York: Cambridge University Press, 2013. https://doi.org/10.1017/CBO9781139198837.

McNeill, H. William. *Europe's Steppe Frontier, 1500–1800*. Chicago: University of Chicago Press, 1964.

Medici, Ann Maria. "Chiudere la porta della schiavitù: Tunisi 1816–1846." In *La Dependenza: Antropologia delle relazioni di dominio*, vol. 1, edited by P.G. Solinas, 159–203. Leece: Argo Editrice, 2005.

Metinsoy, Murat. "Neither Fez nor Hat: Contesting Hat Reform." In *The Power of the People: Everyday Resistance and Dissent in the Making of Modern Turkey, 1923–38*, 234–43. Cambridge: Cambridge University Press, 2021. https://doi.org/10.1017/9781009025775.015.

Miers, Suzanne. "Slave Rebellion and Resistance in the Aden Protectorate in the Mid-Twentieth Century." *Slavery & Abolition* 25, no. 2 (2004): 80–9.

Mirpanjeh, General Esma'il Khan. *Khaterat-i esarat ruznama-yi safar-i Khawrazm va Khiva*. Edited by Safa' al-Din Tabra'iyan. 1370. Reprint, Tehran: Mu'sesa-yi Pazhuhesh va Mutale'at-i Farhangi, 1991.

Mirzai, Behnaz A., dir. *The African-Baluchi Trance Dance*. Ottawa: Social Sciences and Humanities Research Council of Canada, 2012. https://search.worldcat.org/title/african-baluchi-trance-dance-a-documentary-film/oclc/813972994.

–, dir. *Afro-Iranian Lives*. Ottawa: Social Sciences and Humanities Research Council of Canada, 2007. https://doi.org/10.1080/00210862.2017.1269454.

– *A History of Slavery and Emancipation in Iran, 1800–1929*. Austin: University of Texas Press, 2017.

Mirza Sami'a, Muhammad Sami'. *Tazkarat al-Muluk*. Annotated by Dabir Siaqi. 1368. Reprint, Tehran: Sepehr, 1989.

Mitchell, Timothy. *Rule of Experts: Egypt, Techno-Politics, Modernity*. Berkeley: University of California Press, 2002. https://doi.org/10.1525/9780520928251.

Montana, Ismael M. *The Abolition of Slavery in Ottoman Tunisia*. Gainesville: University Press of Florida, 2013. https://doi.org/10.2307/j.ctvx0729p.

Moore-Harell, Alice. "Slave Trade in the Sudan in the Nineteenth Century and Its Suppression in the Years 1877–80." *Middle Eastern Studies* 34, no. 2 (1998): 113–28. https://doi.org/10.1080/00263209808701225.

Mrad Dali, Inès. "From Forgetting to Remembrance: Slavery and Forced Labour in Tunisia." In Frith and Hodgson, *At the Limits of Memory*, 191–208.

– "From Slavery to Servitude: 'Blacks' in Tunisia." *Cahiers d'études africaines* 45, nos. 3–4 (2005): 935–55. https://doi.org/10.4000/etudesafricaines.5704.

Mu'ayyir al-Mamalik, Dust 'Ali Khan. *Yaddashthaei az zendegani-yi khususi-yi Naser al-Din Shah*. 1362. Reprint, Tehran: Nashr-i Tarikh-i Iran, 1983.

Murad Khani, Amir Husayn. *Sara-yi Agha Bahram*. 1399. Reprint, Tehran: Daneshnama-yi Tehran-i Bozorg, 2020.

Mustaufi, 'Abdullah. *Sharh-i zendegani-yi man: Tarikh-i ejtema'i va edari-yi daura-yi Qajar*. 3 vols. 1377. Reprint, Tehran: Zavvar, 1998.

Najmabadi, Afsaneh. *The Story of the Daughters of Quchan*. Syracuse, NY: Syracuse University Press, 1998.

Nakash, Yitzhak. *The Shi'is of Iraq*. Princeton, NJ: Princeton University Press, 1994. https://doi.org/10.1515/9780691190440.

Nashat, Guity. *The Origins of Modern Reform in Iran, 1870–80*. Urbana: University of Illinois Press, 1982.

Noori, Masoud, and Zahra Azhar. "Shī'ī Ideas of Slavery: A Study of Iran in the Qājar Era before and after the Constitutional Revolution." *Journal of Islamic Law* 3, no. 1 (June 2022). https://ssrn.com/abstract=4206107.

Ochsenwald, William. "Muslim-European Conflict in the Hijaz: The Slave Trade Controversy, 1840–1895." *Middle Eastern Studies* 16, no. 1 (1980): 115–26. https://doi.org/10.1080/00263208008700428.

– "Ottoman Arabia and the Holy Hijaz, 1516–1918." *Journal of Global Initiatives: Policy, Pedagogy, Perspective* 10, no. 1 (2016): 23–34.

Olney, James. "'I Was Born': Slave Narratives, Their Status as Autobiography and as Literature." *Callaloo*, no. 20 (Winter 1984): 46–73. https://doi.org/10.2307/2930678.

Omar ibn Said. *A Muslim American Slave: The Life of Omar Ibn Said*. Translated and edited by Ala Alryyes. Madison: University of Wisconsin Press, 2011.

Oualdi, M'hamed. *Un esclave entre deux empires, Une histoire transimpériale du Maghreb*. Paris: Seuil, 2023.

Peirce, Leslie P. *A Spectrum of Unfreedom: Captives and Slaves in the Ottoman Empire*. Budapest: Central European University Press, 2021. https://doi.org/10.7829/j.ctv1c3pdg0.

Peters, Francis E. *The Hajj: The Muslim Pilgrimage to Mecca and the Holy Places*. Princeton, NJ: Princeton University Press, 1994. https://doi.org/10.1515/9780691225142.

Pétriat, Philippe. "Caravan Trade in the Late Ottoman Empire: The 'Aqīl Network and the Institutionalization of Overland Trade." *Journal of the Economic and Social History of the Orient* 63, nos. 1–2 (December 2019): 38–72. https://doi.org/10.1163/15685209-12341504.

"Pictures, Jewish Representatives in Parliament: Sayyid 'Abdullah Behbehani." [In Persian.] 7Dorim. https://www.7dorim.com/tasavir/namayandeh_bebahani/.

Polak, Jakob Eduard. *Persien, das Land und seine Bewohner*. 2 vols. Leipzig: Brockhaus, 1865.

Poussier, Anaël. "Les représentations identitaires de l'État mahdiste: L'autorité provinciale Au Soudan-Est et Les tribus bija (1883–1898)." *Cahiers d'Études africaines* 60, no. 240 (4) (2020): 851–72. https://doi.org/10.4000/etudesafricaines.32302.

Prestholdt, Jeremy. "Portuguese Conceptual Categories and the 'Other' Encounter on the Swahili Coast." In *Conceptualizing/Re-conceptualizing Africa: The Construction of African Historical Identity*, edited by Maghan Keita, 53–76. Leiden: Brill, 2002. https://doi.org/10.1163/9789004474758_005.

Qur'an. Tehran: Salihi, 1354.

Raghavan, Susheela. *Handbook of Spices, Seasonings and Flavourings*. 2nd ed. Boca Raton, FL: CRC Press, Taylor & Francis, 2006. https://doi.org/10.1201/b13597.

Reilly, Benjamin. *Slavery, Agriculture, and Malaria in the Arabian Peninsula*. Athens: Ohio University Press, 2015. https://doi.org/10.2307/j.ctt1rfsnxf.

Robinson, Ronald, and John Gallagher. *Africa and the Victorians: The Official Mind of Imperialism*. London: Macmillan, 1963.

Roe, Alan. "The Old *Darb al Arbein* Caravan Route and Kharga Oasis in Antiquity." *Journal of the American Research Center in Egypt* 42 (2005–6): 119–29.

Roger, Fouquer. *Le Docteur Adrien Atiman: Medecin-Catechiste au Tanganyika, sur les traces de Vincent de Paul*. Paris: Conde-sur-Escaut, 1964.

Sadid al-Saltana Kababi, Muhammad Ali. *Bandar Abbas va Khalij-i Fars*. 1368. Reprint, Tehran: Donya-yi Kitab, 1989.

Sa'dvandian, Sirus, and Mansureh Ettehadieh, eds. *Amar-i dar al-khalafa-yi Tehran*. Tehran: Nashr-i Tarikh-i Iran, 1368.

Schacht, Joseph. *An Introduction to Islamic Law*. Oxford: Clarendon Press, 1964.

Searcy, Kim. "The Sudanese Mahdi's Attitudes on Slavery and Emancipation." *Islamic Africa* 1, no. 1 (Spring 2010): 63–83.

Segal, Ronald. *Islam's Black Slaves: The Other Black Diaspora*. New York: Farrar, Straus and Giroux, 2001.

Shaw, W.B.K. "Darb al Arba'in, the Forty Days' Road." *Sudan Notes and Record: University of Khartoum* 12, no. 1 (1929): 63–71.

Shell-Duncan, Bettina, and Ylva Hernlund. *Female "Circumcision" in Africa: Culture, Controversy, and Change*. Boulder, CO: Lynne Rienner Publishers, 2000.

Sheriff, Abdul. *Slaves, Spices and Ivory in Zanzibar: Integration of an East African Commercial Empire into the World Economy, 1770–1873*. Athens: Ohio University Press, 1987. https://doi.org/10.1515/9781782049784.

Sikainga, Ahmad Alawad. *Slaves into Workers: Emancipation and Labor in Colonial Sudan*. Austin: University of Texas Press, 1996.

Silverman, Eric K. "Anthropology and Circumcision." *Annual Review of Anthropology* 33 (2004): 419–45. https://doi.org/10.1146/annurev.anthro.33.070203.143706.

Simpson, Edward, and Kai Kresse, eds. *Struggling with History: Islam and Cosmopolitanism in the Western Indian Ocean*. New York: Columbia University Press, 2008.

Sindawi, Khalid. "Ḥawza Instruction and Its Role in Shaping Modern Shīʿite Identity: The Ḥawzas of al-Najaf and Qumm as a Case Study." *Middle Eastern Studies* 43, no. 6 (2007): 831–56. https://doi.org/10.1080/00263200701568220.

Sohrabi, Nader. *Revolution and Constitutionalism in the Ottoman Empire and Iran*. New York: Cambridge University Press, 2014. https://doi.org/10.1017/CBO9780511977190.

Solieman, Nashwa M.S., Marwa Farouk Hafez, and Ahmed Mohamed Khattab. "Reconstructing the Ancient Caravan Route of Darb Al-Arbain in Greco-Roman Egypt: Heritage Value and Tourism Potential." *Journal of Association of Arab Universities for Tourism and Hospitality (JAAUTH)* 16, no. 2 (June 2019): 202–24. https://doi.org/10.21608/jaauth.2019.196205.

Solinas, Pier Giorgio, ed. *La Dependenza, Antropologia delle relazioni di dominio*. Lecce: Argo Edizioni, 2005.

Sulivan, G.L. *Dhow Chasing in Zanzibar Waters*. 1873. Reprint, London: Dawsons of Pall Mall, 1967.

Tabari, Azar. "The Role of the Clergy in Modern Iranian Politics." In *Religion and Politics in Iran: Shi'ism from Quietism to Revolution*, edited by Nikki R. Keddie, 47–72. New Haven, CT: Yale University Press, 1983.

Taifa, Sima. *Agha Bahram*. 1399. Reprint, Tehran: Daneshnama-yi Tehran-i Bozorg, 2020.

Taj al-Saltana. *Khaterat-i Taj al-Saltana*. Edited by Mansureh Ettehadia and Sirus Saʿdvandian. 1361. Reprint, Tehran: Nashr-i Tarikh-i Iran, 1982.

Toledano, Ehud R. ed. *African Communities in Asia and the Mediterranean: Identities between Integration and Conflict*. Trenton: Africa World Press, 2012.

– *As If Silent and Absent: Bonds of Enslavement in the Islamic Middle East*. New Haven, CT: Yale University Press, 2007.

– "Enslavement and Freedom in Transition." *Journal of Global Slavery* 2, nos. 1–2 (2017): 100–21. https://doi.org/10.1163/2405836X-00201002.

– "Expectations and Realities in the Study of Enslavement in Muslim-Majority Societies." [Review of *Slavery, Agriculture, and Malaria in the Arabian Peninsula*, by Benjamin Reilly.] *The Journal of Interdisciplinary History* 48, no. 3 (2018): 385–92. https://www.jstor.org/stable/48556364.

– *Slavery and Abolition in the Ottoman Middle East*. Seattle: Washington University Press, 1998.

Troutt Powell, Eve M. *Tell This in My Memory: Stories of Enslavement from Egypt, Sudan, and the Ottoman Empire.* Stanford: Stanford University Press, 2012. https://doi.org/10.1515/9780804783750.
– "Will That Subaltern Ever Speak? Finding African Slaves in the Historiography of the Middle East." In *Middle East Historiographies: Narrating the Twentieth Century,* edited by Israel Gershoni, Amy Singer, and Y. Hakan Erdem, 242–61. Seattle: University of Washington Press, 2011.
Van Rossum, Matthias, Alexander Geelen, Bram van den Hout, and Merve Tosun. *Testimonies of Enslavement: Sources on Slavery from the Indian Ocean World.* London: Bloomsbury Academic, 2020. https://doi.org/10.5040/9781350140318.
Walz, Terence. *Trade between Egypt and Bilād as-Sudān 1700–1820.* Cairo: Institut français d'archéologie orientale du Caire, 1978.
Warner-Lewis, Maureen. *Archibald Monteath: Igbo, Jamaican, Moravian.* Kingston: University of the West Indies Press, 2007.
Wills, C.J. *In the Land of the Lion and Sun, or Modern Persia.* London: Ward, Lock, 1891.
– *Persia as It Is.* London: Sampson Low, Marston, Searle & Rivington, 1886.
Wilson, Arnold T. *The Persian Gulf.* 1928. Reprint, London: George Allen & Unwin, 1959.
Winnebeck, Julia, Ove Sutter, Adrian Hermann, Christoph Antweiler, and Stephan Conermann. "The Analytical Concept of Asymmetrical Dependency." *Journal of Global Slavery* 8, no. 1 (February 2023): 1–59. https://doi.org/10.1163/2405836X-00801002.
Witzenrath, Christoph. "Negotiating Early Modern Transottoman Slaving Zones: An Arab in Moscow." In Conermann et al., *Comparative and Global Framing of Enslavement,* 167–84.
Zdanowski, Jerzy. *Slavery and Manumission: British Policy in the Red Sea and the Persian Gulf in the First Half of the 20th Century.* Reading: Ithaca Press, 2013.

Index

Notes: The letter *f* following a page number denotes a figure and the letter *m* a map. In subheads, "MQ" refers to Mahboob Qirvanian.

ʻAbdul Hamid II (sultan), lix
ʻAbdul Karim (Shaykh), 62
ʻAbdul Mottaleb, grave of, 51, 51n11
ʻAbdul Rasul, 71, 82
Abyssinian "Galla" slaves, xxxiii
Aden protectorate, xx
African Americans, enslaved: identity transformations, xxvii; slave narratives, xxvi, xxvin54
African slave trade in Iran: education of slaves, xix; employment of, xviii–xix; freed slaves, xx–xxi, xxv, xxxiv–xxxv; gender roles, xix; income of slaves, xix; justification for, xviii, xviiin8; marriages of slaves, xxiii; new identities, xix–xx; population of slaves, xxiii; post-emancipation era, xxv; punishments, xx; racial and ethnic groups, xxxvi–xxxvii; slave sales, xviii; slave-master relationship, xix–xxi, xxv, xxxv. *See also* slave-master relationship; slave trade
African soldiers, xlvi, 33

Africans, categorization of, xxxii–xxxiv, xxxvi–xxxvii
agricultural slavery, xix, xxiii
Ahmad (son of MQ), xxx, lxxv, lxxix, lxxx*f*, lxxxi*f*
Ahmad Shah Qajar (king of Iran), lix, lxx
Ahmed Bay (Tunisia), xxxviii
ʻAlawi as MQ's term, 51n9
ʻAli (Hajj), 82
ʻAli (Shaykh mujtahid), 65, 98
ʻAli, shrine of, liv
Alliance school (Tehran), lxii, 64n13
Amanullah Khan (prince), sister of, 100
Amir Atabak school, lxxvi
Amir Hajj, 52–3, 54
Amir Jabal, 55
al-ʻAmuli, Baha al-Din (Shaykh), 103
Aqdas (daughter of MQ), lxxv*f*
Arabia. *See* Ottoman Arabia; Saudi Arabia
Arabs in North Africa, xxxii
Arafat, Mt. (Arabia), xlix, xlixn126
al-ʻAraqain, ʻAbdul Husayn Sayyid, lxxiv, 103

118 Index

Arfa, Hassan (General), xxviii
Asghar, 'Ali, lxxix
Askar (boss of wagon shop), 69
asymmetric dependency, xxxv–xxxvi
Atiman, Adrian, xxvii
'Atiqechi, Muhammad, lxxix
Atlantic world slavery: conditions of enslaved people, xxxv; differences from Islamic world, xx, xxiii
autobiographies: African American slave narratives, xxvi, xxvin54; as literary genre in Iran, xxviii; slave narratives as historical documents, xxv–xxvi

Bagh-i Takht-i Muhammad Khajou (Shiraz), 101–2
Bahrain, xxxiv
Bahr al-'Ulum, Husayn (Ayatullah) (Hajj Aqamir Bahr al-Ulum Rashti), lv, 58
Bakhtiyari, 'Ali Qoli Khan, lxix–lxx
Bakhtiyaris, lxix–lxx, 83
Baqir, Muhammad, 99
Baquaqua, Mahommah Gardo, xxvii
Baskerville, Howard, lix
Bastam, Hasan, 63
Bazaz the merchant, lxv, 82
Behbehani, 'Abdullah (Ayatullah), lvii–lix, lviiin151, lviiif, lix, lxxiiin169, 59–60
Behbehani, Javad (Shaykh), 99; grandchildren of accompanied by MQ, lxxiii, 98
Behbehani, Muhammad (Ayatullah), lxxiii, lxxiiin169, 93
beliefs. *See* customs and beliefs
Berbers, xxxii
Bilad al-Sudan, xxxviii
bodyguards, xix, xxxiii–xxxiv
Boraida, xxxiv
Borazjani, Karbala'i 'Ali, 99

Bozorg, Hajj Aqa, daughter of, lxv, 82
Brazil, labour demand, xvii–xviii, xviiin2
bread shortage, 83, 84
Britain/British: capture MQ for questioning, lxxiii; deferment to 'ulama', xxiv; liberation of slaves, xx–xxi; occupation of Sudan, xlvi, 33; outlawing of slave trade, xxi–xxii, xl, xlv, xlvii, ln130, 32–3, 37–9; passport, lxi, 62; patrols evaded by traders, 32–3, 37–9; support for Qajar dynasty, lix
Brussels Conference Act (1890), lxi

cafre (unbeliever), xxxii–xxxiii
Campbell, Gwyn, xxxv
caravanserais, lxii, 64
Chanpina (mother of MQ), 4–8
Christian nations, sale of slaves, xxi
circumcision: as Islamic tradition, xlixn129; of MQ, xlix, 48; in Saljmattyah, xlii–xliii, xliiinn101–2, 17
clientage relationship (*wala'*), xx, xxxv
clitoridectomy, xlii–xliii, xliiin101
clothing: on forced migration, xlii, 12, 28–9; MQ's choice of, lxxviii; in Ottoman Arabia, l, ln131, 48; in Saljmattyah, xlii, 17; in Tehran (European style), 80, 80n41
customs and beliefs: blessings from water in mouth, 78; celebrations of war victory, 19; chant with *khayzaran*, liii, liiin139, 54n17, 55; devotional practices, xlix; *dorr* stone, 78, 78n40; Eid al-Fitr celebration, 43; firing guns in celebration, lxii, 65, 65n15; about Jabal al-Noor, 44; *mahmal* procession, liiin138; military processions, lxxvi; palm reading,

24; processions, liii, 52–3, 54; sacrifice of castrated rooster, 57; scarification, xxxi*f*, xxxii, lxiv, lxxvii, 12, 78; singing at treasury house, 33–4

Damghani, Farajullah Khan, xxi
Dashtestani, Muhammad (Shaykh), lxxiv, 99
Dashti, ʿAbdul ʿAli (Shaykh), lxiv, 71, 75, 81–2
al-Daula, Abulfath Mirza Salar, lxviii
al-Daula, ʿAli Arshad, lxvii–lxviii
al-Daula, Anis, lxivn160
al-Daula, Arshad, 82
al-Daula, Mushir, bridge of, 100
al-Daula, Muvasiq, 84
al-Daula, Qavam, 103
al-Daula, Salar, 82
al-Daula, Sulat, lxxiv, 101, 102
Divshali Langarudi (Gilani), Shaʿban (Shaykh Ayatullah), ln134
Dom people, xxxvii–xxxviii
domestic service, slaves employed in, xix
domestic violence, 47
Douglass, Frederick, xxvi

education:
- Alliance school in Tehran, 64n13
- literacy rates among slaves, xxvi
- of Mahboob: Qurʾan school (*maktab*), xlix, lii, lv, 47–8, 52, 57–8; Shiʿi seminary, lxxvi, 58
- for MQ's daughters, lxxvi
- schools in Ottoman Empire, lv
- of slaves in Iran, xix
Egypt: African soldiers, xxxiii; carriage of ʿAʾisha procession, liii, 54; *mahmal* procession, liiin138; wedding of Princess Fawzia, lxxv–lxxvi

Eid Ghadir Khom, 84–5
Ethiopians, xxxiii, xxxiv
eunuchs, xix, liv, lxivn160, lxv*f*, 55
Europeans, racial classifications by, xxxii–xxxiii, xxxvi

family names in Iran, lxxviii
Farsiya (Iran), 70
Fatema Zahra, shrine of, 53
Fawzia, Princess (Egypt), lxxv–lxxvi
female genital mutilation, xlii–xliii, xliiin101
food(s):
- in Africa: sesame (*sekda*), xxxiin65; sesame seeds, 6
- in Ottoman Arabia: milk and bread with jam, 43; rice and lentils, xlviii, 40
- on forced migration: bread, 39; bread and milk, xliv, 25; bread and water, 22, 23, 26; camel liver, 26; dates, rice, and milk, 37; desert herbs, xlvii, 36–7; jungle fruits and plants, 14; rice and water, xlvii, 38; roasted coffee beans, 38; sesame seeds (*sekda*), 10; sugar cane, 27, 33; tea as rarity, 30; water and flour, 9–10
France/French: labour demand, xvii–xviii, xviiin2; slave trafficking, xxii, xxxviii
freed slaves, xx–xxi, xxv, xxxiv–xxxv

gender relations: assault of *kaniz* prevented, 41; domestic violence, 47; separate spaces for men and women, xxxii, lxiii, 23, 68, 81; travelling harem, 27; women travelling, 77. *See also* gender roles; slave-master relationship

gender roles: education for MQ's daughters, lxxvi; integration of freed slaves into society, xxi; slave employment, xix, xliv. *See also* gender relations

Gharavi Rashti (Gilani, Amlashi), 'Allama Mirza Habibullah, ln134, lxi, lxvn161

Gharavi Rashti (Gilani, Amlashi), Ishaq (Shaykh Ayatullah): family of, ln134; and Iranian Constitutional Revolution, l–li, lvii; move to Iran, lxxiiin169; MQ and family stay with, lxxiii, 97; photo, lxviii*f*; purchases MQ, l, 49–51; return to Iran (1911), lxi; return to Iran (1921), lxxiii–lxxiv, 98–101; sees MQ off at Ba'quba, 63; visitors to, 57

Gharavi Rashti (Gilani, Amlashi), Isma'il (Shaykh Ayatullah): death of, lxx, 84; death of father-in-law, lxix; family of, lxvn161; MQ lives in house of, lxv; MQ travels with, lix, 59; MQ travels with family of, 85–6; MQ travels with in Kermanshah, 68; MQ's relationship with, lxvii; photo, li*f*; in Tehran, lxivn160, 81–2; travels of, 59–60

Ghulam, 'Anbar, 54

Hadandawa people, 35–7, 35n8
hajj (pilgrimage). *See* pilgrimage (hajj)
Hajj Akbar, 52
Hajj 'Ali, lxv, 82
Hajj Mahdi, the brother of Hajj Reza, 99
Hamadani, 'Ali (Shaykh), lxiii, 70–1, 72–3
Hamadani, Mirza Ibrahim (Shaykh), lv, 58
harems, slaves employed in, xix

Hasani, 'Abdul 'Azim, grave of, 95
al-Hawza al-'Almiya seminary (Najaf), lxxvi
Hijaz (Arabia), xxiii
Hindi, Mirza Muhammad, 62
Husayn Abad (Iran), 71–3

Ibn Sa'ud, liiin138
Ibrahim Beyk Effendi, 44
Ikhwan (Brethren), liiin138
'Imad al-Din (Shaykh), lxv, 82
income of slaves in palace, xix
India, xxii
Indian Ocean slave narrations, xxvi
Indians, sale of, xxi
infectious diseases, xxxiii, lxx
Iran: abolition of slavery, xxiv–xxv; borders, lxii; economic system, xxv; family names mandated, lxxviii; MQ's trails in, 94*m*; parliamentary government established, xxiv; political changes, lxvii–lxxi; racial and ethnic groups, xxxvi–xxxvii; World War I, lxxviii. *See also* African slave trade in Iran; Iranian Constitutional Revolution
Iranian Constitutional Revolution, l–li, ln132, lv–lx, lxi–lxii, 59–60. *See also* Iran
Iranians enslaved, xxiv
Iraq: Constitutional Revolution, 59–60; MQ's trails in, 94*m*. *See also* Qirvanian, Mahboob, life trajectory, Iran to Iraq; Qirvanian, Mahboob, life trajectory, Ottoman Arabia and Iraq
Isfahan (Iran), xxiii, 103
Islamic law (shari'a), on slavery, xix–xxii, xxxiv–xxxv, xxxivnn76–7, lvi. *See also* 'ulama

Jamal (Shaykh of Mecca), xxii–xxiii
Jedda (Arabia), 40–2
Joma Mosque (Shiraz), 101

Kalhor, Davood Khan, lxii, 65–6, 65n16
Kangavar (Iran), 69–70
Karbala' (Iraq), lxi, 61, 97
Karbala'i, 'Abbas Lari (Shaykh), son of, lxiii
Karbala'i, 'Abbas Lari (Shaykh), son-in-law of, 68
Karim, Robat, 84
Karrshid, son of ruler of Saljmattyah, 19
Kashan (Iran), lxxiv
Kazemiyah (Iraq), lxi
Kermani, 'Abdul Karim, 60
Kermani, Ojan Qasim, liii, liv, 55
Kermanshah (Iran), lxiii, 67–8
Khadija bint Khovaylid, grave of, 51, 51n11, 53, 53n14
Khan, Reza, 99
Khanaqin (Iraq), 64
Khartoum (Sudan), xlvi, 33
Khartoumi, 'Abdulrahman, xxi
Khatami, Muhammad Amir, lxxix, lxxx*f*
Khauja, 'Ali Ruzekhan (Mulla), 99
khayzaran, liii, liiin139, 54n17, 55
Khurasan (Iran), 84
Khurasani (Heravi, Kafaee), Mirza Ahmad (Ayatullah): arrival in Tehran, lxiv; asks MQ to depart Tehran, 85; called Ayatullahzadeh by MQ, lxin157; MQ in care of, lxi; respect shown to, lxi–lxiii, 64, 66–8, 74; travels with MQ, 62–8; visits by, 81–2; visits to, 71–2, 75–6
Khurasani (Heravi, Kafaee), Mirza Muhammad, lxxi, 87
Khurasani (Heravi, Kafaee), Muhammad Kazem (Ayatullah Mulla): burial place, lxin158; Constitutional Revolution, lvii; death of, lxix, 83; enemies, lxiii, 77; family, lxi, lxv, lxvn161, 63; photo, lx*f*; student of, lxxiiin169; unity of Ottomans and Persians, lix
Khurasani (Heravi, Kafaee), Zahra, lxv, lxxi
kinship ties. *See* networks
Kurdish people, 65–6, 70
Kurdish province of Iran, lxii–lxiii, 64–8

Lari, Husayn, 68
literacy rates among slaves, xxvi

Mabot Mahdi (sultan), xlvi, 33, 33n7
Madagascar, labour demand, xvii–xviii
Mahallati, Murtaza (Shaykh), 101
mahmal procession, liiin138
maktab (Qur'an school). *See* education, of Mahboob
malaria, xxxiii
Malkum Khan, Mirza, lvii
Mansour (son of MQ), lxxiv, lxxviii–lxxix
maritime activities, slaves employed in, xix
Mascarenes, labour demand, xviiin2
Mashhad (Iran), lxx
Mashq Square (Tehran), lxiv
Ma'someh (wife of MQ). *See* Yosufgar, Ma'someh (wife of MQ)
Ma'someh, Qom (Iran), 75–6, 96, 104
Mas'oud (son of MQ), lxxv, lxxvi
Massicault, Justin, xxxviii
Mazandarani, 'Abdullah (Ayatullah Shaykh): family in Najaf, liii, 55; and Iranian Constitutional Revolution, l–li, ln132, lvii; photo, lx*f*; purchases MQ, l, 49–51; unity of Ottomans and Persians, lix

Index

Mecca (Arabia): bodyguards of rulers, xxxiv; at inauguration of hajj, xlix, 47; *mahmal* procession, liiin138; slave trade, xxii–xxiii, ln130

Medina (Arabia): bodyguards of rulers, xxxiv; description, 53–4; processions, liii, 52–3, 54

military: African soldiers, xxxiii; slaves employed in, xviii

Mina (Arabia), xlix, xlixn125

Mir Fendereski, grave of, 103, 103n13

Mir Sayyid ʿAlaʾ al-Din, grave of, 101, 101n9

Mir Sayyid Muhammad, grave of, 101, 101n8

Mirdamad, grave of, 103

Mirpanjeh, Esmaʿil Khan (General), xxviii

Mirza Ibrahim, lxiv, 81–2

Mirza Mohsen (mujtahid), lxx, 84

Mirza-yi Shirazi. *See* Taqi Shirazi, Mirza Muhammad (Ayatullah)

Miyan Kotal (Iran), 100

Monar Jonban (Isfahan, Iran), 103

Monteath, Archibald, xxvii

Moore, Arthur, lix

Moore, Samuel, xxvii

Mozaffar al-Din Shah Qajar (king of Iran), lvii, 65n16

Mr. Muhammad, 82

Muhammad, Prophet, 44, 53

Muhammad ibn ʿAbdullahi (Imam Mahdi), xlvi, 33n7

Muhammad Ali (Egyptian ruler), xxxiii

Muhammad ʿAli Shah Qajar (king of Iran), ln132, lix, lxvii–lxviii, lxviii–lxix, 83

Muhammad Reza Shah Pahlavi (king of Iran), lxxv–lxxvi, lxxix

Muhammad Shah Qajar (king of Iran), xviiin8

mujtahids, xxiv, xxivn43, ln133, lvii. *See also* ʿulamaʾ

al-Mulk, Asif, lxxiv, 100

Mushir al-Daula bridge, 100

music: celebrations of war victory, 19; chant with *khayzaran*, liii, liiin139, 54n17, 55; daily drums and chanting, 33–4; at inauguration of hajj, xlix, 47; *ney* played in coffee house, 76; traditional African, xlviii

Najaf (Iraq): Constitutional Revolution, 59–60; importance of, liv

Najd (Arabia), 54–5

Naraqi, Mirza Shahab al-Din (mujtahid), lxxiv

Nasara: attack on MQ's village, 4–5, 7–8; forced migration of enslaved people, 8–12; as term, xxxiin66, xxxviii

Naser al-Din Shah, lxivn160

networks: enslaved and freed slaves, xx; kinship ties, xxv, xxvn49; in post-emancipation era, xxv; slaves in maritime activities, xix; in urbanized regions, xxv. *See also* slave-master relationship

Nori, Mirza Hasan, lxxiii

North Africa, race and enslavement, xxxii

Nour al-Din (Hajj), lxxiv, 103

Nubia, xliv, xlivn107

Nubians, xxxiii

Nuri, Mirza Hasan, 97

El-Obeid (Sudan), xlivn106

Olney, James, xxvin54

Omani Arabs: labour demand, xvii–xviii, xviiin2; slave trade, xviii, xxii
Omar ibn Said, xxvin54
Oromo people, xxxiii–xxxiv
Ottoman Arabia: MQ's trail in, 59*m*; opportunities to male slaves, xlix; slave markets, xlviii–xlix, l, ln130, 48–9; slave trading, xxii–xxiii, 40–2. *See also* Saudi Arabia
Ottoman Empire: abolition of slavery, xxii–xxiii; First Constitutional Era, lvi; MQ's trail in, 59*m*; relations with Iran, lv–lvii; religion and status, xxxvi; schools, lv; slave-master relationships, xx; Tanzimat reforms, lvi–lvii, lvin143; Tunisia, xxxviin87; World War I, lxx; Young Turk Revolution, lix
Ottoman Iraq. *See* Iraq

"pagans," xxxii
passports, lxi, 62
Pemba (Mozambique), xvii–xviii, xviiin2, xxii
pilgrimage (hajj): caravan attacks, liii, 52–3; *mahmal* procession, liiin138; Mecca during days of Mina and Arafat, xlix, 47; rituals, xlixnn125–6
pilgrimages: in Mashhad, 87; Maʿsomeh, Qom, 75, 76, 96, 104; Shah ʿAbdul ʿAzim, 95; Shah Cheragh, 101
Pol-i Khaujo (Isfahan), 103
Portuguese labour demand in Brazil, xvii–xviii, xviiin2
processions: carriage of ʿAʾisha, liii, 54; carriage of Zeynab, liii, 52–3, 54; *mahmal*, liiin138; military, lxxvi
public administration, slaves employed in, xix
Punishment Committee (Iran), lxx

Qafqazi Mujahedin, 83
Qajar kings, deferment to ʿulamaʾ, xxiv
Qarabaghi, Bahram (Agha), lxivn160, lxv*f*
Qasr-i Shirin (Iran), 65–7
Qazal Rabat (Iraq), 63, 63n10
Qirvanian, Mahboob:
– autobiography: genealogy, xxxvii–xxxviii; historical context, Africa, xxxvii–xl; historical context, constitutional revolutions, lv–lx; historical context, forced migration to Middle East, xl–xlviii; historical context, MQ's expulsion, lxxii–lxxiii; historical context, Najaf, Ottoman Iraq, liv–lv; historical context, Ottoman Arabia, xlviii–liv; historical context, Ottoman Iraq to Iran, lxi–lxiv; historical context, return to Iran, lxxiii–lxxiv; historical context, Tehran, lxiv–lxxii; importance of, xxv–xxxvii; manuscript, xxx, xxxvii, lxxivn173; significance of, lxxix, lxxxi–lxxxii
– characteristics: education, xxxvii, xlix, liv–lv, lxxv–lxxvi, 47–8, 52, 57–8; generosity, 69, 78–9; kindness for pigeon, 100; overview, lxxvii–lxxix; religious devotion, xxxvii, lxxviii–lxxix; scarification, xxxi*f*, xxxii, lxiv, lxxvii, 12, 78; work ethic, lxxvi–lxxvii
– family and personal: in Africa, 4–10; Ahmad (son), xxx, lxxv, lxxix, lxxx*f*, lxxxi*f*; Aqdas (daughter), lxxv*f*; Chanpina (mother), 4; death of MQ, lxxvi, lxxix; death of MQ's daughter, 84; employed as translator at royal wedding,

124   Index

Qirvanian, Mahboob (*continued*) lxxv–lxxvi; employment, lxxv; financial troubles, lxxii–lxxiii, 85, 88, 90; genealogy, xxxvii–xxxviii, 3–4; identity transformations, xxvin54, xxix–xxx, xxxv; Mansour (son), lxxiv, lxxviii–lxxix; marriage and children, lxix, lxxiv–lxxv, lxxix, 83; Ma'someh (wife), lxxii–lxxiii, lxxvi, lxxvii, lxxviif; Mas'oud (son), lxxv, lxxvi; Rashdan (father), 3, 4; Zamalah (brother), 5
- life journey (overview), xxiii, lxxxiv*m*
- transition from bondage to freedom, xxxiv
- *See also* Qirvanian, Mahboob, life trajectory

Qirvanian, Mahboob, life trajectory:
- in Africa: enslavement, xxxviii–xl, 7–8; fleeing home in Kidelan, 5–7; genealogy, xxxvii–xxxviii, 3–4; invasion of Nasara, 4–5
- Africa to Middle East: from El-Obeid to Khartoum, 31–4; evading British patrol, 32–3; evading British search patrol, 37–9; forced migration from home, xl–xlvii, xliin99, 8–12; identity transformations, xlii, xliin98, xliv, 17–18, 23–4; from Khartoum to Jedda, 34–7; from new town to Sous Aqsa, 21–5; from Saljmattyah to new town, 20–1; in Saljmattyah, xlii–xliii, 12–19; from Sous Aqsa to El-Obeid, 25–31; scarification, xxxi*f*, xxxii, lxiv, lxxvii, 12, 78; at Sous Aqsa, xliv, 24–5
- to Iran: customs and beliefs observed, 78–80; death of MQ's daughters, lxix, lxx, 84; expulsion from Mashhad, lxxii–lxxiii, 88–90; financial troubles, lxxii–lxxiii, 91–3; genealogical chart of the 'ulama' served by MQ, lxxii*f*; identity transformations, liv–lv; from Kermanshah to Qom, 68–75; in Kurdistan, 65–8; marriage to Ma'someh Yosufgar, lxix, 83; move to Mashhad, lxxi, 85–8; MQ's trails in Iran and Ottoman Iraq, 94*m*; from Ottoman Iraq to Iran, first journey, lxi–lxiv, 61–4; from Qom to Tehran, 76–8; in Qom, 75–6; in Tehran, first time, lxiv–lxxi, lxvi*m*, lxvii*m*, 80–5; in Tehran, second time, 90–1; titles of respect used by, lxvi–lxvii
- Iran to Iraq: return to Iraq, lxxiii; from Tehran to Shah 'Abdul 'Azim, 95–7
- Ottoman Arabia and Iraq: circumcision, xlix, 48; constitutional revolutions, lv–lx, 59–60; education in Mecca, xlix, lii, 47–8, 52; education in Najaf, liv–lv, lxxvi, 57–8; identity transformations, xlviii–liv, 42–3, 49–51; from Jedda to Mecca, 42–3; from Mecca to Medina, 51–3; from Mecca to Ta'if, 44–7; in Medina, 53–4; MQ's trail in Ottoman Empire and Arabia, 59*m*; in Najd, liii, liiin139, 54–5, 55; from Najd to Najaf, 55–8; slave market in Mecca, 48–9; slave trade in Jedda, 40–2
- return to Iran: departing Kashan, 103–4; employment, lxxv; in Isfahan, 103; in Shiraz, 101–2; from Najaf to Shiraz, 98–101; from Ottoman Iraq to Iran, second journey, lxxiii–lxxiv
- trail from Tunisia to Iran, lxxxiv*m*

- trail in North Africa (1903), xli*m*
- trail in Ottoman Empire and Arabia, 59*m*
- trails in Iran and Ottoman Iraq, 94
- trans-Saharan trade routes, xxxix*m*
- *See also* Qirvanian, MahboobQom (Iran), lxiii

Qur'an school (*maktab*). *See* education, of Mahboob

race: and enslavement, xxxii–xxxvii, xxxvi–xxxvii; MQ's observations on, xxxii; MQ's term for, lxxviin175
Ras al-Khaimah, xxxiv
Rashti, Ishaq (Shaykh Ayatullah). *See* Gharavi Rashti (Gilani, Amlashi), Ishaq (Shaykh Ayatullah)
Rashti, Isma'il (Shaykh Ayatullah). *See* Gharavi Rashti (Gilani, Amlashi), Isma'il (Shaykh Ayatullah)
religious affiliation and enslavement, xxxii–xxxiii
religious conversion: examples of, xxvii; of MQ, xxix, lii, 50–1; and status, xxxvi
remedies. *See* traditional medicine
Reza Shah Pahlavi (king of Iran), xxiv–xxv
Russia: occupation of Iran, lxi; support for Qajar dynasty, ln132, lix, lxvii–lxviii, lxix–lxx, 83
Russian-Ottoman War, 84

Sabzish castle (Iran), 64
Saljmattyah (Morocco), xlii–xlv, 14–19
Salmasi, Mirza Ahmad, 62
Salmasi family, lxi
al-Saltana, Nusrat, lxxiv, 100, 101, 102
al-Saltana, Samsam, lxix–lxx, 83
al-Saltana, Shu'a, lxviii, 83
Saudi Arabia: establishment, 40n1; slavery abolished, ln130; turban and Hijaza clothing, l, ln131. *See also* Ibn Sa'ud; Ottoman Arabia
Sayyid 'Abdullah, 99
Sayyid Habib (merchant), lxiii, 68
Sayyid Muhammad, 99
scarification, xxxi*f*, xxxii, lxiv, lxxvii, 12, 78
schools. *See* education
Sepah Salar, Husayn Khan, lvi
Shah, Ahmad (Shaykh), 81–2
Shah 'Abdul 'Azim (Iran), 95
Shah Cheragh (Iran), 101
Shahab al-Din, Mirza (Mujtahid), 103
Shahrudi, Ahmad (Shaykh), lxv, 82, 86
Shahzadeh 'Abdul 'Azim (Iran), 79–80
Shi'i leadership. *See* 'ulama'
Shiraz (Iran), 101–2
Shirazi, Qavam al-Mulk, 101
Shushtari, Asadullah (Shaykh), lv, 58
Shushtari, Muhammad 'Abdulnabi, liv, 57
slave employment: categorization of Africans, xxxii–xxxiii; gender roles, xix, xliv; in Middle East, xxxv; in various sectors, xviii–xix, xxxiii–xxxiv
slave-master relationship:
- freed slaves, xx–xxi, xxv, xxxiv–xxxv
- in Iran, xix–xxi, xxv, xxxv
- opportunities to male slaves, xlix
- treatment of slaves in Iran: corporal punishment, lxiv, 78–9, 100

slave-master relationship (*continued*)
- treatment of slaves in Ottoman Arabia: assault of female slave, 41; corporal punishment, 46–7, 48; kindness shown to MQ, lii–liii, 41–2, 49; opportunities to male slaves, xlix
- treatment of slaves on forced migration: clothing, 12; corporal punishment, 18, 22, 34; inspections of, 10; kindness shown to MQ, 14–19, 23; mistreatments of female slaves, xliv, 22; scarification, xxxi*f*, xxxii, lxiv, lxxvii, 12, 78; yoked, xliii*f*; yoked and chained, xl, xlii, 10; yoked and tied, 11
- *See also* African slave trade in Iran; food(s); gender relations; networks; slave trade

slave trade: in Africa, xliii*f*; MQ's general trail from Sousse to Tehran, lxxxiv*m*; MQ's trail in North Africa (1903), xli*m*; Ottoman Arabia, xxii–xxiii, xlviii–xlix, 40–2, 48–9; trans-Saharan trade routes, xxxix*m*. *See also* African slave trade in Iran; slave-master relationship

slave traders: categorization of Africans, xxxii–xxxiii; evasion of British detection, xxii, xlv, xlvii; Hadandawa, xlvi–xlvii, xlviin115, 35–7, 35n8

slavery and race, xxxii
slavery in Iran, xvii–xxv
slavery in Middle East, xxiii, xxxv
Somaliland/Somalis, xxi–xxii
Sous Aqsa (Morocco?), xliv, xlivn105, 29–30
sub-Saharan Africans ("Nubians"), xxxiii
Sudan as term, xxxviii
Sudanese, xxxiv
Sudanese nationalist movement, xlvi
al-Sultan, Rashid, lxviii, 83
Sultan Abad (Iran), 73–4
Swahili coast, xxxii

Tabataba'i, Muhammad (Sayyid), xxiv, lvii
Tabriz (Iran), ln132
Ta'if (Arabia), 45–6
Taima people, xxxiii
Takht-i Folad cemetery (Isfahan), 103, 103n12
Taqi Shirazi, Mirza Muhammad (Ayatullah), lix, lixn153, lxii, 59
Tehran (Iran): MQ's quarter, lxvii*m*; political changes, lxvii–lxxi; population, xxiii; public squares, 81, 81nn42–43; and surroundings (1920), lxvi*m*
Tehrani, Mirza Husayn, lvii
Toledano, Ehud, xx, xxxv
traditional medicine, xlvii, 38. *See also* infectious diseases
trans-Saharan trade routes, xxxix*m*
travel and transportation:
- to Iran: caravanserais, lxii, 64; carriage damaged, 88–9; carriages, 61–3, 64; dangerous roads, lxiii, lxxi, 69–70, 73, 87; Mo'azzam bridge, 62, 62n5; pack animals, 67; stagecoaches and horse changes, 76–7; towers to protect road, lxii, 66; wagon and carriage, 68–9; wagon wheel stuck in mud, 71–2
- Iran to Iraq: pack animals, 96
- on forced migration: donkey, 32, 41; MQ's trail North Africa, xli*m*; riding camels, 27–8; ship, xlv, 31–2, 38–9; trans-Saharan trade routes, xxxix*m*; walking, xl, xlii, 13–14; walking or riding, xlv,

30; walking with pack camels, 25–6; walking with traders on camels, 37–8; walking yoked, xliii*f*; walking yoked and chained, xl, xlii, 10; walking yoked and tied, 11
– Ottoman Arabia and Iraq: camels, one injured, 44–5; camels and carriage, 51; caravans attacked, liii, 52–3; riding camels, 42
– return to Iran: bridge of Mushir al-Daula, 100; ship, 98
tribute, 37, 52–3, 54
Tunisia, xxxvii, xxxviin87, xxxviii
Turk, Ibrahim (Shaykh), 68
Turk, Muhammad, 74
Twelver Shi'i Muslims, liin136
typhoid, lxx, 84

'ulama': genealogical chart, Iranian Shi'i, lxxii*f*; influence on MQ, xxviii; MQ's term for, 51n9; religious capital of Shi'i sect, xxiv; role in politics, lvii; on slavery and abolitionism, xxiv–xxv, ln130; source of term, xxviiin62; support for Young Turk Revolution, lix. *See also* Islamic law (shari'a), on slavery
United States, slave narratives, xxvi, xxvin54
urban settings, slaves employed in, xix

wars, 18–19, 29–30, 84
World War I, lxx, lxxviii

Yafar Khan. *See* Yapram Khan Armani
Yapram Khan Armani, lxviii, 82, 82nn47–8
Yar Muhammad Khan, lxxiv, 102, 103
Yosufgar, Ma'someh (wife of MQ): death, lxxvii; marriage and children, lxix, lxxiv–lxxv, lxxix, 83; after MQ's death, lxxvi; photo, lxxvii*f*; in Tehran, lxxii–lxxiii;
Young Ottomans, lvi
Young Turks, lix

Zamalah (brother of MQ), 5
Zanzibar, xvii–xviii, xviiin2, xxii
Zayandeh Rud dam, 103

www.ingramcontent.com/pod-product-compliance
Lightning Source LLC
Chambersburg PA
CBHW020409080526
44584CB00014B/1251